TURKEY

Second Edition
1993

TABLE OF CONTENTS

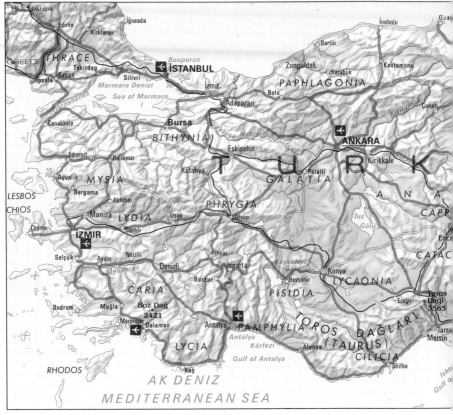

TURKEY

©Nelles Verlag GmbH, München 45
  All rights reserved

Second edition, completely revised
1993
ISBN 3-88618-401-3
Printed in Slovenia

Publisher:	Günter Nelles	**Translation:**	J. Clough, A. Fenner,
Chief Editor:	Dr. Heinz Vestner		E. Goldmann,
Project Editor:	Dr. Heinz Vestner		J. L. High, R. Rosko
Editor:	E. Knutson,	**Cartography**:	Nelles Verlag GmbH,
	Ch. Grimm		Freytag & Berndt,
Color Separation:	Priegnitz, Gräfelfing		Wien
DTP-Exposure:	Printshop Schimann	**Printed by**:	Gorenjski Tisk, Kranj

- 02 -

MAP LIST

Please note: in some cases the spelling of the place names on the maps is not the same as in the text, because the spelling on the maps is according to UN guidelines, whereas the usual English spelling is used in the text.

HISTORY
AND CULTURE

The Land

The Asia Minor Peninsula, situated between the Black Sea and the Mediterranean, essentially corresponds to the territory of the modern-day Turkish state. Its differing climatic zones provide appealing variety, ranging from areas of citrus and olive cultivation in the south to the extremely cold winters of East Anatolia, where wolves howl and temperatures of minus 40 degrees C are not unusual. The enchanting salt desert located in Central Turkey features an exceptional and interesting array of plants. To the north, the Black Sea coast has the allure of a year-round mild and temperate climate. Almost miraculously, it is still relatively untouched. The hazelnuts sold everywhere in Europe during the Christmas season grow here.

Turkey's most developed region is the Aegean coast with its Mediterranean climate. The region in the southeast, along the border to Syria, is also quite intriguing. In the foothills of the Taurus Mountains one can catch sight of camel caravans on their journeys, while from the heights there are breathtaking vistas of gleaming, sun-filled valleys. The highest Turkish mountain is located in the eastern part of the country, the permanently snow-covered 5165-meter-high Mount Ararat, shrouded in legend since ancient

Preceding pages: Miniature of the conquering of Constantinople by the Turks. The inner city of Istanbul with its prominent Galata Tower. A man's world in the yard of a tea house in the Seljuk caravanserai in the bazaar of Urfa. Pamukkale glistens peacefully in the early morning light. The many-breasted Artemis in the Seljuk Museum.

times. Today it is the destination of many amateur explorers looking for Noah's Ark. Although there are no navigable watercourses in Asia Minor, there are several rivers. The lakes of the east are quite impressive, particularly Lake Van. By and large, Asia Minor is a mountainous land with a highly-articulated topography. Gentle and inviting in the western reaches, it becomes rugged and inaccessible in the east, a real challenge for adventurers.

In the Beginning

In the early dawn of human history Asia Minor was already inhabited. Even the people of the Stone Age considered this region to be an ideal crossroads for their trade in obsidian, a rare volcanic glass which they worked into tools and idol figures. There are two primary deposits in Cappadocia, at Çiftlik and Açigöl. Palestine, Cyprus and Crete were supplied from Çiftlik. Açigöl delivered obsidian to northern Asia Minor and southern Anatolia.

At that time in the Fertile Crescent, the western section of which extends into southern Turkey, the transition from the hunter-gatherer and nomadic existence to agricultural society took place. In this region, early human beings began to domesticate wild plants. The bifarious barley, emmer and spelt wheat, wild peas and lentils which flourished in Asia Minor from the west up to the slopes of the Taurus Range provided the initial cultivated stock. The breeding of livestock also had its beginnings here. Goats and wild cows were captured by prehistoric hunters and then domesticated. Towards the end of the last ice age crops which were dependent only on rain could be grown on the precipitation-rich mountain slopes. This attracted settlers early on, before irrigated agriculture along the Nile, the Indus, and in Mesopotamia was invented.

These cultural achievements are generally ascribed to humans of the subspecies *homo sapiens sapiens.* Archeological discoveries from the Karain Cave in southwestern Turkey are evidence that during the mid-Paleolithic (Mesolithic) Age the *homo sapiens neandertaliensis* was still living in the region. In the preceding warmer periods between the ice ages, they had lived in the open, not seeking out caves for shelter until the colder periods came. In these, the two subspecies coexisted. Recent research provides strong indications that they did not fight against each other, but interbred.

Protective roofs as shelters have been discovered in Beldibi and Belbasi near Antalya. The humans living there in the Mesolithic were already using vessels made of stone. Haçilar, in the area of Burdur, and Çatal Hüyük-East are the most significant locations for archeological discoveries from the pre-Ceramic Late

Above: An artistic reconstruction of burial rites during the Hittite era in Turkey.

Stone Age. At these sites, the bones of domesticated dogs and sheep have been found. The earliest art objects are groups of reclining figures made of clay. Paradoxically, the invention of ceramics took place in the pre-Ceramic Neolithic Age. It is air-dried, i. e., not yet fired ceramic.

Early Settlements

During the Ceramic Neolithic Age, humankind began to group together in urban settlements. In Çayönü in southeastern Asia Minor near Diyarbakir and in Sakçagözü, buildings were constructed which were entered by way of ladders. Amulets, seals, monotone grayish-black ceramics as well as woven mats are the remnants left by these first urban dwellers. Colorful wall paintings and bas-reliefs with depictions of animals and hunting from Çatal Hüyük East, as well as images of women, show the new possibilities of artistic expression in these cities, the societies of which had now developed a division of labor.

This was also the period when metal-working began, as evidenced by beads of copper and lead. Textiles began to be produced, and artisans invented a slowly- rotating potters' wheel. The products of Haçilar, Çatal Hüyük-West and Can Hasan were especially well-made. The ceramic objects found in Haçilar feature bizarre patterns, painted reddish-brown on a yellowish background and polished to a gleam. Among the decorative and symbolic motifs used by the artists are the swastika, zig-zagged lines and mouflon heads.

Clay bricks and wood were employed in the construction of buildings. In Haçilar, rooms were grouped around a central court. Some buildings had stone foundations and walls painted with colored whitewash. In Can Hasan there were two-storied residential blocks with defensive walls. Artisans in these cities produced jewelry and weapons made of copper. In the arts and religion, the full-figured statues of the Great Mother Goddess played an important role.

The Bronze Age

The transition from the Stone Age to the Bronze Age is called the "Stone-and-Copper Age" (Chalcolithic), during which daily life was eased with utensils and tools of copper. Later, a method of alloying tin and copper was invented. This new material, bronze, was very hard and ideally-suited for the fashioning of weapons and other equipment.

At the beginning of the Early Bronze Age I, the northern and western regions of Asia Minor were increasingly settled. Asia Minor has an abundance of sites with archeological finds from the transition period between the Late Copper Age to the Early Bronze Age. The most important of these in southwest Asia Minor is Beycesultan. Here the *megaron* buildings, houses with entry halls connecting to rectangular rooms with fireplaces,

were unearthed. Similar architecture was excavated in layer I of Hisarlik (Troy-Ilion); complementary finds of urban culture from the Early Bronze Age come from Yortan, Babaköy, Semayük and Kültepe. An abundance of precious metal finds was unearthed in layer II of Hisarlik, which Heinrich Schliemann erroneously believed to be the Troy of Homer. Today it is known that this layer dates from the second half of the third millennium B.C., whereas the Trojan War didn't take place until the 13th century B.C. Many scholars do not equate Hisarlik with Troy since it is only certain that it used to be called Ilion (which many other places in this region are called as well). This still does not prove that it was the Ilion which later became Troy.

During the third millennium B.C., metal craftsmanship experienced a tremendous upswing. Works of fantastic beauty and elegance representing the highest standards of available technology were created. The centers of this art were Hisarlik (Troy II), Dorak, Horoztepe and Alaca Hüyük. The region's abundance of metals attracted merchants from Mesopotamia and Syria to Asia Minor. As a result, cities were established: Tarsus in Cilicia, Gedikli and Tilmen Hüyük near Islahiye.

The *megaron* construction style continued to be popular during the second phase of the Early Bronze Age. The cities were heavily secured with fortification walls and other military edifices. In western and southern Anatolia, the deceased were interred in large ceramic vessels called *pithes* graves. Royalty was the exception: They were laid to rest in stone chambers. In Dorak, to the south of the Sea of Marmara, the graves of nobility were found to contain statuettes made of electron (an alloy of gold and silver), figures of silver or bronze, highly-ornamented weapons and the oldest known *kelim*. The city's prosperity was derived from trade with Egypt and the islands of

the eastern Mediterranean. Conceivably, the scratch-drawings which have turned up in Karatas are pictographic characters. If this is so, an early form of script is still awaiting decipherment.

During the Early Bronze Age III, metal was being produced on a large scale, and a number of ore mines and smelters were built. In the meantime, the technologies in use here had reached the stage where it became possible to mine quite economically. Small principalities were established. In the south of Turkey, Tilmen Hüyük and Gedikli, at the foot of the Taurus Range, were the trading crossroads for routes to Syria. In the realm of architecture, the *megaron* continued to be dominant; it now appeared in the city of Kültepe in Cappadocia as well. The walls of these structures were coated with white plaster. In Beycesultan and Kültepe, the residents made offerings upon

Above: Figure in relief in the Hittite Museum in Ankara. Right: Another relief from the time of the Hittites (Yazilikaya).

altars, behind which there was a sacrificial ram with horns. The facility was designed for the libation, a cultic pouring out of liquids. An unusual artifact from this era is a dagger with an iron blade discovered in Alaca Hüyük.

Luwians, Hittites and Assyrians

Toward the end of the third millennium, and during the beginning of the second millennium B.C., Indo-Aryan tribes emigrated into Asia Minor. The Luwians came in from the west through the straits of the Dardanelles. The Hittites probably migrated in from the east.

The city of Nesha was the starting point for the development of the Hittite state. The Kussara kings Pitkhana and Anittas conquered the region and dethroned the native rulers. The Hittites derived their name and the designation of their language, Kaneshite, from the city of Nesha. The designation "Hittite" is arbitrary; its intent was the " rediscovery" of a people mentioned in the Bible. From Nesha, the Hittites extended their dominion over central Anatolia, conquering Hattusas and destroying it. They defeated the most powerful ruler in Anatolia, the Grand Duke of Buruschandra.

Not only was the immigration of these Indo-Aryans of historical significance, the establishment of Assyrian trading settlements in Anatolia was of equal importance. The Akkadian (Assyrian) word *karum* means port or transferpoint. The most significant place of this kind is the *karum* Kanis at Kültepe. The Assyrian merchants of the 19th and 18th centuries B.C. adapted themselves to the indigenous customs and habits, marrying women from Kanis as well. The trading partners of these Assyrians were local princes who exchanged copper for tin, lead and textiles. Then, alongside the clay brick and half-timbered structures indigenous to Anatolia, the construction of buildings with a square ground plan and

corner towers began. In Beycesultan, a tremendous palace complex was excavated which measures up in every respect to similar ones in Crete. It has stone foundations and interlocking rooms, interior courtyards with decorative columns, and an extremely elaborate subterranean system of canals which either heated or cooled the palace's rooms according to need.

The close relations which were developed with Mesopotamia in the first half of the second millennium B.C. led to the adoption of cuneiform script in Cappadocia and the utilization of cylinder seals. The latter were used to seal containers filled with goods for trade, attesting to the origins and/or owner of the wares and guaranteeing payment, just as credit cards do today.

The conquest of Babylon by King Mursilis I in 1531 B.C. is evidence that relations did not always proceed peacefully. During the 13th century B.C., the Hittites even defeated the Egyptians at Kades.

Hattusili I (1590-1560 B.C.) founded Hattusas anew after it had been destroyed and abandoned 200 years earlier. He elevated it to the capital city of the unified Old Hittite Kingdom. Thanks to the excavations of German archaeologist Kurt Bittel, we are now very well informed about the ruins of Hattusas, located next to the present-day village of Bogazköy.

As far as fine arts go, the most important carvings of this era were reliefs. In Alaca Hüyük, the fragments of an oversized statue were discovered. Craftsmen fashioned clay steers approximately 90 cm tall. Painted red, they represented the sacred cattle of the storm god and served as ritual vessels. The vase paintings of this period are particularly interesting: Some details, such as the way faces are depicted, are similar to those of Minoan works. The images, however, are unmistakably of a Near Eastern, religious nature. On the Inandik vase, the Bitik Vase and a pitcher from Eskiypar, for example, the *hieros ganos* – holy wedding – is portrayed. The pictures show an unveiling as

well as various acts of sexual intercourse performed in public as a fertility rite by the city's ruler and the high priestess.

The New Hittite Kingdom was founded by Suppiluliumas I in the first half of the 14th century B.C. Hattusas continued to be the capital city. During the 13th and 12th centuries B.C., towards the conclusion of Hittite history, the fortress there was greatly expanded and a new city was laid out alongside the lower city to the south. It was surrounded by a wall which included gates guarded by figures of kings, sphinxes and lions. During this period, the rock of Büyükkale was also included in the defensive installations, and it was connected to the city by way of a bridge. Five temples are known to have existed in Hattusas. The oldest of these was dedicated to the storm god and his mate, the sun goddess Arinna. The imperial seat in Büyükkale has been very carefully researched. It

Above: Some art is for posterity, such as this ancient relief carved in a cliff in Myra.

consisted of a great system of columned halls between which were various courtyards and residential structures. Among the better-known archeological finds here are the figures of a female deity with a disc-shaped headdress and a mountain god with unnaturally large ears. The procession of deities in the main chamber of Yazilikaya forms a unique documentation of the realm of Hittite gods. The deities – opulently attired and carrying their typical attributes and weapons – are portrayed in reliefs which have been carved right into the rock. In the art of making seals, cartouches in Hittite hieroglyphic script appear once again. Among the most popular motifs is the winged sun disc, borrowed from the Egyptians and later used by the Assyrians and Persians.

The Iron Age

Northern sea-going peoples brought Hittite history to an end around 1200 B.C. They advanced from the Aegean into Asia Minor, Lebanon (where they were known as *Philistines*) and Egypt. They destroyed Hattusas. This was made possible by their technological superiority. They brought two innovations onto the world stage: The first was the two-wheeled, horse-drawn battle chariot, the other was equipment and weapons made of iron. With these, they brought on a technological and economic as well as political revolution. Their expansion precipitated a migration of peoples. Their precise identity, where they came from and what sort of people they were as individuals has not been researched yet.

The Aramaeans

The West Semitic Aramaeans founded their own city-states in southern Asia Minor during the period around 1000 B.C. The most important of these were Meliddu (Matalya), Kummuhu (Commagene), Gurgum (Maras), Hatti (Karkemis) and the still little-researched Tabal to the northwest of Malatya. The Aramaeans adopted much from the older indigenous cultures because, as nomads, they had not developed their own tradition in the realm of fine arts. Their visual arts and architecture correspond to the examples of their predecessors. The arts of these Aramaic principalities are often somewhat erroneously designated as "Late Hittite" creations. While based upon Hittite tradition, they also incorporate elements which point to Assyrian and Mitannian influences. Among the more outstanding products of this culture are their orthostastic sculptures (stone slabs for wall decoration),

The Kingdom of Urartu

During the 9th century B.C., the Urartians began to acquire political power in eastern Asia Minor. These people came from the northern mountainous regions and were apparently descendants of the Hurrians, who ruled part of the Near East in the second millennium B.C. The Urartian kingdom had its greatest victories during a period of internal weakness for the Assyrians. This was exploited by Argishti I (about 770 B.C.) followed by his son Sarduri II (about 750 B.C.). Despite heavy battles with the Assyrians, the Cimmerians and the Scythians, the Urartians were able to hold their own on into the 6th century B.C.

Lake Van is situated in the center of the former Urartu; located in its vicinity are the important Urartian sites of Tushpa and Çavustepe. The Urartaeans were renowned as masons and architects. Their temples were surrounded by columned courtyards and walls. They were also skilled engineers. Under King Menua they built an aqueduct 51 kilometers in length, from Gürpinar into the Van plain, which is still in use today. Their tightly-organized state bristled with fortifications and bunkers, was criss crossed with good roads and amply equipped with armament depots and supply storehouses. Among the typical products of Urartian handcraftsmanship are bronze belts embossed with lions.

Numerous pictorial elements, such as the tree of life, were either borrowed from or are related to Assyrian art. Alongside portrayals which adhere closely to nature are many which are rather abstracted. Embossed helmets, forged metal cauldrons and bronze handle attachments with images of people and beasts are common archeological discoveries from the Urartian excavations. The Urartian kingdom extended east from Turkey into Armenian regions.

The Phrygians

The Phrygians became the inheritors of the Hittite culture in Central Anatolia. They ruled the region to the north of the Halys River and to the west as far as the area of Eskisehir. One of their kings during the 8th century B.C. was named

Mita. It is he who has become known to us through Greek legend as Midas – the king whose very touch turned everything into gold. The most important cities were Gordion, Midas-City and Bogazköy. Additional settlements included Alaca, Alisar and Pazarli. Most of what we now know about the Phrygians has resulted from recent excavations. The German archeologist Kurt Bittel researched Bogazköy; American crews carried out digs in Gordium, uncovering a significant palace complex. Some structures were designed as *megara*, and several had mosaic floors. The entire grounds were secured with fortification walls.

The primary reverence of the Phrygians was reserved for the goddess Cybele, who was worshipped in rock sanctuaries. Supposedly, during sacrificial ceremonies her priests castrated themselves in frenzied raptures in order to offer up their most important possession to the goddess. The goddess herself is portrayed as smiling.

The geometric tomb and temple facades in the neighborhood of Eskisehir and Afyon are both famous and well worth seeing. Among the handcrafted articles characteristic of Phrygian culture are fibulae (garment clasps) and pitchers in the form of animal heads. These products were exported to the western Mediterranean and Near East.

Phrygian culture faded with the invasion of the Cimmerians shortly after 700 B.C., although the empire continued to exist for some time afterwards.

The Lydians

In the course of the 7th century B.C., the Lydians became dominant in western Asia Minor. They minted coins, a practice which was soon taken up in both Greece and Persia.

Right: The head of Medusa in Didyma, a reminder that the Greeks were here.

The capital city of the empire was Sardis. Long-distance trading routes led from there to the Mediterranean and Persia. The river which flowed through the capital city is said to have contained an abundance of gold; nonetheless, the city's inhabitants owed their affluence to skillful trading and sophisticated politics. They brought handcraftsmanship to higher technical and aesthetic perfection in their factory-like workshops.

The most famous Lydian king was Croesus, whose wealth was so proverbial that his name now stands for any rich man. Croesus ruled from 560-546 B.C. He was defeated by the Achaemenian "King of Kings", Cyrus the Great of Persia. Thereupon, the Lydian realm became a *satrapy* (province) of Persia; Sardis was then the *satrapy*'s administrative seat.

Greek Colonies

During Greece's archaic period, which lasted from the ninth to the sixth century B.C., Greeks sailed away from their homeland in all directions. Many of them founded colonies on the Mediterranean coastline of Asia Minor. They were impelled to make their journey in search of trade and wealth by increasing population pressures at home. They returned with new knowledge – of the alphabet, for example – and new gods, such as Cybele, and thus stimulated the cultural development of the mother country.

The Greeks included in process this were the Aeolians, Ionians, Dorians and Achaeans. The Ionians founded a league of cities to which Miletus, Ephesus, Smyrna and others belonged. The Dorians did the same with Halicarnassus (Bodrum) and Knidos. Tarsus developed on the southern coast of Asia Minor. According to legend, Homer is supposed to have come from Smyrna. Many of the great "Greek" philosophers, historians and thinkers had their origins in Asia Minor. Thales and Anaximander came from Mi-

letus, from Ephesus the renowned Heraclitus, and Herodotus, the renowned historian, was born in Halicarnassus.

The Achaemenians

During Greece's archaic and classical periods, trade routes through Asia Minor connected Greece with Persia. The colonies in Asia Minor were unable to retain their independence for very long; they came under Persian hegemony after the Lydian interlude. However, they were able to retain the greater part of their autonomy under the new rulers. They still had their own local prince or king, as did other lands in the Achaemenian empire, although they were represented abroad by the "King of Kings", the Achaemenian ruler. The empire was divided into *satrapies* (provinces), which were administered by *satraps*.

It then came to pass that Ionian architects and builders co-created – inspired by the *Artemision* of Ephesus – the Achaemenian royal seats of Pasargadae,

Persepolis and Susa, where kings like Cyrus, Darius, Xerxes and Artaxerxes held court.

Several of the cities under the hegemony of the city of Miletus rebelled against Darius I in 499 B.C. in order to avoid having to pay taxes, but they were subdued in 494 B.C. A small number of reinforcement troops moved into Asia Minor from Athens, so that, as even Herodotus conceded, the Greeks provoked the Persian Wars themselves. In the course of these hostilities, the Achaemenians advanced into Europe and destroyed Athens.

Religious freedom as well as the freedom to live where one chose existed in the Achaemenian empire. During this time the Jews, liberated by Cyrus, returned from Babylonian captivity to their homeland. This sort of tolerance went so far that although rebellious kings were indeed punished, their dynasties were never obliterated. As a result, the rulership of the Achaemenians was hardly considered foreign domination; ulti-

mately, one had only to pay his tributes and obey the laws.

This realm was carefully observed by the "eyes and ears of the King" and woe to the corrupt judge or deceitful official! They were shown no mercy. The judge Sisamnes, a member of the royal court, rendered an unfair sentence, whereupon King Cambyses had him flayed. His skin was cut into strips which were used to upholster a chair. His son Otanes was placed upon this chair and warned that he should consider with each ruling whose place he had taken.

Trade flourished during the Achaemenian era, and all of Asia Minor was connected with the surrounding lands by an outstanding network of roads as well as postal and courier services.

Although Caria was not independent, it enjoyed special liberties. The most fa-

Above: More Greek remnants, the Ionic temple near Kütakya. Right: The Romans left a lasting mark with this aqueduct near Istanbul.

mous ruler of this area was Mausolus (377-353 B.C.). His renowned tomb was considered in antiquity to be one of the Seven Wonders of the World; it is also the origin of the modern word "mausoleum".

Although the Greeks were able to keep the Persians out of Europe with their victories at Marathon, Salamis and Platea, they were unable to pull themselves together for an attack on the Achaemenian empire. The shock over the destruction of Athens was still too great, so the honor of conquering the Persians and bringing their rule to an end was left to the Macedonian Alexander.

Alexander and Hellenism

Alexander, son of King Philip of Macedonia, passed the Hellespont with his host in 334 B.C. In the following year, the military organization of Darius III, the last of the Achaemenians, suffered a heavy defeat at Issus. Issus is located near Iskenderun, a city which (as is true of a variety of others) owes its name to Alex-

ander, since *Iskender* is the Arabic equivalent. From there, Alexander's army advanced further to the south and east. In the ensuing years, it conquered the entire-known world. Alexander had his generals marry Persian princesses and laid plans to develop Babylon into a gigantic world capital.

It goes without saying that the Greeks were not exactly enchanted with such notions. They were disgruntled with Alexander because he had adopted Oriental customs and forced them up on his men. Especially degrading in Greek eyes was the practice of *proskynesis* – groveling in the dust before the ruler.

In his megalomania, Alexander even wanted to reshape the Macedonian mountain of Athos into a gigantic figure of himself, in the right hand of which a city for ten thousand inhabitants would be built. He entrusted this task to a young unkown, Dinocrates, whose eccentric behaviour had impressed him. Imitating Hercules, Dinocrates appeared naked with a lion's pelt, club and a garland of poplar. The two megalomaniacs took a liking to each other and Dinocrates was put in charge of the construction of Alexandria in Egypt.

Alexander's early death, in Babylon on June 13, 323 B.C., put an end to plans for remodelling Athos. For some twenty years, the *diadochi* – his successors – fought for pieces of his vast domain. Ptolemy received Egypt, Seleucus won Mesopotamia and Persia, as well as the eastern section of Turkey. Lysimachus received Thrace and western Turkey. Pontus was ruled by Persian princes of the Mithridates dynasty; in Cappadocia, the rulers belonged to the Ariarathes Dynasty. In Pergamum (Bergama), Philataeros, an officer of Lysimachus, developed a state of his own. The altar dedicated to Zeus, once located in Pergamum but now in Berlin on the Museum Island, is quite possibly the most imposing all-around work of Hellenistic art. The local custom of writing on animal skins, thus replacing the transitory papyrus with durable leather, is the origin of the word "parchment" – a corruption of the town's name.

Alexander's true legacy is not of a political, but rather of a cultural nature. Greek was now spoken and written from Greece to India. Religions and philosophies mingled with each other, as did the fine arts and architecture. The result was a multifarious, syncretistic entity familiar to us as Hellenism – which has also enjoyed a tenacious afterlife. Hellenism as an open-minded and liberal world view and lifestyle survived the empires of the Seleucids, Parthians, Sassanids and Romans, and not until the expansion of Islam was it pushed back to Byzantium, its last bastion.

The Romans, Parthians and Sassanids

The Attalid dynasty of Pergamum ended in 133 B.C. with the death of its last king, Attalus III. Having no male heir, the ruler bequethed his lands to Rome. Thus, the Pergamene kingdom became the Roman province of *Asia Propria*. Large numbers of Roman citizens migrated there in order to exploit the new trading opportunities. Local principalities also continued to play an important role, among them the realm of Antiochus I of Commagene, who erected the colossal statues atop Nemrut Dagi during the first half of the first century B.C.

The presence of the Romans in Asia Minor provoked Mithridates VI, a Pontic king, to declare war in 88 B.C. After battles with Sulla, there came a period of temporary peace in 85 B.C. Lucullus (general and progenitor of the gourmet) conquered Mithridates, and the kingdom of Pontus was incorporated into the Roman Empire. Defeated, but by no means despondent, Mithridates founded a new kingdom on the Crimean Peninsula. His son, Pharnaces II, attempted to reconquer Pontus, only to be defeated by Caesar on August 2, 47 B.C. This event at Zela (Zile) led to Caesar's renowned proclamation: *"Veni, vidi, vici"* ("I came, I saw, I conquered").

When Augustus closed the gates of the Janus Temple, it signaled the beginning of a long-lasting peace in Asia Minor. With the Parthians, the Hellenized successors of the Achaemenians, he concluded a treaty in the year A.D. 20 which brought an end to the Roman sphere of interest along the Euphrates. Excepting isolated skirmishes on the borders, Asia Minor experienced a relatively quiet period under the *Pax Romana* for almost 200 years afterwards. Ikonion (Konya) and Ankyra (Ankara) became new nodal points for transportation and trade. Robust stone bridges were constructed, some of which are still in use today. Trade and the arts flourished in such Hellenistic cities as Ephesus. The Christianization of Asia Minor was begun by Paul in A.D. 47. He founded a variety of congregations in the trading settlements of Asia Minor. The new religion was adopted particularly by the poor and oppressed. In the course of time, Christianity eclipsed the Mithras cults and various other religions promising resurrection and redemption. In the year A.D. 197, heavy battles broke out once again with the Parthians; Septimius Severus was able to resolve these in Rome's favor.

In time, the successors of the Parthians, the Sassanids, generated new and larger headaches for the Romans. This Persian dynasty sought to reestablish the great empire of the Achaemenians. Sapur I (A.D. 241-272), a Sassanid king, was victorious over three Roman emperors: Valerian, Gordian and Phillipus Arabs. The Sassanids conquered Antioch, Tarsus and Cappadocia.

The Roman emperor Diocletian (A.D. 284-305) had to battle against symptoms of domestic disintegration while externally commanding a war of attrition on two fronts, against the Germanic tribes in the west and the Sassanids in the east.

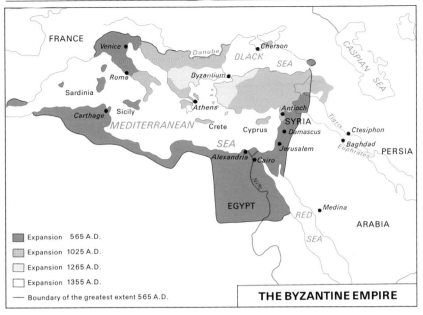

Expansion 565 A.D.
Expansion 1025 A.D.
Expansion 1265 A.D.
Expansion 1355 A.D.
— Boundary of the greatest extent 565 A.D.

THE BYZANTINE EMPIRE

Following this important emperor's abdication, Constantine emerged from a struggle among his rivals as absolute monarch. He guaranteed the Christians unhampered practice of their religion and, soon after his arrival in Asia Minor, convened the Council of Nicaea (A.D. 325) in which the Aryans were adjudged to be espousing heresies and the divinity of Jesus Christ was dogmatized.

In the year A.D. 330, Constantine proclaimed Byzantium, the city at the Straits of Bosphorus which had been founded by the Dorians, the new capital of the Roman Empire. He dubbed the city *Nova Roma*. The emperor personally supervised the expansion of the city, which was renamed Constantinople after him. He had numerous statues by Greek sculptors from other cities in Asia Minor, as well as Athens and Rome, brought in to decorate the new metropolis.

The relocation of the capital city was also to have beneficial effects for Christianity: People in Rome were conservative and still too close to the old gods,

whereas in Asia Minor Christianity had already established roots.

The Byzantine Empire
(395-1453)

Constantine's decision was a political and military consequence of an eastward shift in the center of gravity in the Roman world. He laid the foundations for the capital of an empire which, in over one thousand years of its existence, was to blend together Christian teachings, Roman civilization and statecraft, Hellenic culture and a number of Oriental elements. At the zenith of its power, it extended from the Straits of Gibraltar all the way to the Caucasus region.

Theodosius I was the last of the Roman emperors to rule over the entire empire. In A.D. 392, during his brief period of absolute monarchy, Christianity was declared the state religion. When he divided the Roman Empire between his sons Arcadius and Honorius shortly before his death in A.D. 395, it was an attempt to

27

Above: A mosaic of Christ the Redeemer in the Kariye Cami Museum in Istanbul.

overcome administrative difficulties. However, this measure led instead to the establishment of two distinct empires.

The Western Roman Empire collapsed into chaos as a consequence of the Germanic invasions and then, with the conquest of Rome in 476, ceased to exist. Now there was only one Roman capital left: Constantinople. The Eastern Roman Empire of that time encompassed the eastern Mediterranean region, Syria, Palestine and Anatolia up to the Euphrates River. Constantinople became the center of the civilized world.

Up until Justinian I's assumption of power (527-565), the history of the Byzantine Empire was, however, one uninterrupted series of intrigues and rebellions. The population was splintered into a number of parties; in the emperor's court one bloody palace revolt came hot on the heels of the last, and the clergy was bogged down by fruitless discussion.

A change in the taxation system resulted in clashes between merchants and landowners in 491. In 513 the Thracian commander brought his troops and fleet to the city walls and laid siege to the capital. Finally, in the course of the Nika Rebellion of 532, the rival Blues and Greens (named for the colors of their charioteer teams) roiled and, in the process, set the entire city on fire. Many of Constantinople's greatest monuments went up in flames, among them the Hagia Sophia.

Byzantium achieved its first Golden Age under Justinian I, who came to the throne with the goal of restoring the empire's unity. With the assistance of his generals Belisar and Narses, he won back regions which had been lost. In North Africa, he subdued the Vandals; in Spain and Italy, the Goths. By paying tributes, he bought peace with the Sassanids as well as the attacking Slavs and Avars. With the aid of his enterprising wife, Theodora, and Belisar, Justinian I delivered the Nika Rebellion a bloody defeat, thus reestablishing peace and order.

From that time on, Theodora would have to be considered co-ruler. Thanks to the *Secret History* by Procopius we know only many of the details of her controversial life. She grew up as the daughter of a bear-keeper in Constantinople's circus. After turbulent years in the circus and a dubious theater in the city's suburbs, she started out on an adventurous journey through the Orient. After her return, she encountered Justinian, who was at that time heir to the throne. Euphemia, the mate of the presiding Emperor Justin, did everything within her power to prevent the marraige, but Justinian prevailed. It has been claimed that Justinian's triumph in this matter was among the greatest exertions of will in his life, and that without Theodora's qualities his regime wouldn't have survived its first five years. According to the chroniclers, Justinian distinguished himself with mental obsessiveness and tireless hard work. Theodora exceeded him in her sober pragmatism, sense of realism and personal courage.

Justinian gave the empire an authoritarian, although moderate and enlightened, political system, as well as new administrative laws. In his person, worldly and clerical power were united, although the Patriarch of Constantinople continued to be the chief administrator of the church. The capital city was perceived as the earthly counterpart of Heavenly Jerusalem, the empire that of God's Kingdom. The emperor was Christ's representative on earth. With these guiding precepts, he had important churches within his realm decorated with mosaics portraying him as the equivalent of Christ with a nimbus and in place of the apostles – the members of his imperial court (such as in San Vitale and San Apollinare Nuovo in Ravenna).

Justinian led his capital city of Constantinople to unprecedented splendor. He had the buildings which had been destroyed in the fury of civil war replaced with magnificent new structures. The engineering and creative services which he exacted at that time from his architects, master builders and artists, the development of magnificent church and palace buildings, and the creation of numerous charitible services and defensive installations swallowed immense sums of money ... not to mention the wars which were being fought. There is a legend according to which Nestorian monks smuggled silkworms out of China and started breeding them in Asia Minor. Justinian is reputed of being able to replenish his exhausted treasury to some degree through his monopoly on the production of silk.

His successors were unable to continue with the restoration of the Roman Empire towards which Justinian had aspired. The empire was then concentrated in the countries of the eastern Mediterranean region, principally comprising Asia Minor and the coastal areas of Greece. The Slavs and Avars advanced towards the Balkans and stood within threatening distance of the capital. The Persian Sassanid Empire conquered Syria, Palestine and Egypt's breadbasket in a matter of a few years, while the organization of the Byzantinian state suffered its final collapse during civil war. In A.D. 610 Herakelius (610-641) ascended to power. He carried out a thorough reform of the administrative apparatus and succeeded in fending off the Avars in a large-scale field campaign, as well as delivering a final defeat to the Sassanids.

A completely new and increasingly threatening power profited from the weakening of Byzantium through the struggle with the Sassanids: Islam. Bearing in mind the bequest of their prophet Mohammed, who had died in 632, the Islamic hosts plunged headlong into the Holy War. At the speed of the wind they conquered Egypt and the oriental provinces, including the holy city of Jerusalem, thrusting ahead towards Asia Minor and establishing a solid foothold for themselves in Antioch. The Sassanid empire was able to offer the Arabs little resistance, and even Byzantium could not stop the invasion. The Islamic armies advanced to Constantinople and laid siege to the city. Constantine IV Pogonatos (668-685) was able to achieve a sea victory over the Arabs partly through the use of Greek fire, a substance with the ability to burn on water. This enabled his forces to break the blockade of the city. Nonetheless, the Arabs continued to move through the Anatolian countryside, plundering and pillaging as they went. The cities tried to protect themselves with the construction of defensive fortifications. Not until the emperors of the Macedonian dynasty (867-1056) was there success at finally pushing – and keeping – the Arabs out of Asia Minor.

During the 8th and 9th centuries, a grave internal political and religious crisis shook the empire, endangering the domestic stability of the state as well as the Byzantine culture. The conflict was triggered by an edict against the worship of icons (730), which split the people and clergy into two parties. Leo II (717- 741) supported the iconoclastic movement, pointing out the prohibition of idolatry in the Old Testament.

All depictions of human beings were forbidden as a result. Crosses, plants and birds were permitted as symbols of belief and creation, however, we have been handed down the observation from one critical contemporary, so that the house of God had been transformed into "a vegetable garden and birdhouse". Iconoclasm was waged with ever-increasing vehemence. A council convened by Constantine V (741-775) ordered the destruction of all icons, illustrated manuscripts and depictions of the human figure in churches. Empress Irene pushed through the reintroduction of icons; her successor proceeded to rescind this decision. In

843, the dispute was ended in favor of the artistic images with a festive ceremony in the Hagia Sophia.

The second major flowering of the empire began following Basileios I's (867-886) ascension to the throne. A consistent policy of expansion led to brilliant successes over the Arabs, Bulgarians and Russians. A portion of Armenia was annexed as well. The Christianization of the Slavic peoples during the 9th and 10th centuries contributed to the patriarch of Constantinoples' accretion of power. A split occurred between the eastern and western churches, which had become noticeable long before the separation was officially carried out. The papacy was an outgrowth of the Episcopate of Rome, and the *papa* (pope) thus claimed to rule over all of Christianity. From the viewpoint of the Byzantine emperor, this position of power belonged exclusively to the patriarchs. There were also differences in dogma between the two supreme clergymen. By means of mutual excommunications, the pope and patriarch consummated the final split into the Roman Catholic and Greek Orthodox Churches.

Following the iconoclastic dispute, a sort of cultural renaissance took place, particularly in the capital cities. The legacy of ancient Greece was contemplated. Classical education, philosophy, literature and the sciences gained in importance; the arts were also revived. Rulers in Western Europe commissioned Byzantine architects, painters and mosaic artists: Byzantine luxury goods, including sumptuous fabrics, gold and ivory work, enjoyed popularity. In the realm of architecture, a new type of church was created – the cruciform domed basilica – which appeared from then on to the end of the Byzantine Empire.

The successors of the Macedonian dynasty were unable to maintain the predominance the empire had assumed. Southern Italy was lost to the Normans; the Turkish Seljuks invaded Armenia. It

Right: The famous whirling dervishes, here in a "sema" performance in Konya.

didn't take long before the latter had forged ahead to the Aegean Sea and the Mediterranean coast. The empire did succeed in forcing the Seljuks back to Central Anatolia in 1097 with the assistance of the army of the First Crusade, which was underway with the mission of liberating Jerusalem. Despite an accord between Byzantium and the crusaders, by the terms of which all reconquered territory was to be incorporated into the Byzantine Empire, the crusaders established small independent realms of their own around Antioch and Edessa. On their campaigns into the Holy Land, they erected several mighty fortresses which are today among the most impressive of Asia Minor's historical monuments. In the Fourth Crusade, devoted to the liberation of the Holy Sepulcher, the knights captured Constantinople in order to depose the emperor. During one of the bloody palace revolutions, Emperor Alexius III Angelos (1195-1203) had had his brother, Isaac II Angelos, blinded and driven from the throne. The son of the

victim had approached the commander of the crusaders for help. This help was successful to the extent that Isaac II Angelos was re-coronated with much pomp and ceremony in the Hagia Sophia in the presence of his son, Alexius IV Angelos. However, the emperor and his son, who served as co-ruler, had to seek reconciliation with the Holy See as reciprocation for the assistance they had received. The Greek Byzantinians rebelled against this. Alexius IV was murdered; Isaac II lost his throne.

After the final break with the Byzantinians, the crusaders plundered Constantinople (1204) and destroyed many art treasures. At that time a Byzantine eyewitness to the plundering wrote: "Even the Saracens (Arabs) are merciful in comparison to these creatures who carry the cross of Christ on their shoulders." Following Western European examples, the crusaders founded the Latin Empire in the vicinity of Constantinople, while a sort of government-in-exile was set up in Nicaea.

By the time Michael VIII Palaeologus of Nicaea succeeded in winning back Constantinople in 1261, the city had utterly lost its political significance. The Venetians and Genoese had completely taken over the empire's foreign trade activities. Furthermore, the Turkish Seljuks were advancing inexorably, until finally the Byzantine state consisted of little more than Constantinople. Its last emperor, Constantine XI Palaeologus, met his demise in fighting for the city in 1453, after he had celebrated the last church service in the Hagia Sophia together with the Greeks and Latins.

The Seljuk Empire (1071-1307)

The history of the Seljuks began in the steppes of Asia north of the Aral Sea. Members of one of the Oguz Turkmen

Above: Süleyman the Magnificent (1494-1566), the sultan who not only presided over a Golden Age in the Ottoman Empire, but also led armies to the gates of Vienna.

tribes, they migrated to an area north of Iran around the 7th century. As a result of their conquests of Arab territory, they came into contact with Islam, which they eventually embraced.

Towards the middle of the 11th century, Tughril, the founder of the empire, conquered the Iranian interior and marched for Baghdad, which was shaken by riots at the time. In the year 1055, he assumed protectorate authority over the city and the entire Abbasid caliphate. In this manner, the Seljuk empire became the most powerful state in the Near East.

His successor, Alp Arslan, extended the empire to Mecca and, in 1071, inflicted a crushing defeat on the Byzantine army at Manzikert, not far from Lake Van. Now the path was clear to Asia Minor for the hosts of Turkish horsemen. In a short while they reached the Mediterranean coast and the Aegean Sea. Alp Arslan's successor, Süleyman, succeeded in gaining a foothold in Nicaea. He elevated it to his residence and established the first Seljuk state on Asia Minor's soil. Masud I, Süleyman's grandson – forced to retreat to central Anatolia by the Byzantines – founded the first Sultanate of Rum in Konya.

From that moment on, it could lay claim to being the most important national entity in Asia Minor. The word *Rum* was derived from "Rome", which was synonymous with "west". The rulers of the Anatolian branch of the Seljuk dynasty took on the name Rum Sultans in order to distinguish themselves from the Iranian Seljuks.

At the beginning of the 13th century, the Rum Seljuks managed to push ahead to the coast again and became engaged in maritime trade. Under Sultan Kaikubat I (1219-1236), the Seljuk empire achieved its greatest power and experienced a singular flowering of the arts and sciences. The sultan had lived for several years as an exile in Constantinople, thereby coming into contact with Byzantine culture.

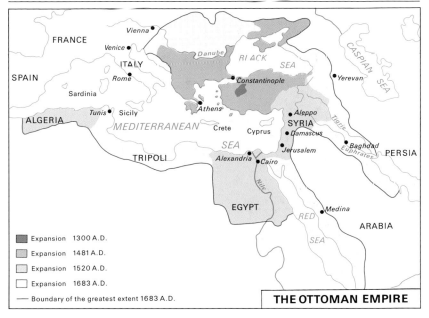

Expansion 1300 A.D.
Expansion 1481 A.D.
Expansion 1520 A.D.
Expansion 1683 A.D.
— Boundary of the greatest extent 1683 A.D.

THE OTTOMAN EMPIRE

In his capital city of Konya, he appointed scholars, poets and artists from Islamic countries.

The art of the Seljuks abided by Koranic law, although an early Turkish folk tradition evolved as well, melding Asian, Arabic, Persian, Armenian, and Greek-Byzantine elements into a unique style. The extensive architectural legacy of the Rum Seljuks consists of sacred buildings such as mosques and *türbes* (burial chapels of the nobility) as well as the immense fortress-like caravanserais along the trading routes. These served as both inns and roadhouses, as well as having the task of securing the highways. The larger of these facilities, which were established by the sultans, provided every manner of comfort and luxury to the traveling merchants. They were equipped with mosques, baths, kitchens, sleeping and living rooms, apothecaries, repair workshops, warehouse halls and stables. In addition, the Seljuks sponsored many Koran schools and hospitals. Also worthy of note are the multifaceted

and highly-developed applied arts in ceramics, woodcarving, relief work, coins and textiles. The art of making knotted carpets, an invention of nomadic tribes from interior Asia, achieved broader distribution due to the Seljuks. During this period, Anatolia must have been a leading center in the crafting of hand-knotted carpets.

Notwithstanding these extraordinary achievements in artistry and craftsmanship, when seen from a different perspective the penetration of the Turkish nomads resulted in the economic decline of Asia Minor, the decay of agriculture, and, particularly, the degeneration of urban culture. The Rum Seljuks never seriously attempted to eradicate Byzantium.

The invasion of the Mongolian hordes under Genghis Khan brought the brief blossoming of the Seljuk empire to an end. By 1241, the Mongols had seized Erzurum; in 1243, the Seljuks were vassals of the Mongols. In 1277, the Mamelukes attacked Anatolia. The Mameluke sultans were descendants of former

33

enslaved Turkish soldiers, and resided in Cairo. They fought the Mongolians and occupied the crusaders' city of Antioch. The Rum empire disintegrated into complete anarchy, even though it was formally under the sway of the Mongolian Khan in China. The last Seljuk ruler was assassinated in 1307.

The Ottoman Empire (1300-1923)

With the collapse of the Seljuk sultanate, the Oguz prince Osman of Eskisehir seized upon the opportunity to annex the surrounding principalities one after the other. In 1300, he wrenched several cities in northwestern Asia Minor from the Byzantine emperor and advanced as far as Bursa. When he died in 1324, the Ottoman Empire extended to the southern shores of the Sea of Marmara. His son Orhan succeeded in the conquest of

Above: The conquest of Constantinople in 1453 looks simpler than it really was in this miniature.

Bursa, which he then elevated to be his royal seat. He organized the first standing Osmanli army and founded the renowned Janissary corps. Orhan moved more energetically against the cities still occupied by the Byzantines, and soon had the entire coastal region up to the Straits of Bosphorus in his hands. Relations with Byzantium were not exclusively hostile, however. John Cantacuzenos, aspirant to the Byzantine throne, requested 6000 armed horsemen from Orhan so that he could prevail in his ambitions. In exchange, he gave Orhan his daughter's hand in marriage.

Following the fall of his father-in-law in 1355, Orhan issued troops over the Dardanelles and pushed ahead to Adrianople (Edirne). His son and successor, Murat I (1362-1389), managed to secure the Thracian possessions and make Edirne into the capital city of the Ottoman empire. Territoral expansion into eastern Europe made the relocation of the capital seem advisable. With their victory over the Serbs and Bulgarians at Kosovo in the year 1389, the Ottomans achieved supremacy over the Balkans: Murat, however, was assassinated in his tent by a Serbian deserter.

His son Beyazit (1389-1402) inherited a secured empire and the strongest military power in southeastern Europe. He was determined to conquer Constantinople, which by that time could only be reached by sea. Before he could realize that goal, a new horde of Mongols invaded Anatolia. Their commander, Tamerlane, pushed far into the interior of the land, plundering and murdering as he went. In 1402, there was a battle at Ankara in which Beyazit's troops suffered a devastating defeat. The sultan and his son Musa were taken prisoner. Tamerlane went back to Asia in order to conquer China, and soon released Prince Musa from captivity: Beyazit died as prisoner in 1403.

Then an embittered battle between brothers flared up within the royal family over the succession to the throne. After years of chaotic conditions, Mehmet I and Murat II were able to reestablish the unity of the Osmanli sultanate, an effort fostered by the beginnings of decay within the Mongolian empire following Tamerlane's death.

When Murat II died in Edirne in 1451, he bequeathed his 19-year-old son a consolidated empire. Mehmet II conquered Constantinople in 1453, renamed it Istanbul and made it his capital city. With the relocation of the governmental seat, he wanted to make clear that the Grand Sultan was stepping in as political and cultural successor to the Byzantine Emperor. As the latter had done, he retreated into his palace and governed as absolute ruler, surrounded by an elaborate, ceremonial court.

Mehmet II, who assumed the title "Lord of Both Continents and Both Seas", continued with his forefathers' policy of conquest. He sent his troops as far as the Crimean and south Italy, earning the appellation *Fatih* ("the Conquerer"). In domestic politics, he consolidated the empire by means of firmly establishing the responsibilities of the imperial offices and enacting the Fratricidal Law, according to which, an Ottoman ruler could have his brothers executed as soon as he had ascended to power. The measure was supposed to ensure that the sultan would be succeeded instead by his ablest son.

Beyazit II (1481-1512) assumed power and achieved merit particularly in the construction of bridges and roads. Leonardo da Vinci presented the sultan with plans for a bridge over the Golden Horn. He attempted to enlist the help of Michelangelo for the project, but the latter refused. At any rate, the construction of numerous mosques with a variety of ancillary buildings was realized, as was a library in Amasya with some 20,000 volumes, which is still being used today.

Beyazit's son and successor, Selim I (1512-1520) extended the Ottoman empire towards the east and southeast by conquering Armenia and twice (at Aleppo and Cairo) achieving victory over the Mamelukes: he subjugated Syria, Palestine, Egypt, Persia and Mecca, and transferred the caliphate of Egypt to Istanbul.

The most important figure ever to have occupied the Ottoman throne was Süleyman II (1520-1566). He led Turkey on its advance into Hungary, which couldn't be braked until it had reached Vienna in 1529. With this and his maritime victories over Carl V, Süleyman II brought the Turks to the zenith of their power. Corresponding to the requirements of a large state, he organized the legal system and administrative functions anew, earning himself the name *Kanuni* ("legislator") among his subjects. According to the new laws, the way to higher office now stood open to Muslims of non-Turkish heritage. These posts could be awarded and rescinded by the sultan alone. The grand vizier was his representative in all matters of civil and military nature. In the realm of culture as well, Süleyman did tremendous things. He loved courtly pomp and splendor and was therefore known in Europe as *The Magnificent*. As master builder he far overshadowed his predecessors. He renovated the dilapidated Byzantine water-delivery system, erected mosques and bridges, and had the Topkapi expanded into a palatial city surrounded with a wall.

With Sinan, the "Michelangelo of the East", he had at his side an inspired architect. European travelers of the 16th century reported with great enthusiasm on the magnificence of the Ottoman imperial city, although the "lesser arts" also flourished in the studios of the Topkapi Palace. Among the most impressive examples of these creations are ornamented weapons, carpets, calligraphy and illustrated books.

In the choice of his successor, Süleyman was less fortunate. Following old paternal custom, he had several of his sons and grandsons executed in order to secure the throne for Selim II, the son of his favorite wife Roxelana. Selim II went down in history as the "prunkard". Achmet, who ascended the throne in 1603, introduced a somewhat less bloody method of shutting out his rivals, although for the Ottoman dynasty it proved to be disastrous. He had the princes brought up in the "golden cage" of the harem, where they were in the company of over-indulgent mothers, eunuchs with their plots and intrigues, and concubines. In this environment they frequently turned into neurotic, weak- willed and effeminate individuals whose tastes leaned more toward luxury and a life of pleasure than toward coveting the throne and coping with the inconveniences which now and

Right: Mustafa Kemal, later known as Atatürk, during the failed British landing at Gallipoli in 1915.

then accompany the wielding of power. As a result, Mehmet IV (1648) wasn't able to bring himself to accompany his troops on the Second Siege of Vienna (1683). He had his grand vizier executed for the defeat. Furthermore, his son, Süleyman III, who came to power in 1687 after 40 years in the harem, requested a little while later to return to his comfortable prison.

Incapable rulers and harem intrigues were not the only forces weakening the empire. There were revolts by the powerful Janissary corps, growing corruption, and increasing restlessness amongst the major feudal lords of Anatolia. Bit by bit, the formerly proud empire was lost. When the Second Siege of Vienna remained unsuccessful, a veritable tide of wars washed over Turkey: Budapest, Belgrade and Peloponnesia fell, Austria expanded at the expense of the Turks, the Crimea went to Russia, and Egypt was lost to the French under Napoleon.

Several rulers attempted to counteract the internal dissolution of the empire by the introduction of reforms modeled after European examples. In 1826, Mahmut II (1808-1839) took drastic measures to shut out " once and for all " the Janissaries, who were opposed to any innovation. He assembled the elite troops on the parade grounds and had gunfire opened on them. 4000 soldiers died then and there, while thousands more were hunted down in the cities and provinces. Under pressure from the major powers, upon which Turkey had become more and more dependent, Mahmut conceived of an Ottoman empire with equal rights for all subjects regardless of religion or ethnic heritage; despite this liberalization, Serbia and Bulgaria demanded their independence. In order to deal with the empire's financial crisis, the government brought foreign capital into the country, conceding numerous monopolies and special privileges in exchange. Europe's influence over Turkey grew.

Abdül Hamit II (1876-1909) finally summoned Muslims from around the world to join together in battle against European predominance. Although he came to power as a reformer, he soon began espousing reactionary policies with which he hoped to save the disintegrating empire. He annulled the constitution and mobilized an omnipresent secret police in order to smother even the first signs of opposition. His policies ran aground on the aggressive pan-Turkish nationalism of the "Young Turks", emanating from Paris. They founded the "Committee for Unity and Progress" and toppled the sultan in 1909. The new sultan, Mehmet Rashad V, was lacking both power and influence.

Turkey in the 20th Century

Following the military collapse of the Ottoman Empire in the First World War, the English, French and Italians occupied portions of the Asia Minor Peninsula, while the Greeks landed in Izmir under British protection. According to the wishes of the victorious powers, the territory under the dominion of the sultanate was to be limited to central and northern Anatolia, as well as the vicinity surrounding Istanbul.

In 1919, General Mustafa Kemal appealed for resistance to the conditions of the ceasefire, calling for the formation of an independent state including Asia Minor in its entirety. On the 23rd of April, 1920, a new parliament convened in Ankara. The Grand National Assembly declared itself the representative of the nation and entrusted executive power to Mustafa Kemal. The new government failed to gain recognition abroad. On August 10th, the sultan's authorized representative signed the Treaty of Sèvres, which among other things stipulated the division of Anatolia into French, British and Italian zones of influence. The year hadn't even ended when an offensive by the Greeks triggered the Turkish War of Independence. It brought great losses to both sides, ending with a victory for

Mustafa Kemal and the flight of the Greeks from Asia Minor.

In the ensuing Peace Treaty of Lausanne, the independence and sovereignty of the new Turkish state were recognized, and its international boundaries determined. Furthermore, a resolution was passed which was most unfortunate for those affected, stipulating that the Greek population of Anatolia was to be exchanged for the Turkish inhabitants of Greece.

On October 29, 1923, Turkey was declared a republic, with Mustafa Kemal holding the office of president until his death in 1938. Sustained by an unshakable faith in progress, he proceeded to modernize Turkey. He abolished the caliphate and decreed new criminal, trade and civil laws, replacing the Islamic-based legal standards which had been in effect until then. Among the numerous, sensational reforms he enacted were the separation of religion and state, the dissolution of the Order of Dervishes, the introduction of the metric system, the Gregorian calendar, the Latin alphabet and the right to vote for women, the abolition of polygamy, and the legal obligation to take a surname. Because of its central location, Ankara was selected as the capital and underwent large-scale development into a major modern city.

After the death of Atatürk ("Father of the Turks" – this title was bestowed upon him by the National Assembly in 1934 for his service to the nation), Ismet Inonü, his old comrade-in-arms and co-worker of many years, assumed power of government. With considerable skill, he steered his country through the confusion of World War Two, declaring war on Germany in February 1945 so that upon the conclusion of peace, Turkey would stand

on the side of the victors. After the war, the calls for free elections could no longer be ignored. These took place in 1950, delivering the newly-founded Democratic Party of Adnan Menderes an overwhelming victory, after it made out the promise of free enterprise and the end of state economic control. In 1952, Turkey became a member of NATO. The unconditional affiliation of the new government with the foreign policy of the western powers, an ambitious program of industrialization and the foreign debt which accompanied it, as well as the devaluation of the currency resulted in considerable social unrest.

In 1960, the army carried out the first of three military coup d'états within the next two decades. Menderes and some of his secretaries of state were imprisoned and condemned to death. In the period which followed, there was a variety of coalition governments: These, however, were unable to follow through with all of their announced reforms. When the conduct of the Turkish government regarding Cyprus strained foreign relations, the domestic scene was threatened by terrorism from right-wing extremist groups, and unemployment and mounting inflation brought about a chaotic state of affairs, the generals staged another coup in 1980.

They drafted a new constitution, which was adopted with 92 percent of the vote in a 1982 referendum. The ANAP ("Fatherland Party") of Turgut Özal emerged as the strongest party from the elections of 1983. In 1989, Özal became the eighth president of the Republic of Turkey. Consistent with its western-oriented policies and economy, Turkey has aspired for years towards full membership in the European Community.

In the parliamentary elections of Autumn 1991, the "Party of the Proper Path" was the strongest. Its chairman Süleyman Demirel formed a coalition government with the Social Democrats.

Right: Under the watchful eye of the history of the Ottoman Empire, a Turk stands in the shadows of the splendid Dolmabahçe Palace.

CITY ON THE BOSPORUS

ISTANBUL

ISTANBUL

Since Greek and Roman times, Europe and Asia, Occident and Orient, have converged on the Bosporus. Legend has it that King Byzas of Megara founded the city of Byzantium in 667 B.C. on the long, rocky peninsula stretching between the body of water called the Golden Horn and the straits known since antiquity as the Bosporus. After the city had been fought over as a trading station for centuries, its hour had come at last when the Emperor Constantine made Byzantium the capital of the Roman Empire in A.D. 330, thus fulfilling his hopes of a second Rome. The city was now christened Constantinople after him. Later, the emperor Justinian (527-565) raised Constantinople to eminence as the spiritual center of Christendom by erecting the splendid Church of Hagia Sophia (the name is Greek for "Divine Wisdom"). Justinian's reign is considered the Golden Age of the Byzantine Empire, which at that time spread from the Euphrates River to what is now the Rock of Gibraltar, and from the Alps to the Nile. However, it was the devastation of the city by the crusaders in

Preceding pages: The silhouette of Istanbul, marked by a forest of minarets, glows in the evening sun.

1204 which ultimately spelled the beginning of its decline. A last brilliant Byzantine era followed before the Ottoman sultan Mehmet II captured the city in 1453. Constantinople soon had a new name: Istanbul. Nevertheless, it remained essentially a cultural melting pot.

Hagia Sophia

When Emperor Justinian entered the Hagia Sophia on December 27th in 548 to consecrate it, he was overwhelmed by the unprecedented size and splendor of the basilica. He gave thanks to God and cried out: "Solomon, I have surpassed thee!" This magnificent church, standing as it does on the city's highest hill, was to embody the center of the Christian world as a symbol of spiritual and temporal power. In just five years a domed structure was erected by the renowned architects Anthemius of Tralles and Isidorus of Miletus. With a dome 55.6 m high and 32 m in diameter, and walls pierced by rows of windows, the church of Hagia Sophia has always seemed so luminously light that the historian Procopius enthusiastically described the dome as suspended from heaven on a golden chain. The Justinian Hagia Sophia is standing on ruins. In 404, the church which had been erected by Emperor Constantine burned down. The five-aisled basilica built by the Emperor Theodosius II and completed in 415 was destroyed in the Nika Insurrection (see "Hippodrome"). Excavations have uncovered remains of the vestibule which can be seen in front of the central entrance of Hagia Sophia.

Above the main entrance to the narthex, the **Emperor's Portal**, a mosaic depicts its donor, the Emperor Leo VI (886-912), kneeling before Christ. Above it in medallions are the Virgin Mary and the Archangel Gabriel. The mosaic is among the earliest of the Hagia Sophia. Unfortunately for art historians and art lovers, the splendid Justinian mosaics were destroyed by the iconoclasts (729-843). This group of fanatical religious purists regarded image worship as a return to the heathen cult of idols.

On the left, a ramp over which Justinian's empress Theodora had herself carried in a litter, leads to the **gallery,** which is well worth seeing. The right-hand gallery contains a moving *deesis* (prayer) mosaic in the empress' loge. Such scenes were typically Byzantine. This one probably dates back to the early 13th century. It depicts Christ Pantocrator ("ruler of all"), his hand raised in a gesture of blessing, the Virgin Mary and John the Baptist at his side. Before Hagia Sophia was made a museum in 1934 by Kemal Atatürk, the figurative mosaics, which had been covered by a thick layer of plaster since the days of Süleyman the Magnificent, were uncovered. Across from them in the floor is the slab covering the grave of the Venetian Doge Enrico Dandolo, who led the Fourth Crusade and destroyed the city in 1204. On the end wall of the right-hand gallery, the emperor and empress are portrayed as donors, carrying the standard attributes of purse and deed. To the far left there is a good view of the apse mosaic: the Virgin Mary is portrayed seated, holding the Infant Christ on her knee (9th century). From left to right an imposingly hieratic procession of

emperors and empresses unfolds: Constantine IX Monomachus and Zoe with Christ Pantocrator (11th century); then John II Comnenus and Irene with the Virgin Mary and Child (12th century); to the far right, Alexius, the son of John II Comnenus.

Back at the Emperor's Portal, one enters the sumptuously-decorated **nave** of the church. The green granite columns down the sides are from ancient Ephesus, the red porphyry columns in the corner niches from Baalbek, and the marble panels on the walls from the Isles of Marmara. The Byzantine basket capitals bearing the monograms of Justinian and Theodora look indeed like filigree. The lunettes on the side walls are decorated with representations of the major Byzantine saints. Slightly to the right of the apse, in which the altar stands, the spot where the emperors were crowned is marked by a colorful plate mosaic. In the Byzantine era this holy place was considered to be the navel of the world, the *omphalos.*

After taking Constantinople in 1453, Mehmet II made Hagia Sophia the main mosque, turning it into a Muslim place of worship. A prayer niche facing Mecca, known as a *mihrab*, was built into the apse wall at a slight angle. To the left of the apse is the mid-19th century, octagonal sultan's loge, designed and built by the Swiss architect Gaspar Fossati. It stands on ancient columns. It can be entered from outside. In it the sultan could remain undisturbed at prayer. To the right of the apse rises the *minber*, the pulpit from which the sermon is given on Friday. On the marble rostrum before it, the muezzin himself prayed after summoning the faithful from the mosque's tower, the minaret. On huge round plaques suspended in the central bay, the names of Allah, Mohammed and the first caliphs are in gold on a green background. Green is the holy color of Islam. The two large marble vessels under the

rear gallery, at which Islamic worshippers could perform their ablutions, came originally from heathen Pergamum. They are said to have been Alexander the Great's coffers of state. The "weeping column" (left, rear) is considered by the faithful to work miracles.

Looking up, one spots fine ornamental gold mosaics under the galleries and in the narthex. On the right **side portal**, accessible from the narthex, a mosaic depicts the Virgin Mary and Christ Child. At their side are Constantine with a model of the city, and Justinian with a model of the church (10th century). One leaves the church through an ancient bronze door (2nd century B.C.) from Tarsus, the city where the Apostle Paul was born. Outside, on the left, is the Justinian baptistery, now the last resting place of several sultans. To the right across from it stands a handsome purification fountain in the ornate Turkish rococo style.

Above: Stillness for reflection in the Hagia Sophia in Istanbul. Right: The Blue Mosque.

The path now leads to Sultan Ahmet Square. Glancing back at Hagia Sophia, one sees the powerful buttresses which have been supporting it since the Ottoman era and cannot overlook the four minarets – added by various sultans over the course of a century.

The Sultan Ahmet Camii, the renowned **Blue Mosque**, now awaits you. *Cami*, which is pronounced "jami", meaning "mosque" in Turkish. In 1609, Sultan Ahmet I commissioned Mehmet Aga, a pupil of the famous Turkish architect Sinan, to build a new principal mosque. Its six minarets and impressive pyramid of domes were intended to counterbalance Hagia Sophia. To emphasize the preeminence of Mecca, which also had six minarets, Sultan Ahmet commissioned a seventh minaret for Mecca.

One enters the outer courtyard, surrounded by an openwork wall, through a gate to the left side portal, through which sightseers are expected to enter the mosque. The front of the mosque, to the right, faces west towards the At Meydani,

which was once the Byzantine Hippodrome. On this side are the main door and the inner forecourt, surrounded by a colonnade roofed with cupolas. The forecourt contains the purification fountain, called *sadirvan* in Turkish. Devout Muslims are expected to live by five precepts, the "Five Pillars of Islam": Faith, prayer, almsgiving, fasting and pilgrimage. Prayers must be said five times daily at prescribed times. Before praying in the mosque, believers perform ritual ablutions, washing face, hands (to the elbows) and feet (to the knees) at the fountain in the courtyard of the mosque. In Turkey, non-Muslims may also enter mosques but they must remove their shoes at the entrance. Women should also cover their hair with a scarf.

In the interior of the Blue Mosque, massive gray marble columns, appropriately termed "elephant legs", support the weight of the dome. The more than 20,000 tiles from Iznik, ancient Nicaea, which cover the lower walls and the ladies' loge in the gallery gave the Blue Mosque its name. They are alive with superb floral designs – tulips, carnations, roses, hibiscuses, cypresses – all stylized to form ornamental patterns in shades of blue, green and brown. The white marble *mihrab* contains a piece of the sacred Black Stone from the Kaaba in Mecca. The white marble *minbar* is a replica of the *minbar* at Mecca.

Whenever there was not enough room in the mosque at Friday noon prayers, the forecourt also became a place of worship. This caused little or no inconvenience because – thanks in part to the elevation of the *minbar* – the Friday sermon could be heard through the open doors. All the major religious and political meetings took place in this courtyard under the reign of the sultans. This was where the major Islamic festivals, the sugar and sacrificial festivals, *seker bayrami* and *kurban bayrami*, were celebrated. Even more important, this was the spot from which pilgrimages to Mecca started.

The translucency of the *mihrab* walls in the Blue Mosque turns sunlight into

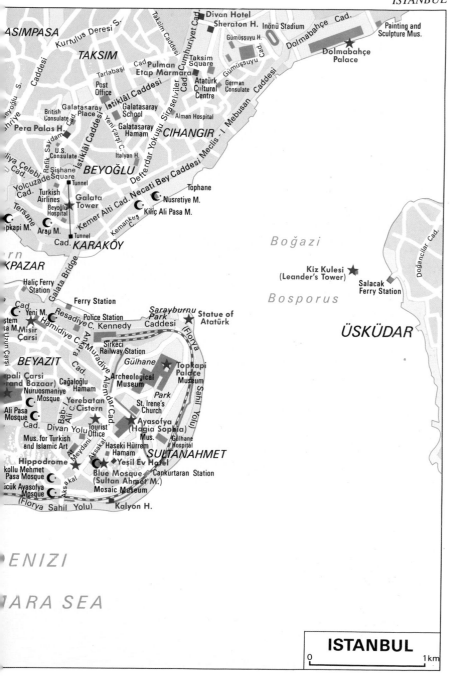

ISTANBUL

0   1 km

dancing colors, inspiring an almost Gothic feeling of space. One leaves the mosque through the left side portal. You can turn right down the restored bazaar street to the **Mosaic Museum.** The massive foundations of the Blue Mosque rest on what little remains of the Byzantine imperial palaces. A few floor mosaics in the Mosaic Museum nevertheless convey some idea of their former grandeur.

From the Mosaic Museum an alley leads down to the **Küçük Ayasofya Camii,** little Hagia Sophia, or the Church of Saints Sergius and Bacchus. This small church was built by Anthemius of Tralles between 527 and 536 as a study for its great namesake. The foundation legend is depicted in an elaborate frieze. The story is that Justinian had conspired against the Emperor Anastasius I, who therefore wanted to execute him. In a

Above: A hodgepodge of styles, including Antique, Byzantine and Ottoman, can be observed in such a secular place as the Hippodrome in Istanbul.

dream, St. Sergius interceded with the emperor on Justinian's behalf. Justinian subsequently built the little church as an offering of thanks. Unfortunately, nothing else remains of its fine mosaics.

One reaches the **Sokollu Mehmet Pasa Camii** by way of the Mehmet Pasa Sokagi. *Sokak* means "alley". Sokollu Mehmet Pasa, a Bosnian, was one of the mightiest grand viziers in the Ottoman Empire. This mosque, which he commissioned in 1571, is one of Sinan's more mature works (see "Suleymaniye"), and is truly noteworthy for its splendid tiles from Isnik.

The street leads uphill to the At Meydani or **Hippodrome.** In the Byzantine era, the Hippodrome was the hub of public life. Built in 203 by Septimius Severus according to the example of the Circus Maximus in Rome, the Hippodrome was enlarged under Constantine I to seat 100,000. Here the great chariot races as well as circuses and gladiatorial battles were held. The imperial family could watch the spectacles in comfort from their loggia on the eastern tiers of seats. The Hippodrome was the scene of two major bloody revolts.

Here, the bloody Nika Insurrection was crushed by Justinian's general, Belisarius. "Nika", meaning "Conquer!" in Greek, was the cry of spectators at the races, supporters of charioteers in either blue or green garb. Known accordingly as the Blues and Greens, these competing factions corresponded to rival divisions in the urban militia. Generally more interested in sports than politics, the groups united in 532, went on a rampage, and sought to overthrow the emperor. Large parts of the city were devastated – and Justinian nearly lost his throne – before Belisarius succeeded in confining the rioters in the Hippodrome and slaughtering 30,000 of them.

On this same spot, Sultan Mahmut II massacred the Janissaries who were rebelling against his reforms in 1826. In the early Ottoman Empire the sultan's elite troop, the Janissaries, were accorded special privileges. Recruited by compulsory levy from Christian families in subdued territories, they received a special education as Muslim converts at the sultan's court. The reforms of Mahmut II aimed at putting an end to their disproportionate power.

Ancient testimony to the past grandeur of this square stands on its central axis, the *spina*. In the reign of Constantine, the serpent column from the Apollo Sanctuary at Delphi was brought here. It was cast from bronze arms captured by the Greeks from the Persians at the Battle of Plataea in 479 B.C. In 390, the Emperor Theodosius I added an obelisk of the Pharaoh Thutmose III (1504-1450 B.C.). The imperial family is portrayed in bas relief on the marble base, where the erection of the obelisk is depicted. A reminder of more recent events is the Kaiser Wilhelm fountain, which was presented by the German Kaiser to Sultan Abdül Hamit II in 1895.

Along the west side of the square stretches the **Ibrahim Pasa Sarayi** (*Saray* means "palace" in Turkish), a tranquil oasis where the noteworthy Museum of Turkish and Islamic Art is housed. Ibrahim Pasa was grand vizier under Süleyman the Magnificent. A dubious action of the sultan in the Topkapi Palace put an end to the great man's all too meteoric career.

The first tour ends in front of Hagia Sophia on the east side of Sultan Ahmet Square, at the **Haseki Hürrem Hamami.** Roxelana, who was Süleyman the Magnificent's favorite wife, commissioned the architect Sinan to build this Turkish bath in 1556. It is symmetrically divided into men's and women's sections. A side street leads from here along the east front of Hagia Sophia to the **Fountain of Ahmet III,** a beautiful early 18th century piece of Turkish rococo at the entrance to the Topkapi Palace. There are, in addition, several carefully-restored wooden houses near the Haseki Hanim Hürrem Hamami and the wall enclosing the Topkapi Palace. Such traditional wooden houses gave the city its character until well into the 1950s. Today, modern functional concrete buildings have radically changed the cityscape.

The Topkapi Palace

The **Topkapi Sarayi,** the Palace of the Cannon Gate, named after a Byzantine Gate on the side facing the sea, was the seat of the Turkish sultans for centuries. Through the **Bab-i-Hümayun,** the Gateway to the Empire, one enters the first of the four spacious courtyards of the sprawling palace precincts. The Ottomans were only too well aware of how to make good use of Seraglio Point. They settled on the site of the acropolis of ancient Byzantium. The earliest buildings here date back to the 1460s, in the reign of Mehmet II. The latest was built about 1839, before Sultan Abdül Mecit I made

the Dolmabahçe Palace his residence. In its heyday, from the mid-16th to the mid-18th centuries, the palace housed about 5000, which meant that it was really a small walled city. An army of domestics dressed in the costumes of their trades served and supplied the palace.

In the first courtyard, which is now a parking area for buses, were the storerooms and the bakery. The courtyard also served as a parade and drill ground for the Janissaries. To the left of the gate is the Church of **Hagia Irene**, which was consecrated to Blessed Peace in 300 and is one of the city's earliest churches. In the reign of Theodosius I, the important Second Ecumenical Council (381) met here to lay the foundations of the Christian faith. After being destroyed in the Nika Insurrection, the Church of Hagia Irene was rebuilt by Justinian. The Ot-

Above: The "Tugra," the signature used by the Ottoman sultans. Right: Not everyone was allowed to pass through the doors to the harem in the Topkapi Palace.

tomans used it as an armory. One of the porphyry sarcophagi in the church vestibule is said to have been Constantine the Great's last resting place.

One reaches the second courtyard and the Palace Museum through the **Bab-i-Selam,** the Gate of Salutation. Flanked by turrets, the gate was built by Süleyman the Magnificent in 1524. It reflects the admiration for European castles which the sultan had felt on his campaigns in the Balkans and Hungary. The gatehouse was capacious enough to serve as a prison for men condemned to death, and the heads of those executed were displayed above it on pikes. The most striking building in the second courtyard, and a distinctive feature of the palace's silhouette, is the **Kubbealti** on the left. This was the assembly room of the Ottoman council of state, the *divan*.

Behind the Kubbealti is the entrance to the mysterious and long-inaccessible harem. The Turks learned polygamy from the Arabs. The harem was not very large, however, until the era of Süleyman the

Magnificent in the 16th century because the sultans' numerous campaigns hardly left them time for private life. In its prime the harem had 400 rooms. Only a few of them are currently open to visitors. Going through the black eunuchs' compound and passing the princes' schoolrooms, one arrives in the quarters of the odalisques. These were slaves who lived in the harem as concubines and were waited on by servants of lowlier status. Women who bore the sultan sons became favorite "wives", but the most important female in the household was the *valide sultan*, the mother of the present ruler. The fact that her sumptuous apartments were right next to his hints at the extent of her influence. Some rooms in the harem are exquisitely decorated with tiles and intarsia, in particular the so-called "Gilded Cage". Here – in virtual seclusion – the crown prince awaited the day when he might strap on the Sword of Osman to obey the law of Fratricidal.

Along the right side of the second courtyard, the **palace kitchens** contain a superb collection of Far Eastern and European porcelain. Through the **Bab-i-Saadet**, the Gate of Bliss, one reaches the third courtyard. Also called the Gate of the White Eunuchs, this portal was the jealously-guarded public entrance to the sultan's private realm. Only particularly prominent guests were received in the **Arz Odasi**, his audience hall, right behind the gate. At the center of this courtyard is the **Library of Ahmet III**, decorated with exquisite tiles and mother-of-pearl and ivory intarsia. The **Treasury**, which is located on the right side of the courtyard, contains fabulous treasures such as the famous golden Topkapi dagger set with emeralds and the "Spoonmaker Diamond". Devout Muslims consider the **Collection of Relics** the greatest treasure. Here objects belonging to Mohammed and his early comrades-in-arms have been preserved. Sultan Selim brought them back from his campaign to Mecca, Medina and Egypt in 1517. Other rooms worth visiting in this courtyard house the sultan's imperial robes, the

Gallery of Miniatures which contains calligraphy and portraits of the sultans and a **clock collection.**

At the tip of Seraglio Point lies the garden of the **fourth courtyard**. It boasts a superb view over the Golden Horn, the Bosporus and the Sea of Marmara. During the 18th century "Tulip Period" (*lale devri*), when a tulip craze swept the Ottoman Empire, the sultan and his wives enjoyed glittering parties on moonlit April nights here amid flowering tulip beds. In the **Circumcision Pavilion** to the far left, a major event in the young princes' lives took place, the first step towards adulthood. In front are the magnificent **Baghdad and Erivan Pavilions.** Murat IV (162-340) built them with the plunder garnered from his Persian campaign. The most recent building in the Topkapi Palace is the **Mecidiye Pavilion**, at the right, which Sultan Abdül Mecit had built shortly before moving into the

Above: The covered bazaar in Istanbul is one of the places to go to see local color.

Dolmabahçe Palace in 1839. Tired visitors can take refreshment on the terrace or in the restaurant there. If you seek quiet, it is advised to eat lunch before or after the usual hours. Sultan Ibrahim (1640-48) could dine pleasantly under the gilded baldachin of the **Iftariye** on the far side of the garden. But during Ramadan, the Muslim month of fasting, he had to wait until a white thread was found to be indistinguishable from a black one to partake of his meal (*iftar* = evening meal during Ramadan).

Once again in the first courtyard, we pass through a side gate to the **Museum of Oriental Antiquities**. The earliest peace treaty in history, which was concluded between the Hittite King Hattusilis II and the Egyptian Pharaoh Ramses II in 1269 B.C., can be seen here. Here is also the **Archeological Museum** with the famous Alexander sarcophagus, and the **Cinili Kösk**, a small castle built by Mehmet II. Its decoration reveals Seljuk and Persian influence. Below it is **Gülhane Park,** a zoological garden accessible only to the sultan's family in Ottoman times. Today it is a public park. On Sundays, especially, it is noisy and colorful. Leaving the park and heading for the water, one can cross **Sarayburnu Park** and watch the busy ship traffic on the glistening waterway. The exit from the other side of Gülhane Park leads to the right along the outer palace wall to the **Sublime Porte.** In the Ottoman era it was synonymous with the Turkish government. Until 1923 it was the entrance to the precincts of the grand vizier. Following the street downhill, one reaches **Sirkeci Station**, last stop of the fabled Orient Express on the European side. A ferry from Karaköy goes to Haydarpasa Station on the Asian side. From there one can travel on eastwards with the Baghdad Railway.

Around the Bazaar

Ankara Caddesi leads up from Sirkeci Station past **Valilik,** the impressive residence of the governors of Istanbul Province, to Cagaloglu District, which is both the center of the Turkish press and the carpet merchant's headquarters. To the left in the direction of Sultan Ahmet Square is the famous **Yerebatan Sarayi,** the sunken "castle" that Emperor Justinian had built to supply the city with water. Visitors can descend into the restored cistern. They find themselves venturing into an enchanted world of illusory dancing lights and music.

Again on Sultan Ahmet Square, you can turn west into the heavy traffic of Divan Yolu, originally a Byzantine boulevard. At the corner of Ankara Caddesi stands the **Mausoleum** *(türbe)* **of Mahmut II** (1808-39). It was he who crushed the Janissary rebellion on the Hippodrome Square. Across from the mausoleum is the **Köprülü Library,** well stocked with the books and documents of this family of statesmen that was so influential in the 17th and 18th

centuries. Down the street is the "burnt column", called **Çemberlitas** ("banded stone") by the Turks on account of the iron rings supporting it. Surmounted by a golden statue of the sun god Apollo, as whom Emperor Constantine was fond of representing himself, it formed the center of the magnificent Forum of Constantine, a vast ancient square. Flanking the square is the **Nuruosmaniye Camii,** the city's first 18th century Baroque mosque. This mosque is not a further development of the single-domed structures perfected by Sinan. The purity of classical Ottoman architecture, revealing structural relationships, has here yielded to dainty ornamental forms disguising the breadth of the mosque. The street diagonally across from Pasa boasts the **mosque** and *türbe* of **Kara Mustafa,** Grand Vizier of Mehmet IV. Since he proved to be unable to take Vienna in 1683, he was beheaded by the sultan.

To the right as one proceeds down Divan Yolu, the bazaar unfolds, extending to the Golden Horn. Its western boundary is the **Dove Mosque of Beyazit II,** who was son of Mehmet the Conqueror. The doves are said to descend from a pair the sultan bought from a beggar. Beyazit, who was devoutly conservative, tended to take Islamic rather than Byzantine architecture as his model. The splendid Moorish gate above the square leads to the **Istanbul University.** Behind it was once the first palace of Mehmet II (before the sultan moved to the Topkapi), and later the Ottoman Ministry of War. Back when most city houses were built of wood, the fire alarm was spread from the **Beyazit Tower,** now a weather station.

Beyond the university the vast complex of the Süleyman Mosque, **Süleymaniye Camii,** crowns the city's fifth hill high above the Golden Horn. The three greatest architects of the Ottoman era were named Sinan; the most famous of them is sometimes referred to as "the Turkish Michelangelo". It was he who

was commissioned, by Süleyman the Magnificent to build this, perhaps Istanbul's finest mosque. Started in 1550, it took seven years to complete. In emulation of Hagia Sophia, its central axis is emphasized by two semidomes supporting the central dome, with four supporting pillars far off to the sides. Without attempting to surpass the dimensions of Hagia Sophia, Sinan's domed structure, with its light-flooded spatial conception, conveys to one lingering within a feeling of floating in inner peace. Hollow blocks in the dome ensure ideal acoustics for common prayers, as well as for the sermon. A sophisticated ventilation system once drew off air, sooty from countless oil lamps, through a small gauze-covered window in the rear portal. The soot trapped in the gauze was used as the basic ingredient of the sultan's ink.

Above: The inner walls of the Rüstem Pasa Mosque are covered with intricately painted tiles. Right: The Topkapi offers a view of the Golden Horn and the Bosporus.

In the mosque's southern outer courtyard are the *türbe* of Süleyman and his favorite wife, the Russian Roxelana. Sinan's *türbe* is to the north, outside the wall around the mosque. An extensive *külliye* precinct surrounds the mosque. The term *külliye* refers to the charitable institutions belonging to a mosque, in this case a Koran school *(medrese)*, a hospital, baths, a public kitchen *(imaret)*, lodgings for travelers and the homeless, and a bazar. In the narrow alleys west of Süleyman's mosque, one can still spot some fine examples of the wooden houses typical of old Istanbul.

Returning to the street in front of the university, Cadircilar Caddesi, booklovers may enter a paradise, the **Sahaflar Çarsisi,** or book market. Beyond it, on the left side, is an entrance to the world of the **Kapali Çarsi,** the bazaar. All the riches and enchantments of the Orient await visitors in the thousands of shops here. One is likely to be invited to a glass of tea, for the bazaar is a delightfully hospitable place. Each guild used to have its own lane. Some of this still remains. At the heart of the bazaar are the small goldsmiths' and silk merchants' shops. Further out are more humble materials including readymade clothing. Then come the open streets with the workshops of tin and coppersmiths and joiners.

Down at the bottom on the Golden Horn, diagonally across from Galata Bridge, is the L-shaped building which houses the Egyptian Bazaar, the **Misir Çarsisi.** The scent of spices, herbs, dried fruits, freshly-roasted coffee, smoked fish, mingling with the perfume of all sorts of exotic essences, is intoxicating. Over the vaulted entrance, the famous Pandeli Restaurant caters to the famished as well as the discriminating. From the right side gate of the Egyptian Bazaar, an alley leads to the **Rüstem Pasa Camii.** Rüstem Pasa, grand vizier and son-in-law of Süleyman the Magnificent and enormously rich, commissioned Sinan to

build this gem in the bustling bazaar quarter on the Golden Horn. It is decorated with marvelous Iznik tiles. The visitor reaches the forecourt, supported by vaulted shops beneath, and the entrance to the mosque by climbing a narrow stair.

Outside the hours of prayer, one is at leisure to study the imaginative painting of the individual tiles as well as the bands and surfaces composed by them. The arabesques show a great variety of flowers, but tulips particularly intrigued the tile painters since they seem stylized by nature.

Across the street from the spice bazaar at the end of Galata Bridge rises the **Yeni Valide Cami,** a late 16th century mosque commissioned by the mother of Sultan Mehmet III. This part of Istanbul is considered the liveliest. Here traffic converges to cross the Golden Horn or, coming from the other side, disperses. Here passengers from the Bosporus ferries and numerous bus lines meet, creating endless waves of pedestrians. Here pedlars mingle with the crowds, hawking their wares, and all are surrounded by flocks of pigeons pecking, and unperturbed by the chaos.

The Golden Horn

The Golden Horn, named after its hornlike shape and the golden shimmer it assumes at sunset, stretches 7 km from Galata Bridge to its two tributaries, "The Sweet Waters of Europe". Its mud is thought to conceal great treasures: As a natural harbor it was often the site of hefty sea battles. When the city of Constantinople fell in 1204, the crusaders breached the sea wall from here. In 1453 Mehmet II had his ships drawn on a wooden slipway across Pera ridge to the Golden Horn, and attempted to take the city from here. The defenderrs had blocked the natural entrance to the harbor with a heavy chain. For centuries groves along the Golden Horn concealed the summer residences and pavilions of the upper class. When the city became industrialized, the once-sparkling waters of the Golden Horn turned into a sewer. In recent years, radical redevelopment of the shoreline has given it an air of romance again. Small boats depart from **Haliç Iskelesi** behind the Chamber of Commerce on the Old City quay on excursions up the Golden Horn, stopping at particularly attractive spots on the Bosporus or the Princes Islands. You can also take one of scheduled ferries that stop at Galata Bridge.

The Fener district, from the Greek *phanari* ("lighthouse"), lies beyond **Atatürk Bridge,** the second of three bridges spanning the Golden Horn. About 30 years ago this was still a bustling Greek quarter. Attending mass in the Greek Orthodox **Patriarchal Church**, Hagios Georgios, one is among the few worshippers left. The Neo-Gothic **Church of St. Stephan the Bulgarian** stands on the shore between Fener and Balat. It was built of cast-iron parts brought down the Danube from Vienna. In the adjacent Balat (an incorrect rendering of "palace" parts of the Byzantine **Tekfur Sarayi**, also called the Palace of Constantine, have been preserved. In the 1400s, Spanish Jews sought refuge in this quarter from the pogroms of the Inquisition. In the old Ahrida Synagogue, the holy service is still held in Hebrew or the ancient Ladino dialect.

About on a level with **Haliç Bridge**, the third bridge spanning the Horn, the Byzantine inland fortifications intercept the seawall. At this point **Eyüp** begins. This surburb was named after Mohammed's standard bearer, Eyüp Ensari, who fell in front of the walls during the first siege of the city by the Arabs (674-78). After the Ottomans took the city, a monument was erected to him here. In its mosque, Eyüp Sultan Camii, the sultans girded on the sword of Osman upon ascending the throne, a rite corresponding

Right: Daily life in Fatih. Far right: The mosaic in the Fethiye Mosque.

to the European coronation ceremony. Behind the *türbe* on the slope extends a vast Muslim graveyard. Many devout Muslims wanted to be buried near this meritorious intercessor.

It is a delightful walk from here to the **Café** of the Turkophile French writer, **Pierre Loti** (1850-1923). The novelist cultivated his romantic muse in Eyüp during the mid-19th century. It is a pleasure to gaze at the distinctive skyline over a cup of mocca or tea. All Istanbul lies at your feet.

Along the City Wall

Once again at the city wall, the path follows the inland fortifications to the **Edirne Gate**, the Byzantine Charisius Gate. About 20 km of largely preserved walls around the Old City bear testimony to the strength of its defences. In 1453, Mehmet II stood before this mighty bulwark to launch his decisive assault on the Romanos Gate a short distance to the south, now the Topkapi or Cannon Gate (not to be confused with the Topkapi Palace on Seraglio Point). Until then, the walls had withstood siege and earthquake for the past 1000 years. Because the sultans also depended on the protection which the walls afforded, they repaired them. But building the railway along the Sea of Marmara damaged them severely.

The **Mihrimah Camii** rises to the right beyond the Edirne Gate. Mihrimah, the daughter of Süleyman the Magnificent and wife of the grand vizier Rüstem Pasa, was in a position to commission Sinan to build a mosque. The master's touch is unmistakable.

Across from it, a short street leads to another Istanbul gem, the **Kariye Museum,** better known as Chora Church. The splendid mosaics in the outer and inner narthexes graphically illustrate the lives of Christ and the Virgin Mary. The early 14th century frescoes in the parecclesion, or funerary chapel, south of nave

also enchant literate people of modern times. Around the church is another group of restored wooden houses. Tey are best enjoyed from a cosy tea garden.

The path now leads once again from Edirnekapi either along Fevzi Pasa Caddesi (*cadde*, pronounced "jadde", means "street") into the city, or further along the inland fortifications towards the Sea of Marmara. Going into the city one passes Vefa Stadium on the left, once the open Well of Aetius, to reach the **Sultan Mehmet Fatih Camii.** After taking the city, Sultan Mehmet II commissioned his first mosque to be built on the ruins of the Church of the Apostles of Constantine I. Destroyed by an earthquake in 1766, the mosque was rebuilt. The Fatih Mosque adjoins the largest *külliye* complex in Istanbul.

Via Darüssafaka Caddesi you can reach the **Sultan Selim Camii** a short distance to the north. Süleyman the Magnificent commissioned it in honor of his father, Selim the Grim, who had incorporated the holy Muslim lands of Arabia

into the Ottoman Empire. Sinan's predecessor, the Persian architect Acem Ali, built it. Covered by only one dome, the interior is strongly reminiscent of early Ottoman cubic structures.

One street to the west is the **Fethiye Camii,** once the Church of the Theotokos Pammakaristos (Joyous Mother of God). Mehmet II left this church to the Patriarch Gennadios, who opposed the Pope. Not until 1591, during the reign of Murat III, was it turned into the "Mosque of the Conquest" to commemorate Ottoman conquests in Azerbaijan and the Caucasus. The fine 14th century mosaics which have been exposed in the dome depict Christ and the 12 Apostles.

Further in towards the city, the 4th century **Valens Aqueduct** runs along the left side of the main road. It brought water from the Belgrade Woods to the north of the city to wells within the city limits. The modern complex off to the right is Istanbul's City Hall, **Belediye Sarayi.** Across from it is the **Sehzade Camii,** the Princes' Mosque, commissioned by Sü-

leyman the Magnificent in 1544 as a memorial to his son Mehmet. The boy had died of smallpox a year earlier and is buried in a *türbe* in the mosque's garden along with several of his siblings. Other prominent tombs here include those of the grand viziers Rüstem Pasa and Ibrahim Pasa. As this was Sinan's first major mosque, it is considered a kind of "apprenticeship". It has a central dome supported by four semidomes. By continuing along the main road (Sehzadebasi Caddesi) one arrives again at the university campus.

It is worthwhile to follow the **inland fortifications** downhill from Edirnekapi to the Sea of Marmara. Across from the *Topkapi*, the Cannon Gate, life in what passes as a modern caravanserai can be observed around the clock, for there the huge **bus station** is located. Big fluorescent signs announce departures to destinations in all directions. However, in-

Above: The Galata Bridge is almost always swarming with people.

stead of camels, donkeys and horses, powerful air-conditioned buses transport modern travelers.

Following the wall almost to its southern tip, one reaches the **Golden Gate**, built in the 4th century by Theodosius I. The Via Egnatia led from it to imperial Rome. Once a free-standing triumphal arch, it was integrated into the fortifications built by Theodosius II in the 5th century. Four of the towers of **Yedikule** date from this period; three more were added in the 14th century by the Ottomans. It therefore received the name "Castle of Seven Turrets". Under the Ottomans, Yedikule served first as a treasury, then as a state prison. One enters the walls via a narrow entrance to the left of the castle.

The road past the entrance continues on to **Imrahor Camii,** the Byzantine Church of St. John built in 463 by Studios, an affluent patrician. Many princes of the imperial line were educated in the monastery founded by Studios. Unfortunately, only fragments of wall and floor mosaics suggest the former splendor of these buildings.

Fiorya Sahil Yolu, the coastal road, takes you to **Kumkapi,** a section of the city beyond the railway footbridge. This old fishermen's quarter has a wealth of cosy seafood restaurants. Narrow streets lead uphill from Kumkapi to the university. Sahil Yolu takes one back to Seraglio Point and the Golden Horn. Since the Marmara shore has been cleaned up, a trip along the scenic coastal road can be quite an experience. The visitor glides between the skyline of the Old City and the ships plying back and forth on the Sea of Marmara.

The New City

Galata Bridge links the Old City on the right side of the Golden Horn with what is called the New City on the left side. Its districts of Galata (Karaköy) and Pera, which together comprise Beyoglu, were founded in the Byzantine era as a Genocse trading station. After Constantinople had been freed from Rome in 1261, the Byzantine emperor granted the Genoese virtual autonomy under their own governor. Until the mid-19th century, when Abdül Mecit's mother had a wooden bridge built across the Golden Horn, ships handled all traffic. Sultan Beyazit II had planned a bridge in the early 16th century. To this end he contacted Michelangelo, the Florentine sculptor, painter, poet and architect often considered the archetypal Renaissance figure, but nothing came of the project.

The present old Galata Bridge, to be reserved for pedestrians once a new parallel bridge on piers opens, was built by a German firm in 1912. It floats on pontoons. Drawing the center section aside enables even large ships to enter the inner harbor. In the little restaurants lodged under the arches of the bridge, one eats swaying as if on shipboard with a view of the Topkapi.

Going up the Horn on the left bank one reaches the **Arap Camii** on the right, a Dominican church built about 1325 in the style favored by mendicant Italian orders. In 1492 the three-aisled basilica was placed at the disposal of Arabs driven from Spain. On the left, just before Atatürk Bridge, stands the **Azapkapi Camii** (1577), a late work of Sinan's. Its dome supported by eight semidomes is strongly reminiscent of the conception underlying the Selim Mosque at Edirne. The **Galata Tower** on the slope above was built by the Genoese in the mid-14th century as the northernmost turret of their city walls. It houses a nightclub, a restaurant and a café. The view from its balcony is superb.

Further east is the **Divan Edebiyati Müzesi,** once a monastery for the Whirling Dervishes and now the Museum of Divan Literature. Where the mystics once twirled, clothing, musical instruments and calligraphy are exhibited in secularized surroundings.

Istiklal Caddesi, the main artery of the New City, is reached by Europe's earliest underground, a 600 m tunnel railway which was built in 1875. Trade agreements between the Genoese and the Ottoman Empire enabled the Europeans to develop free trade and commerce here and gave the New City international stature. After fires which did extensive damage in 1831 and 1871, Istiklal Caddesi was rebuilt to look much as it does today. Many foreign embassies – consulates since Ankara became the capital in 1923 – commercial houses, and banks grace this street with palatial structures. Christian churches abound. In some of them, mass is still held at Christmas and Easter.

On Galatasaray Square stands the **Galatasaray Lycée,** one of Turkey's elite schools. In 1868 Sultan Abdül Aziz established a modern school on French principles to inculcate progressive European thinking into the children of the affluent who would one day hold admin-

istrative posts. Somewhat above it on a side street is the **Galatasaray Hamami**, a bath built in the 15th century and still in use. Diagonally across from it is the famous **Çiçek Pasaji,** the flower sellers' alley. Little restaurants, called *meyhaneler*, under roofed arcades invite one to linger. Modern shops, restaurants, bars, cafés and cinemas, as well as numerous establishments in the side streets, make the area lively day and night. In recent decades, the shopping and business district has expanded to include Osmanbey and Sisly.

The Istiklal Caddesi ends at **Taksim Square.** Its name is derived from its function as a municipal water distribution point. On the right is the **Atatürk Cultural Center,** the city's modern opera house, where art exhibitions and symposia are also held. The **Atatürk Monu-**

Above: Beyoglu by night, the place to go to see a bellydancing show. Right: The friendliness and hospitality of the Turks can be read in this face.

ment at the center of the square commemorates the decisive Turkish victory over the Greeks in 1922 and the founding of the Republic a year later. International luxury hotels have taken advantage of this propitious location.

To the east are the buildings of the **Technical University.** To the north is the **Military Museum,** which is highly instructive in the war tradition of the Ottoman Empire. An Ottoman martial band (*mehter*) playing traditional instruments gives daily concerts at 3 p.m. International theater and concert performances are given in the **Açik Hava Tiyatrosu,** an open-air theater nearby. The street leading down to the Bosporus passes **Inönu Stadium** and ends at the Dolmabahçe Palace.

The trip from Galata Bridge along the coast of the Bosporus to the Dolmabahçe Palace is also delightful. On the left rises a massive cannon foundry, the 15th century **Tophane,** with its five domes. Diagonally across from it is a *mosque*, a miniature Hagia Sophia, built by the famous architect Sinan in his old age for the naval hero Kiliç Ali Pasa. After the Battle of Lepanto in 1571, in which the Ottoman fleet was decisively defeated, Kiliç Ali Pasa acquitted himself nobly, managing to save the surviving Turkish ships by skillful manoeuvring. In the background rises the **Nusretiye Camii,** commissioned in 1823 by Mahmut II to honor Divine Victory. During his reign the Janissaries were reformed. He also sought to develop and exploit new architectural forms. His architect was Kirkor Balyan, founder of a dynasty of Armenian architects who profoundly influenced 19th-century Ottoman architecture. Kirkor Balyan had studied in Paris. The Nusretiye Camii, a monumental structure with one central dome and high fenestrated partitions, is a curious blend of Turkish Baroque and French Empire.

The Bosporus

Bosporus means "cow crossing" in ancient Greek. According to mythology, Zeus transformed his beloved Io into a cow to save her from the wrath of his jealous spouse, Hera. When Hera sent a gadfly to plague Io, the cow plunged into the Bosporus and swam across. The 32 km of the Bosporus, in Turkish Bogaziçi, link the Black Sea to the Sea of Marmara. The end of the latter is marked by Leander's Tower, although Leander swam not the Bosporus but the Dardanelles. Behind it on the Asian side is **Üsküdar,** ancient Scutari, still thoroughly oriental with its old wooden houses. The first building which visitors notice here is the **Iskele Camii** on the harbor. The mosque commissioned by Mihrimah, daughter of Süleyman the Magnificent, in 1548 was designed by Sinan and it is a variation on the Sehzade Mosque. From **Çamlica Mountain** to the northeast, the views over the city and the straits are superb in the morning and even better at night.

The development of palace architecture reveals the influence of European architecture and lifestyles on the 19th century sultans. The most sumptuous palace of the period is the **Dolmabahçe Palace** on the Bosporus. *Dolmabahçe* means "raised garden". Early in the 17th century Ahmet I had a terrace built up at a beautiful spot on the European shore for a wooden residence which was to be used during the hot summer months. Abdül Mecit I, who found the Topkapi Palace to be old-fashioned, commissioned the Armenian architect Nikogos Balyan to build the present Dolmabahçe on the same site in Turkish renaissance style. The palace, with its 285 rooms, vast throne room and lavish interior, plunged the Ottoman state into debt. On November 10, 1938, Mustafa Kemal Atatürk, the father of modern Turkey, died in this palace.

Farther up the Bosporus is the **Sinan Pasa Camii,** which was built by the architect Sinan in 1555 for Sinan Pasa, admiral of the fleet and brother of Rüstem Pasa, the grand vizier.

In front of it is another work of Sinan's, the **Hayrettin Barbarossa Monument** which was dedicated to Süleyman the Magnificent's admiral of the fleet, who subdued the entire Mediterranean with his navy. The **Naval Museum** on Besiktas Quay is informative on Turkish naval history. The Ottoman galleys which conveyed the sultan to his summer residences on the Bosporus and a map of America, dated 1513 and owned by the Turkish captain Piri Reis, are particularly remarkable exhibits.

Still farther up the Bosporus is the **Çiragan Palace,** where Abdül Aziz died under mysterious circumstances in 1876. His nephew was already mentally deranged by the time he ascended the throne as Murat V, and he was succeeded

Right: The section of the city called Ortaköy Camii lies on the European coast of the Bosporus and is well worth a visit, especially in conjunction with an exploration of Arnavutköy (the "Albanian" village).

in relatively short order by his brother, Abdül Hamit II. The palace burned down in 1910. Recently restored, it has been converted to a luxury hotel.

The **Yildiz Sarayi** above it is an architectural link with the airy Ottoman "park pavilions". Sultan Abdül Hamit II lived almost exclusively in this palace. Fearing assassination, he took extreme precautionary measures on its premises. In 1908 he was deposed by the Young Turks, who were convinced that the sultanate prevented the country from progressing along European lines.

Having passed under the first **Bosporus Bridge,** ceremonially dedicated in 1973 on the 50th anniversary of the Republic, one sees the **Beylerbey Palace** on the Asian side. Built by the Armenian Serkis Baljan, it was the second residence of Abdül Aziz. Here Abdül Hamit II spent his last years, dying in 1918.

The numerous summer residences, called *yali,* on the shores of the Bosporus where meant to be viewed from the water. As in the past, one should choose to go by water between Europe and Asia, by ferry or by small excursion boat.

From Galata Bridge you can head up the Bosporus towards the Black Sea. Since the Black Sea is higher than the Bosporus, the current flowing towards the ship is strong, up to 5 km/h. At its narrowest point, where the Bosporus is only 660 m wide, twin forts were constructed prior to the fall of Constantinople.

Rumeli Hisari is on the European side and **Anadolu Hisari** on the Asian. Their cannons deterred ships from passing, thus preventing the vital provisioning of the besieged city with Black Sea grain.

South of Rumeli Hisari lies **Bebek,** one of Istanbul's most elegant residential areas. Here too, the old airily-built wooden houses, so suited to catching cool Bosphorus breezes, are yielding to modern luxury high-rises. Strict zoning laws are intended to protect the coastline from speculation and over-development, and to contribute to the solution of various traffic problems.

Above Rumeli Hisari, dense greenery all but conceals **Bogazici Üniversitesi,** a renowned institution where instruction is given in English. South of Anadolu Hisari is yet another palace of Sultan Abdül Mecit II, **Küçüksu Palace**. Situated by "the Sweet Waters of Asia" – two streams flowing into the strait – its shady grounds made it favorite with Ottoman excursion parties.

Beyond the second Bosporus bridge, **Fatih Köprüsü,** which was opened to public traffic in 1988, there are fine *yalis* on the Asian shore. **Kanlica** is famed for its delicious yoghurt which is served on the Bosporus ferries. Above Çubuklu is the **Khedive's Castle,** a summer residence that was built at the turn of the century by the Egyptian viceroy, Abbas Hilmi Pasha.

At **Tarabya,** on the European side, many foreign powers built summer residences for their ambassadors because Pera was too stifling during the hot months. To the north, at **Büyükdere,** the Bosporus is at its widest, 3.5 km across. From here the Black Sea is visible. Above Büyükdere, extensive deciduous forests, the Belgrade Woods, are popular with Istanbul residents for day-trips. The main city reservoir is here. After capturing Belgrade, Süleyman the Magnificent settled Serbs here to build and maintain the aqueducts.

Continuing up the Bosporus one reaches **Sariyer**, the second to last stop on the European side before the Black Sea. It has a fascinating fish market and many fish restaurants. In August, the sophisticated town of Sariyer is truly oriental, since summer guests from Arab nations predominate. You can take the bus or a group taxi, a *dolmus*, overland from here to reach the bathing beaches at **Kilyos** on the Black Sea.

The last stop on the European shore is **Rumeli Kavagi,** a sleepy fishing village.

Anadolu Kavagi on the Asian shore is the end of the line. The area to the north of these two towns is a military zone. The 1936 Montreux Treaty permit the passage of merchant and war ships over 15,000 tons, but only from states bordering the Black Sea.

Passage to the Black Sea has been jealously guarded ever since the days of the mythical King Jason and his Argonauts. As the saga relates, they had to obtain the Golden Fleece at Colchis, an ancient country south of the Caucasus. But the basalt cliffs along the coast closed with a tremendous crash on ships trying to sail through.

The Argonauts were able to deceive the rocks, which were known in mythology as the Symplegades, by sending a dove ahead. The rocks crashed together, tearing off only its tail feathers. As they were in the process of reopening, the Argonauts rowed through full speed ahead, leaving behind only a piece of the stern. Since then the rocks have remained in their place, just as an oracle had foretold.

ISTANBUL

(Telephone area code for Istanbul: 1-)

Accommodation

LUXURY: **Istanbul Hilton**, Cumhuriyet Cad., Harbiye, Tel: 131 4650. **Sheraton Istanbul**, Taksim Park, Tel: 131 2121. **Pulman Etap**, Mesrutiyet Cad., Tepebasi, Tel: 151 4646. **Ramada**, Ordu Cad. 226, Laleli, Tel: 513 9300. **Divan**, Cumhuriyet Cad. 2, Taksim, Tel: 131 4100. **Çinar**, Yesilköy, Tel: 573 3500. **Büyük Sahinler**, Mesih Pasa Cad. 73, Laleli, Tel: 511 7363. **Büyük Sürmeli**, Saatçi Bayiri Sok. 3, Gayrettepe, Tel: 172 1160.

MODERATE: **Bebek**, Cevdetpasa Cad. 113-115, Bebek, Tel: 163 3000. **Büyük Keban**, Gençtürk Cad. 47, Laleli, Tel: 512 0020. **Harem**, Ambar Sok. 2, Selimiye, Tel: 333 2025. **Büyük Istanbul**, Akaretler Yokusu 98, Besiktas, Tel: 160 7860. **Washington**, Gençtürk Aga Yoksu Cad. 12, Laleli, Tel: 520 5990.

BUDGET: **Çiragan**, Müvezzi Cad. 3, Besiktas, Tel: 160 0230. **Gezi**, Mete Cad. 42, Taksim, Tel: 151 7430. **Oriental**, Cihangir Cad. 60, Taksim, Tel: 145 1067. **Plaza**, Arslan Yatagi Sok. 19-21, Taksim, Tel: 145 3273. **Rio**, Saitefendi Sok., Laleli, Tel: 528 4708. **Ayasofya Pension**, Sogukçesme Sok., Sultanahmet, Tel: 513 3660. **Hidiv Kasri**, Çubuklu, Tel: 331 2651. **Sokollu Pasa**, Mehmetpasa Camii Sok. 10, Sultanahmet, Tel: 512 3753. **Yesil Ev**, Kabasakal Cad. 5, Sultanahmet, Tel: 517 6785. *CAMPING:* **Ataköy Mokamp**, Sahilyolu Ataköy, Tel: 559 6000.

Hospitals

American Hospital Admiral Bristol, Güzelbahçe Sok, Nisantasi, Tel: 131 4050. **Pasteur Hastanesi (French Hospital)**, Taskisla Cad., Elmadag, Tel: 148 4756. **Alman Hastanesi (German Hospital)**, Siraselviler Cad. 119, Taksim, Tel: 143 8100. **Cerrahpasa Tip Fakültesi (Faculty of Medicine)**, Kocamustafapasa Cad., Cerrahpasa, Tel: 585 2100.

Festivals / Special Events

International Film Days, April 6–19; *Tulip Festival*, April 23–May 1; *Jazz Festival*, May 18–30; *Internat. Marmara Folk Dancing Festival*, May 28–30; *Fatih Festivities*, May 29; *International Istanbul Festival*, June 15–July 31; *Sultanahmet Culture and Arts Festival*, July–August; *Culture Festivities*, July 14–15; *Drama Festival*, July 15–Sept 15; *Istanbul Bi-Annual Arts Festival*, Oct 14–Nov 8.

Museums

Archaeological Museum, Sarayiçi, Osman Hamdi Yoksu, Sultanahmet, open 9.30 a.m.-5.00 p.m., closed Mon. **Atatürk Museum**, Halaskar Gazi Cad. 250, Sisli, open 10.00 a.m.-12.00 noon and 2.00-4.30 p.m., closed Sat and Sun. **Ayasofya Museum**, Sultanahmet, open 9.30a.m.-5.00 p.m., closed Mondays. **Dolmabahçe Museum**, open 9.00 a.m.-5.00 p.m., closed Mon and Tue. **Marine Museum**, Besiktas, open 9.00 a.m-5.00 p.m., closed Mon and Tue. **Military Museum**, Harbiye, open 9.00 a.m.-12.00 noon and 1.00-5.00 p.m., closed Mon and Tue. **Museum of Turkish and Islamic Art**, Ibrahim Pasa Palace, Sultanahmet, open 9.00 a.m.-12.00 noon and 1.00-5.00 p.m., closed Mon. **St. Irene Museum**, Sarayiçi 35, Sultanahmet, open 9.30 a.m.-5.00 p.m., closed Wednesdays. **Municipal Museum**, Saraçhanebasi, open 9.00-11.30 a.m. and 1.00-5.00 p.m., closed Sat and Sun. **Topkapi Palace**, Sarayiçi, Sultanahmet, open 9.00 a.m.-5.00 p.m., closed Tue. **Carpet Museum**, Camii Bahçesi, Sultanahmet, open 8.00 a.m.-5.30 p.m., closed Sun and Mon. **Yildiz Palace**, Yildiz Park, open 9.00 a.m-6.00 p.m. **Yerebatan Palace Museum**, Yerebatan Cad., Sultanahmet, open 9.00 a.m.-5.00 p.m., closed Tue.

Churches

CATHOLIC: **St. Antoine**, Istiklal Cad. 325, Beyoglu. **St. Pasifique**, Büyükada. **St. Luis des Français**, Postacilar Sok. 11, Beyoglu. **Sts. Pierre et Paul**, Kuledibi, Karaköy. *PROTESTANT:* **St. Helena Chapel**, on the grounds of the British Consulate, Beyoglu. **Union Chapel** on the grounds of the Dutch Consulate, Beyoglu. *ORTHODOX:* **Panayia Church**, Büyükada. **Aya Yani**, Burgazada. **Aya Nikolaos**, Heybeliada. **Aya Triada**, Meselik Sok. 11, Taksim. **Aya Efimia**, Dakiköy. **Orthodox Patriarchate**, Sadrazam Ali Pasa Cad. 35, Fener. **Panayia Church**, Emin Nevruz Sok, Galatasaray. *SYNAGOGUES:* **Beth Israel**, Efe Sok. 4, Sisli. **Neve Shalom**, Büyük Hendek Cad. 61, Sishane.

Turkish Cuisine

Turkey is the heir to both Byzantine and Ottoman imperial cuisine. Add to this the influence of Persia, Arabia and the Balkans, and the result is one of the most exciting and diverse kitchens in the world.

The first thing to tell a waiter is what you want to drink. Try *raki*, the national drink which locals refer to as "lion's milk". Mix it with water and let it curdle milky-white.

Next comes the *meze*, or hors d'oeuvres, which range from white cheese, chicken and walnut paste and red hot minces, to fresh beans, cauliflower, leeks, fried eggplant and zucchini. Just pick out what looks good in the large tray filled with small dishes presented by the waiter. Favorite seafood dishes are *karides güveç* (shrimp casserole), *kalkan* (turbot) and *kiliç* (swordfish). Lamb and beef are usually offered as *adana kebab*, *döner kebab*, *iskender kebab* or simply *shish kebab*.

Tatli, or desserts, are also a speciality. If these seem too heavy, opt for the fruit basket. No meal is complete without a cup of Turkish coffee. Have it *sade*, black, *orta*, with one sugar cube , or *sekerli* , very sweet. When you ask for the bill, or *hesap*, don't be surprised if you've been at the table for two or three hours. Dining in Turkey is a social affair and should never be rushed.

Restaurants

FISH: **Antik**, 1. Gaddesi 47, Arnavutköy, Tel: 163 6627. **Doganay Restoran**, Yaliboyu Cad. 26, Beylerbeyi, Tel: 333 0197. **Karaca**, Rumelihisar, Tel: 163 3468. **Sandal**, Çapari Sok. 13A, Kumpaki, Tel: 520 6225. **Yeni Bebek**, Cevdet Pasa Cad. 123, Bebek, Tel: 163 3447.

TURKISH: **Beyti Lokantasi**, Omar Sok. 33, Florya. Tel: 573 9373. **Bab Cafeteria Beyti**, Yesilcam Sok. 24, Beyoglu, Tel: 144 0514. **Dörtler**, Bagdat Cad. 6, Bostanci, Tel: 358 1958. **Haciabdullah**, Sakizagaci Sok. 19, Tel: 144 8561. **Konyali**, Sultanahmet, Tel: 526 2727. **Hacibozanoglu**, Ordu Cad., 214, Laleli, Tel: 528 4492. **Pandelli**, Misir Carsisi, Eminonu, Tel: 527 3909.

INTERNATIONAL: **Abdullah**, Koru Cad., 11, Tel: 163 6406. **Amarcord**, Bagdat Cad. 208, Selamiçesme, Tel: 356 0813. **Merih Wine Cellar**, Kuruçesme 26, Arnavutköy, Tel: 163 5977. **Plaza**, Bronz Sok. 4/A, Maska, Tel: 141 6356. **Rejans**, Olivya Geçidi 15, Galatasaray, Tel: 144 1610. **Ziya**, M. Kemal Oke Cad., 21/1, Nisantasi, Tel: 147 1708. *ITALIAN:* **Flora Pizzeria**, Valikonagi Cad. 9, Harbiye, Tel: 148 7694. **Kral ve Ben Pizzeria**, Istiklal Cad. Turnacibasi Sok. 10, Galatasaray, Tel: 144 9688.

CHINESE: **China Town**, Cevdet Pasa Cad., Bebek, Tel: 163 2082. **Chinese Restoran**, Lamartin Cad. 17, Taksim, Tel: 150 6263. *JAPANESE:* **Yumeya**, Cumhuriyet Cad. 39, Beyoglu, Tel: 156 1108. *KOREAN:* **Seoul**, Nisbetiye Cad. 41, Etiler, Tel: 163 6087.

Transportation

Istanbul is the most important traffic junction in the whole of Turkey, and the result is absolute chaos during rush hours. It's best to plan your wanderings around the city during off-peak traffic times – whether by private car, taxi, bus, boat or *dolmus*, the large shared taxi, which is a unique institution in Turkey.

BUS: **Bus Terminal** *(oto gar)*, Topkapi-Edirnekapi Cad., at the Topkapi Gate. *RAIL:* **Rail Terminal Sirkeci**, Kennedy Cad., at the Galata Bridge. **Rail Terminal Haydarpasa**, Haydar-

pasa, on Istanbul's Asian side. *FERRIES:* **Istanbul – Yalova**, hourly. **Istanbul – Bandirma**, daily 8.30 a.m. from Istanbul, 3.00 p.m. from Bandirma. **Istanbul – Izmir**, Fri 3.00 p.m. from Istanbul, Sun 2.00 p.m. from Izmir. **Istanbul – Samsum – Trabzon**, Mon 5.30 p.m. from Istanbul, Wed 10.00 p.m. from Trabzon. *RENTAL CARS:* **Avis**, main office, Tel: 157 7670. At the Divan Hotel, Tel: 146 5256. At the Hilton Hotel, Tel: 148 7752. Atatürk Airport: Tel: 573 6445. **Hertz**: Cumhuriyet Cad. 291, Tel: 134 4300. Atatürk Airport, Tel: 574 6948. **Europcar**: Cumhuriyet Cad. Taksim, Tel: 150 8888. Atatürk Airport, Tel: 573 7024.

Tourist Information

Atatürk Airport, Tel: 537 7399. In the harbor terminal Karaköy, Tel: 149 5776. At the Hilton Hotel, Tel: 133 9592. Sultan Ahmet Divanyolu Cad., Tel: 522 4903. **Port Authority**: Rihtim Cad., Karaköy, Tel: 144 0207.

Turkish Baths

The *hamam*, or Turkish bath, has long been an important element of Turkish culture and there is nothing more relaxing than spending an afternoon sweating in the steaming bowels of a marble-lined, domed room while attendants scrub you down.

Two favorites in Istanbul are the **Cagaloglu Hamam**, Kazim Ismael Gorken Cad. 34, Cagaloglu (men's section open 7.00 a.m.-9.00 p.m., women's section open 8.00 a.m.-7.00 p.m.), and the **Galatasaray Hamam**, Turnacibasi Sok., Beyoglu (men's section open 6.30 a.m.-8.00 p.m., women's section 8.00 a.m.-7.00 p.m).

Be prepared to spend a couple of hours inside. One enters through a series of increasingly humid and hot rooms, starting with the *sogukluk*, or "cold room" and proceeding into the *hararet*, the "hot room" in the middle of the *hamam*. The domed room, its walls lined by marble basins with hot and cold water spigots, is usually built around the *göbek tasi*, the "stomach stone". Book one of the attendants to give you a massage followed by an invigorating rub-down with a special abrasive mitt that peels the layers of dead skin off your body. Be prepared to tip everyone from the masseur to the tea boy upon departure.

Beaches

Some lovely beaches can be found in the vicinity of Istanbul. Avoid the shore of the Sea of Marmara, or take a boat to one of the offshore islands. More pleasant and less crowded are the Black Sea beaches, for instance **Kilyos** on the European side and **Sile** on the Asian side. The long beach of Sile is the prettier of both, but very overcrowded at weekends.

THRACE
SEA OF MARMARA
NORTHERN AEGEAN

EDIRNE / BURSA

ÇANAKKALE / TROY

AYVALIK / BERGAMA

MANISA / SARDIS

EDIRNE

Thrace, in Turkish, *Trakya*, is the southeasternmost tip of the Balkans or the northwesternmost European part of Turkey. Only 3 percent of the area of Turkey lies in Europe. The other 97 percent compromises Asia Minor and is called Anatolia, from the Greek word *anatole* which means "land of the sunrise".

Thrace has always been a gateway. Two important transitways, one from Bulgaria through the border town Kapikule, the other from Greece through Ipsala, cut across the soft, rolling flatland to the destinations Istanbul and the Bosporus. This trail leads the traveler past sleepy-looking villages which are surrounded by fields of sunflowers and wheat in the summer. In the lower wetlands are ricefields. Icy northeast winds from the Black Sea frequently sweep across the land with few trees in the winter, stopped only by the Ganos Dagi and Koru Dagi mountains in the southwest, which climb to 945 meters. The Gallipoli (Gelibolu) Peninsula on the Dardanelles stretches like a finger into the Aegean Sea. Without the connection

Preceding pages: Fishermen from the sea of Marmara inspect their nets before work.

of the Dardanelles to the Aegean and of the Bosporus to the Black Sea, the Sea of Marmara would be landlocked.

West of the Dardanelles is the mouth of the Meriç, in ancient times the Hebros, which today forms the border with Greece and empties into the Aegean Sea. The river once served as an important waterway, which seagoing ships could navigate quite far inland. In the fertile river meadows, where the Meriç meets the Tunca, Emperor Hadrian founded Hadrianopolis, Adrianople, in the year A.D. 125. Since the Ottoman Empire it has been called **Edirne**.

The history of Edirne is the history of Thrace, written for the most part by migrating peoples and traveling armies. From 314 until 323, the city became the stage for serious confrontations between Emperor Constantine and his enemy Licinius. Constantine eventually overcame his rival at Chrysopolis, today Üsküdar, on the Asian bank of the Bosporus. Emperor Valens was defeated near here by the Goths in 378, but the victors failed to capture the city. It similarly withstood the siege of the Avars in 586. From the 9th through the 11th centuries, however, the Bulgarians plundered it three times. It became involved in the First Crusade in 1101 and the Second Crusade in 1147 in the battles with wealthy Constantinople.

Emperor Frederick Barbarossa established his winter bivouac here during the Third Crusade in 1189. As the Ottomans prepared to attack Constantinople, they tried to cut the city off from its European neighbors: In 1354 they crossed the Dardanelles near Gallipoli (Gelibolu). Edirne became the new capital of the Ottomans in 1367; Murat I moved his residence from Bursa to Edirne. Even after the conquest of Constantinople and the shift of the sultan's residence to the palace of Topkapi, Edirne remained a favorite site of the sultans to rest during their cam paigns in the Balkans.

The city first began to lose stature when the empire did. In the Treaty of Adrianople of 1829, after the Russo-Ottoman war, the provinces of the Danube were lost to the Russians and Greece won its independence. Only through the intervention of the western nations and another war in 1878 could the annexation of Thrace be prevented. With the treaty which concluded the Balkan Wars of 1912/1913, in which Turkey fought Bulgaria, Edirne officially became part of Turkey. From the First World War through 1922, Greece took Edirne once more, but in 1923 the Peace of Lausanne reestablished Turkish possession of East Thrace, bringing peace to the area once and for all.

To many, Edirne is known only as a quick stop after the border crossing. But with all of its winding alleys, bazars, old houses and bridges, it remains in many sections a good example of a typical Oriental city. There is hardly a better spot to study the evolution of Ottoman architecture, from its very beginning to its most venerated golden age. The tour of the city begins at the main square, **Cumhuriyet Meydani**, at the intersection of Kapikule Caddesi, arriving from the Bulgarian border, with Istanbul Caddesi and Saraçlar Caddesi. The latter heads west towards Greece, crossing both the Meriç and Tunca rivers. On the square is

also the old mosque, the **Eski Cami**, built between 1403-14 by the architect Haci Alaettin from Konya under the auspices of Mehmet I. Mehmet I ascended to the throne only after his father Beyazit I had been taken prisoner by the Mongol Tamerlane during the battle of Ankara in 1402, and his brothers had been overcome. In the mosque you can recognize the strong influence of Seljuk pillar-hall mosques, even though, as is already obvious in the slightly older Ulu Cami at Bursa, flat wooden ceilings have given way to stone domes, and masonry columns have replaced the wooden pillars. In the Eski Cami, the diameter of the dome has been broadened to 13 meters (in comparison to 9 meters in the Ulu Cami) and only four additional columns support the 9 domes. Lanterns highlight the middle axis towards the *mihrab*. On the walls are large and beautifully-written words of inspiration from the prophet Mohammed as instruction to his followers, and neo-Baroque floral patterns.

Below the main square is the **bedesten**, a covered market which, through trading in precious stones and costly antiques, was the economic basis for the old mosque. To the north rises the **Üç Serefeli Cami**. Its name is derived from one of the four minarets, which has three galleries. Originally, the mosque had only one minaret (in the northeast) with two galleries. The finished mosque (completed in 1447 by Murat II, the father of the conqueror of Constantinople) has simply one dome with a diameter of 23 meters. It is supported solely by the walls and two columns. The domed arcade of the front garden is already an element of the golden age of Ottoman style, while the smooth outside walls are typical of an earlier period.

The jewel of this assembly of mosques is the **Selimiye Camii**, the Selim mosque, located in the center of Edirne. The son of Süleyman the Magnificent, Selim II, contracted Sinan to build the mosque in

1569. Sinan, who was reportedly born in 1490 in the province of Kayseri,was conscripted into the army at the age of 21 to serve as Janissary during the campaigns of Süleyman the Magnificent, and used to his advantage the opportunity to thoroughly analyze the architectural methods of the conquered territories. Süleyman promoted him at the age of 49 to the position of court architect. At the age of 85, he completed the Selimiye. It is considered his masterpiece.

Two of his earlier mosques, the Sehzade, which is thought of as his apprentice piece, and the famous Süleymaniye, his journeyman piece, are located in Istanbul. It is considered proof of the importance of the city at the end of the 16th century, the high point of the Ottoman Empire and the period of the Balkan campaigns, that such a building would be undertaken in Edirne.

Above: The Selim Mosque in Edirne. Right: Another religious wonderwork in Edirne, the Üç Serefeli Mosque.

As you drive towards Edirne from Istanbul, the Selimiye appears shimmering behind a curve in the road like a mirage in the haze. Each of the 70-meter-high minarets, the highest in Turkey, has three galleries, and each of the two on the right and left of the entrance has three independent spiral staircases. From a forecourt on the main street through a covered bazaar, the *arasta*, you arrive at the outer courtyard. Continuing through a gateway and domed arcade, you will find a vestibule with a beautifully crafted marble fountain in the middle. A Seljuk entranceway leads to the inside of the Selimiye. This was brought from the principal mosque of Birgi, near Izmir, by way of wagons drawn by donkeys.

Once inside the prayer room, a sense of transcendent weightlessness prevails because the dome rests on an octagon of columns, but their clever integration into the walls and side galleries creates the impression of an interior without supports. Since the completion of renovations in the mid-1980s, the effect of the

interior is highlighted by colors such as Sinan would have chosen. It is greater still when light streams through the Romanesque windows in the cupola onto the walls, or emanates from lanterns in the evenings, especially during Ramadan. The *mihrab*, decorated with gorgeous Iznik porcelain, is balanced harmoniously by the delicate marble work of the *minbar* opposite it. The artfully-painted wooden choir gallery with a flowing fountain underneath works as a small distraction from the otherwise central focus of the room.

Somewhat to the east you come to the **Muradiye Camii** of Murat II, from 1436, typically early Ottoman with its cubic shape. At one time it was surrounded by a Dervish monastery, founded by students of the great Mevlana Celaleddin Rumi from Konya. Today, only the headstones with their images of the high Mevlana caps bear witness to that time.

The road leads north past the Üç Serefeli Cami to the Beyazit II complex. Immediately on the left at the beginning

of the road are the remains of a **clock tower** which demarcated the northeast border of the Hadrianic town. The tower itself comes from the Byzantine era; Emperor John III Dukas had it rebuilt in 1123. Diagonally across the way is the so-called "double bath" **Çifte Hamam**, built in 1579 by Sinan for Sokollu Mehmet Pasa.

Over a bridge which crosses the three arms of the Tunca river stands the complex of **Beyazit II Camii** which was built between 1484 and 1488. To protect the mosque from the recurring floods of the Tunca, Beyazit had high dams built. The master builder was Hayrettin, who also supervised the building of the Beyazit mosque in Istanbul. Through the main entrance gate you come first to a spacious outer garden. On the right, a passageway leads to further small courtyards which once housed institutions such as a medical school, pharmacies, and a hospital. The mental hospital consists of a domed common area around a fountain, with niches built into the walls through which doors lead to heated rooms. A very impressed 16th century historian, Evliya Çelebi, described how music was used to heal the souls of the afflicted. Today the rooms are used by the architecture students of the University of Trakya. On the opposite side of the courtyard were kitchens and dining rooms for travelers and the needy. Through a forecourt, the mosque can be entered. With its dome sitting directly on the squared stone of the side walls, it represents the early Ottoman mosque style.

Further up the Tunca lies **Seraglio Island** (Saray Içi) with its sparse remains of once elegant palaces and pavilions from the golden age of Edirne, between the 15th and 17th centuries. The sultans resided here when they were in Edirne. One of the few structures to withstand the time of destruction following the reign of Süleyman the Magnificent is the Tower of Justice, Adalet Casri. Today, for only a short period at the beginning of July, the island comes alive as the site of the *Kirkpinar Güresleri*, a famous wrestling tournament. *Güres* is the national sport of Turkey. Wearing nothing but long black leather pants, their bodies covered with oil, men compete freestyle for the honor of being strongest.

It is worth driving along the dike on the left bank of the **Tunca** to Kapikule Caddesi. The reward is a magnificent view of the silhouettes of Edirne's mosques. Since the riverbank is in a military security zone on the Bulgarian border, photography is forbidden.

Going back to Cumhuriyet Meydani, you can take the main commercial avenue, Saraçlar Caddesi, location of the post office, banks, restaurants, and cafes. On the right side, laid out according to the ancient design, stretches the **Ali Pasa Bazaar** which was built by Sinan in 1569 for the grand vizir of Süleyman the Magnificent, Hersekli Ali Pasa. In the direction of the Tunca, the fish market, **Balik Pazari**, adjoins the bazaar. This is where

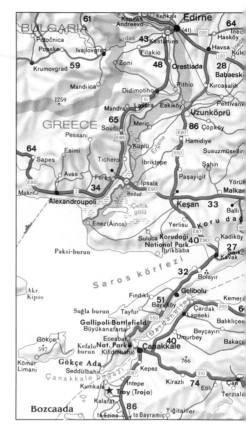

the former Byzantine southeast tower of the city was located.

By the river Tunca are the ruins of Hadrian's wall. Following the road, you cross first the Tunca, then the Meriç before they meet. There is a wonderful tea garden on the right bank of the Meriç. Here one can reflect at leisure upon the stirring history of the region.

Whoever wishes to arrive as quickly as possible on the Aegean coast should choose the road through **Uzunköprü**. The place takes its name from a long Ottoman bridge. Further along the route is **Kesan** and then the **Koru Dagi National Park** with its 350-meter-high pass to the **Dardanelles**. There are two ferries across the straits. One line leaves from **Gelibolu**

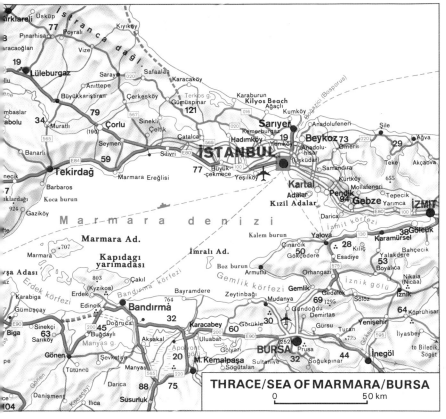

THRACE/SEA OF MARMARA/BURSA

0 _____ 50 km

to Lapseki. Gelibolu, once called Gallipoli, is a pretty little fishing town where the coming and going of the ferries can be viewed while partaking in a meal of fish. The trip from **Eceabat** to Çanakkale is more convenient. Driving along a narrow road away from **Eccabat** on the European side of the Dardanelles, the visitor passes a fortress built by Mehmet II, the **Killitulbahir**, reaching the tip of the **Gallipoli Peninsula**. Here, in 1915, one of the bloodiest battles of the First World War took place, in which 50,000 soldiers were killed. Under the command of the German General Liman von Sanders, Mustafa Kemal, later known as Atatürk, successfully pushed back the advance of the western Allies. Today, the monuments of the Turks, French, British and Australians stand in remembrance.

Those who first want to stop in Istanbul can continue south towards the Aegean on the road along **Izmit Körfezi**, the Bay of Izmit. Because this area has seen so much industrial growth in recent years, it would be wise to take the ferry from **Kartal** to Yalova. **Yalova** has always been a favorite bathing spot because of its thermal springs. The road from Yalova towards Bursa passes a lake, Iznik Gölü.

A detour from **Orhangazi** on the east bank of the lake to **Iznik**, the former Nicaea, is recommended. The name stems from Nicaia, the wife of the Macedonian Lysimacho, a general of Alexander the

Great. Formerly the lake was connected to the sea, which explains the rise in commercial importance of Nicaea during the Roman empire. At that time, a monumental city wall was built, which through the centuries of onslaught underwent considerable changes. The city today occupies only a portion of the area with the walls. The rest is devoted to agriculture. It was in Nicaea that Constantine the Great called into session the first Ecumenical Council in 325, at which the identities of God and Jesus Christ were defined. In 787, the seventh Ecumenical Council met at Nicaea to settle the question of the use of images in the mass. In order for Gottfried von Bouillon to win the city back from the Seljuks in 1097, he had to pull his ships over the land that had filled in the bay, closing it off from the sea. When the Latin rulers took Constantinople (1204-61), the government in exile resided in Nicaea. It was during the time of

Above: Playing cards in a café, the same pastime the world over.

Selim I, the Ottoman ruler, that the city, now named Iznik, once again became celebrated. The sultan returned from military campaigns in Afghanistan and Tabriz with many Persian tradespeople who erected ceramic workshops. In the 16th century there were approximately 600 families working to meet the demand for expensive porcelain in the expanding Ottoman empire.

The most notable sight in present-day Iznik is the **ring of ancient walls**. Three of the original four gates, but especially the Istanbul gate in the north and the Lefke gate in the east, are well-preserved. At the intersection of the streets connecting the gates is the **Hagia Sophia**, the place where the seventh Ecumenical Council took place in A.D. 787. Sections of the church date back to the era of Justinian the Great in the early 6th century. In the northeast lies a soup kitchen, **Nilüfer Hatun Imareti**, which was built in 1388 by Murat I for his mother Nilüfer Hatun. It is now a museum housing a collection of porcelain from that period.

Southeast of Iznik, you will pass the village of **Bilecik** to arrive at **Sögut**, the veritable birthplace of the Ottoman empire. This is where Osman Gazi as leader of the Oghusen tribes established the first permanent settlement. It was the starting point for the campaigns against the Byzantine Empire.

BURSA

When the Ottomans took **Bursa** from the Byzantines in 1326, the city must have struck them as a paradise on earth. The Oghusen tribes embarked at some point in the 11th century from Khorasan in northeast Persia and had rolling steppes to overcome on their way to the west. Bursa, also known as "the green city", is located at the northern foot of Ulu Dagi, the 2543-meter mountain which in ancient times was also called the Bithynian or Mysian Olympus. It is supplied with water by a number of small mountain streams which allow a lush vegetation to thrive. The hot springs in the western part of the city have long made Bursa a popular spa.

It is assumed that Bursa was founded in the year 185 B.C. by the Bithynian king, Prusias I, on the recommendation of the Carthaginian general Hannibal, who apparently spent several years at the court of Prusias. In Roman times, when Pliny the Younger was the representative of Bursa, the baths were expanded. Justinian erected here a palace and the Byzantine empresses came to Bursa to spend the summer and enjoy the spa. After the takeover of the city by the Ottomans, it became the first capital of the young Ottoman empire. Even after the capital was moved to Edirne in 1367, Bursa was lavishly expanded.

In the center of the city, on the recently renovated main square at Atatürk Caddesi, lies the Grand Mosque, the **Ulu Cami**. The legend explains that the contractor, Beyazit I, kept a promise in having this mosque built. Before the battle in Serbian Nicopolis, he swore to have 20 mosques built should he win. This promise was, however, beyond his means. Instead, he built one mosque with 20 domes, the Ulu Cami. The mighty pillars and the domes, which are 9 meters in diameter (quite small when compared with the Eski Cami in Edirne), create the atmosphere of a Seljuk pillar hall. Unusual are the purifying springs under a glass roof in the middle of the mosque. In the darkness of the *mihrab* niche, one sees beautiful glazed tiles that are very reminiscent of their elegant, green Seljuk forerunners and do not yet show the floral extravagance of later Iznik porcelain. To the right rises an artistically carved cedarwood *minbar,* on the sides of which is portrayed the infiniteness of the universe, star-shaped and dotted with semi-circular suns portrayed. In one of the gigantic lines of writing on the walls, the calligrapher was no longer able to control his phantasy. This resulted in abstract representations of Noah's Ark, the interior of a mosque and an Islamic city.

Bursa is very conservative. The pious here take their commitments on Fridays and during Ramadan very seriously. The mosque then becomes the center of society.

Beneath the Ulu Cami lies the **covered Bazaar**. In the **Koza Hani**, directly below the large square, the great silk auction takes place in April. Silkworms are bred in mulberry plantations north of the city in the Nilüfer Valley. After the worms have made their cocoons, these are auctioned off. On the second floor of the Koza Hani, wholesale textile manufacturers present their collections, and in the smaller shops in the bazaar, retailers offer their silk creations. Not only luxury items such as silk and jewelry are offered at the bazaar. Practical items like rubber shoes, towels or black school uniforms with white collars can also be bought. For the hungry, the eating establishments and

restaurants in Bursa offer a delicious specialty, *iskender kebab* – meat from the rotisserie with tomato and yoghurt on fresh pittabread, all smothered in hot butter. Accompany this with *ayran*, a refreshing yoghurt drink. For dessert there is another Bursa specialty which is available in one of the famous *pastahaneler* (pastry-shops) at the main square and in the passages beneath, *kestane* or candied chestnuts.

If you follow Atatürk Caddesi to the east, you come to the endowment complex of Mehmet I (1413-21), the **Yesil Cami**. Mehmet I was the grandfather of Mehmet II, the conqueror of Constantinople. In early Ottoman times, tombs were considered an important part of the mosque complex. The *türbe* of Mehmet I stands sublime above the mosque. The name yesil tomb – *yesil* means green – comes from the green decorations that

Above: Inside the Ulu Cami, a mosque with 20 domes. Right: The tomb of Osman, founder of the Ottoman dynasty.

adorn it. Particularly extravagant is the interior of this mausoleum. Mehmet I was placed to rest in the circle of his family beneath a tiled sarcophagus which is adorned with calligraphy. The body lies buried in the earth according to Islamic convention, its right side facing the *mihrab*, the tiles of which graphically portray the light of Allah.

Below the tomb stands the mosque, built by Mehmet in the so-called Bursa style. The shape is that of an upside-down T. An arch of triumph stretches between the two domes of the main axis, in which the rest of the gold allotted for the construction is walled. According to legend, architect Ilyas Ali did this to preclude the rumor that he had taken the extra gold after Mehmet's death. A stairway leads up to the higher, frontal part of the mosque, the actual prayer chamber. In the middle of the side walls, there are doors to small rooms on the left and right which served as lodging for wandering dervishes, Islamic monks. The domed open sides offered room for Koran lessons and for the dispensation of justice. Above the entrance stands the sultan's loge, following the example of the Byzantine emperor's loge. Behind the barred windows on the right and left are the women's rooms. At a later time, the sultan was praying to Allah to the left of the *mihrab*.

Drinking a *çay* or *kahve*, Turkish tea or coffee, in one of the tea gardens near the mosque, you have a view of the city as far as the valley and can see the **Beyazit Mosque** to the east.

Cutting across the city past Ulu Cami towards the west, the visitor sees a winding road on the left side which leads to the former **Citadel hill**. Remains of the Byzantine wall and a clock tower are still recognizable. Above them are located the tombs of the founders of the Ottoman Empire, Osman I and his son Orhan. The latter took power after the death of his father, shortly after the capitulation of this city.

If one follows the street along the crest of the hill, one reaches a small park with a beautiful view of the **Muradiye**, a collection of sultan's tombs further down, on the other side of the road. Murat II, the father of Mehmet II, contracted this complex, having a final resting place for himself and his family built beside the Bursa-style mosque. Its roof, an artistic carving which stretches out in front of the building, is reminiscent of the roofs of nomad tents. Inside there is an opening in the dome which allows rain to fall on the earth of the graves. This demonstrates the meaning of water to the Ottomans, even in the afterlife. After 1453, more tombs were constructed for the princes who were victims of fratricide or intrigue. Such was the case with the poet Cem Sultan, the favorite son of Mehmet II and the brother of Beyazit II. Not only the dead, but also the living find an oasis of peace beneath the high plane trees, magnolias and cypresses in this resting place, tenderly cared for by the guards.

Most of the hotels in Bursa are located in the western part of the city called **Çekirge.** Following Çekirge Caddesi, the visitor sees two old Turkish baths below on the right. The Yeni Kaplica, the so-called new bath with its sulphurous water, was built in the 16th century by Rüstem Pasa, the grand vizier of Süleyman the Magnificent. The other is the Eski Kaplica which was built in the 14th century by Murat I on Byzantine foundations. The bathers are separated according to sex, although very small boys may be escorted by their mothers. Under high domes, their windows providing natural light, body, mind and soul are purified by the hot water bubbling out of the earth in this damp, steamy environment. After that, it is time for a revitalizing massage and relaxation in the quiet room. The visitor feels like he or she has a new lease on life. In earlier times it must have seemed like paradise after a long ride through the hills. Thermal water also flows from most of the faucets in Çekirge, and many hotels have their own *hamam.*

The main street which runs right through Çekirge leads to the summit region of the **Ulu Dagi**, designated a national park. Informative placards along the way point out the flora typical for the altitude and are an invitation to tarry or take a hike. The Ulu Dagi is a favorite skiing spot for Istanbul society. Ski-lifts and luxury hotels surround the mountain.

Further to the west: Those who wish to go directly to Bergama, the Pergamum of ancient times, should take the road which turns off towards Balikesir after passing Uluabat Gölü, also called Lake Apolyont. From Balikesir, a smaller road heads south through Savastepe and Soma to Bergama.

Those who choose to spend more time in the northwest of Turkey will probably continue to the Aegean via the route

Above: The great Muradiye complex comes awake in the morning sun. Right: Water and hygiene were always important in Turkish culture, as this thermal bath in Çekirge shows.

which runs along the southern coast of the Sea of Marmara and the Dardanelles. To the south of **Bandirma** lies Manyas or **Kus Gölü,** Bird Lake in English, a paradise for birds and ornithologists. In spring this coastal lake, rich in fish, provides the perfect food supply for colonies of herons, cormorants and pelicans, as well as other types of birds. If one follows the sign "Manyas Kuscenneti Milliparki", one arrives at the Bird Paradise National Park. To visit this national park from March to May is truly a special experience. From a wooden watchtower, the brooding habits of the birds can be observed through binoculars. In the winter, the lake is the resting place for migratory birds from the Danube delta. The various birds can be observed more closely in the small, informative museum. These are preserved birds that have died natural deaths. A worthwhile diversion leads from Bandirma north to the Kapidagi Isthmus. On the strip of land that connects the isthmus with the mainland lies what is left of the ancient city of

Cyzicus which was founded by Greeks from Miletus as a colony in the 7th century B.C. and was strategically important for control of the Dardanelles. A decisive naval battle took place here between Athens and Sparta in the year 410 B.C.

Erdek, located in the southwest of the isthmus, is a charming little harbor town. From here motorboats visit a variety of islands, the largest of which is Marmara. On this island's north coast are the famous marble quarries which provided material for the construction of extraordinary buildings in autiquity. Back on the mainland, to the west near Biga, there is a small river to be crossed. In ancient times called the Granicus, today it is called Can Cayi. The first major battle between Alexander the Great and the Persians under Darius III took place on this river in 334 B.C. The Macedonians' decisive victory put most of western Asia Minor under their power.

On a stretch of road that passes through some beautiful landscape one reaches the eastern entrance to the Dardanelles and Lapseki. Lapseki, in ancient times Lampsakos, was founded as a colony on the Dardanelles by Phocaea, today Foça. It served as an important trading stop during the development of the fertile Black Sea coasts. In ancient times, Lampsakos was well known because of its excellent wines and its Priapus cult. The fertility god Priapus, son of Dionysus and Aphrodite, was born here according to legend. He is usually portrayed with exaggerated genitals. Ferries shuttle from Lapseki to Gallipoli.

The Dardanelles stretch 65 kilometers from the Sea of Marmara to the Aegean Sea. At the end of the ice age, the straits were narrow river valleys which filled and became wider and wider as the sea level rose. The Dardanelles today measure 7.5 kilometers at their widest point and 1.3 at their narrowest.

In ancient times they were called Hellespont after Phryxes and Helle, his sister.

The two tried to cross the straits on a golden ram to escape from their cruel stepmother, but Helle fell into the water and drowned. It was the fleece of this ram that the Argonauts had to bring back from Colchis on the Black Sea. The desire to control the Dardanelles was probably also the cause of the Trojan War. In 480 B.C. the Persian King Xerxes crossed the Hellespont on a bridge of ships in order to march against the Greeks. About 150 years later, Alexander the Great came to reclaim the areas taken by the Persians. In 1356, the Ottomans crossed on rafts and first set foot on European soil.

The saga of Hero and Leander, which inspired Friedrich Schiller and Franz Grillparzer to beautiful verse, is set at the outlet of the Dardanelles into the Aegean. Hero, priestess of Aphrodite in Sestos on the European bank, and Leander, a boy of Asia Minor from Abidos, could only find their way to each other through the waters of the Hellespont. Jealous sea gods, as well as the human hunger for power, demanded a sacrifice for love. Leander

drowned in a storm. Hero threw herself into the sea, heartbroken.

ÇANAKKALE

Çanakkale, "Bowl Fortress" in English, gets its name from an earlier reputation for ceramic work. It lies at the narrowest point of the Dardanelles. Before Mehmet II was able to conquer Constantinople, the Dardanelles, like the Bosporus had to be controlled by blockade fortresses. These were **Killitulbahir** on the European side and the **Sultaniye Kalesi** in Çanakkale on the Asian side. The Sultaniye Kalesi is today home to a maritime museum with numerous pieces from the Gallipoli campaign of 1915 (see "Gallipoli Isthmus", page 74). Old cannons still point out over the water from the fortress. In the warm season, you can sit in one of the tea gardens or fish restaurants on the shore road, observe the ships

Above: The fortress of Killitulbahir, keeping a watchful eye on the strategic Dardanelles.

and the sunset, and contemplate this fateful dividing-line between Occident and Orient.

TROY

About 3000 years earlier, a few kilometers to the south, another bitter battle took place – the Trojan War. A small road forks to the right from the main road and leads to Truva, the fabled Troy. For a long time the ruins of Troy lay buried, but in the mid-1800s a businessman from Mecklenburg in Germany, Heinrich Schliemann,began to search for clues to its location in Homer's *Iliad*. Schliemann had learned Greek solely for this purpose. According to his findings, the city should lie northwest of the Zeybek Dagi (Ida Mountains) at the spot where the Küçük Menderes and the Dumrek Çayi, in ancient times the Skamandros and Simoeis, meet. In the *Iliad*, both of these rivers flooded when Achilles tossed the enemies he had killed in a rage into their waters. A small island,

Tenedos, must stretch out in front of the coast, behind which the Achaeans prepared their ruse with the Trojan Horse. Schliemann was able to obtain a permit to excavate from the Ottoman authorities and began to dig a wide and deep valley in the distinctive 40-meter-high hill Hisarlik. This hill was located at a safe distance from the sea, as described in the *Iliad*, yet the entrance to the Dardanelles could be watched from it. Convinced that the legendary Troy would be right at the bottom of the mound, Schliemann dug through the top layers without a great deal of interest until he discovered a treasure that has come to be known as the "Treasure of Priam". This find was brought to Berlin and has not been seen since the Second World War. According to modern dating methods, the treasure was taken from the level Troy II and its date is estimated at between 2500 and 2300 B.C. It follows that the treasure is over 1000 years older than that which Schliemann was looking for, as the Trojan War is thought to have taken place between 1240 and 1230 B.C. In addition to this, we now know that Homer's Troy was not at the lowest level, level I, but rather at level VI or VIIa.

The tour of the excavations begins at a placard of the layout behind an imaginative reproduction of the **wooden horse**. The path along the east wall, which passes through the **east gate**, enters an area which goes back to the Troy VI period (1900-1240 B.C.). Based on the finds at this level, a prosperous city was able to develop over the centuries, which may have motivated the Achaeans to an extended siege. Some researchers, however, consider the Troy VIIa level to be the city of the Trojan War. During excavations behind the east gate, houses built closely together with doubled floors for supplies and hastily built additions were discovered. These features are typical of cities in times of crises. Continuing north, the visitor comes across pieces of the once mighty retaining wall of the **Athena Temple**, built much later in the Hellenistic-Roman age (Troy IX, A.D. 350-400). Because Aeneas, who was able to escape the burning Troy, was considered to be the founding father of Rome, the Romans had Troy gloriously rebuilt. From a platform, the visitor has a beautiful view of the burial mound and the river landscape, the former battlefield, all the way to the Dardanelles.

The path leads down into the deepest levels of the excavation, to **Troy I and II**. At Troy I are the remains of a gate and a house. Beside one of the ramps at Troy II, Schliemann discovered the "Treasure of Priam". To the far west, at a renovated piece of the wall, may be the opening through which the Trojan Horse was pulled into the city. To the south, you can see the so-called **Place of Sacrifice** of Troy VIII (1070-350 B.C) where Xerxes sacrificed his 1000 steers before crossing the Dardanelles. The path to the **Dardanian Gate** leads past a Roman bath on the right and a theater on the left. From this gate, Priam and Helen were witnesses to Achilles' rage at the death of his friend, Patroclus. To avenge his fallen comrade, Achilles killed the man who slayed him, Priam's son Hector, and dragged his corpse behind his chariot around the city walls three times. In the **Odeum**, a small theater where the original rows of seats are still intact, there are often school groups or, ever more frequently, a silent reader enjoying the *Iliad*. This is the end of the tour. Troy is by no means a monumental excavation, but whoever visits it at the beginning of a trip to Turkey – before having become satiated by archeological superlatives – gets a sense of the aura of the place, the *genius loci*.

Perhaps someday the site will support the theory that the battle over the beautiful Helen did not take place in and around a village with a diameter of 180 meters, but that what has been discovered so far

is only the royal court and that most of Troy's inhabitants lived spread out on the outskirts of the excavation.

Some of our fantastic ideas about Troy, destroyed by the raw reality of the excavations thus far, would be restored if this theory could be proven. As strange as the wooden horse at the entrance may strike some visitors, the horse was the symbol of the sea god and earthquaker Poseidon. It is possible that an earthquake helped the Achaeans, battered after ten years of siege, take the city shortly before they returned to Greece.

Leaving Troy, the road continues south. West of Ezine on the coast lies **Alexandria Troas** which was once an important harbor. The Apostle Paul spent time here on his second missionary trip. Today, remains of the Roman spa can still be seen. With a permission from the Governor of Çanakkale, the visitor can take a ferry from the fishery harbor of

Above: A terracotta relief of the Trojan horse with attacking warriors, from about 670 BC.

Odun Iskelesi to **Bozcaada**, in ancient times Tenedos. Here, at the "Gateway to Byzantium", which historically was an important stopover for Arabic and Venetian invaders, the visitor finds a wonderful peace on the quiet beaches and in the town surrounded since ancient times by vineyards.

Beyond Bayramic, to the east of Ezine, lies **Skepsis** where the famous library of Aristoteles was kept. It was later moved to Pergamum and Alexandria.

In **Ayvacik**, a small road branches off to Behramkale, in ancient times **Assos**. An alternative route, which follows the coast down from Alexandria Troas, is recommended only for those seeking adventure since the road is quite bad in parts.

It is best to tackle the town on foot. You can climb up the volcano to the **acropolis** through archaic surroundings. The volcano rises in terraces to a height of 290 meters above sea level. The mosque of Murat I, situated below the acropolis, was built in the 14th century.

Also dating back to the Ottoman era is an arched bridge from the 17th century which you can see below the town, next to the modern road. On the acropolis, the ruins of the Temple of **Athena**, one of the few examples of Doric architecture in Anatolia, bear witness to the Greek past of this area. Assos was founded around 1000 B.C. across from the island of Lesbos as a trading colony by Aeolian Greeks. The city was so important in the 4th century B.C. that Aristotle founded a philosophy school here (348-45). This is where he developed his famous definition of the nature of democracy. The Apostle Paul also stayed in Assos in the year A.D. 58. From the acropolis there is a beautiful view not only of the Greek island Lesbos, but also of the ruins of the ancient city which stretch to the west and the south along the slope. The monumental **west gate** and the **necropolis** remain well preserved. Upon descending, refreshment in one of the cozy fish restaurants near the harbor may be called for. From Assos, the road along the sea continues to Kücükkuyu. Unpaved up till now, it is presently being expanded and modernized.

The ancient landscape of Troas is bordered by the Gulf of Edremit in the south. Stretching along the coast are the Zeybek Dagi, called the **Ida Mountains** in antiquity. The handsome Paris is supposed to have lived here as a reclusive shepherd until Zeus made him the judge of the beauty contest between Hera, Athena and Aphrodite. His judgement in favor of Aphrodite and later on his rub of the beautiful Helen caused the Trojan War.

The coastal road winds beautifully below the Ida Mountains through stone pine forests and olive groves. A short side-trip to **Gürekaplicalari** leads to the warm springs of Artemis which were already popular in Roman times. In the alluvial fan of the Havran River lies **Edremit**, in ancient times named An-

dramittium after Adramys, the brother of King Croesus. One of the oldest colonies on the coast of Asia Minor, constantly fought over and destroyed because of its strategically-advantageous situation, the pleasant town contains hardly any antique buildings today.

AYVALIK

South of Edremit lies Turkey's largest olive-growing area. The center is the harbor city Ayvalik with its oilmills and soap factories. In Ayvalik, the traces of the more recent Greek past can probably best be followed: In 1773 the small city received, by a decree of the sultan, *ferman*, the status of an independent Greek state. The reason was the rescue of Gazi Hasan Pasa by the inhabitants of the city: they saved the hero of the Algiers campaign after the Russian fleet had defeated him at Çesme on his way home. The new status brought with it a tax exemption and a prohibition that forbade Muslim citizens to settle here. Ayvalik, then called Kydonia, grew to a city of 30,000 and developed into a prospering commercial center. A Greek academy was founded. When the Greeks turned against the Turkish government during the wars of Liberation in 1821, Ayvalik was destroyed and its inhabitants expelled. After 1827 the inhabitants were allowed to return from exile, but the former glamor of the city was gone.

After the First World War, the government in Athens, with the support of the allied powers, decided to revive the idea of a greater Greece. On the 29th of May 1919, troops landed on Lesbos and then at Ayvalik. This was the start of a Greece offensive. Under the leadership of Kemal Atatürk, the Greeks were finally defeated at Izmir and expelled from Anatolia in 1923. The Muslim population of the Greek islands and Saloniki was resettled in the cities which were left deserted by the expulsions.

Following the narrow streets of the old city that lead inward from the harbor, you can almost believe that time has stood still. What is now the **Saatli Camii**, a clock-tower mosque, the **Çinarli Camii**, formerly the Agios Yanis church, and the **Taksiyarhis Kilisesi** are all reminders of the short Greek heyday at the beginning of the 19th century. The last building mentioned above is now a museum where one can see scenes of Christ's life depicted on fish scales.

Over a causeway, the visitor can drive to the island of **Alibey**, referred to by its Greek name, Çunda. This is the largest island of the Ayvalik archipelago. The fishing town of the same name, Alibey, counted a population of about 12,000 at the turn of the century; still to be seen from that time is the Greek **Aya Nicola** cathedral, heavily marked by earthquakes and decay.

If you leave Ayvalik towards the south, the road will take you to the **Seytan Sofrasi**, the "Devil's Table", supposedly named after the devil's footprint on this mountain. From the summit, there is a wonderful view of the surrounding islands off the coast. Towards the east lies a clean sand beach that is gradually being discovered as a bathing beach by tourists. Further to the south, the small harbor town of **Dikili** has become a meeting place for the counter-culture scene. From Dikili the famous reliefs of the Zeus altar of Pergamum were shipped to Berlin. Between Dikili and Çandarli, which is dominated by a Venetian fortress, divers can find an underwater paradise that has hardly been explored.

BERGAMA

About 40 kilometers up the river Bakir Çayi lies Bergama, the old Pergamum. Even from a distance one can recognize

Right: Old salt anchored down with his dreams on the island of Çunda.

the acropolis, the mountain fortress of the ancient city. Buildings dating from the period of Greek hegemony cover the hilltop and extend down its slopes; the Roman city is mostly buried under the small town of Bergama.

In ancient times Pergamum was the capital of a kingdom of the same name, a major center of trade for East and West, and one of the most important cities, culturally speaking, of the contemporary world. A small settlement until the 4th century B.C., it began its ascent under Lysimachus (305-281 B.C.), a general and successor of Alexander the Great. In the course of the power struggles after Alexander's death, Lysimachus acquired a remarkable treasure which he secured in the fortress here. The guard of the treasure, Philetaerus, defended it successfully against the Seleucids. Under the rule of his nephew Eumenes (263-241) and his grandson Attalos I (241-197), who appointed himself king and gave the Attalid dynasty its name, Pergamum grew into an important center of power.

The defeat of the Celtic Galatians and the support of the Romans in the battle at Magnesia at Sipylus in 190 B.C. helped to strengthen the borders of the kingdom and secured the benevolence of the Romans. This made an undisturbed development – most notably under Eumenes II (197-157) – possible. Even infringements of the Bithynian King Prusias II during the reign of Attalos II (159-138) could not, thanks to the help of Rome, stop the ascent of Pergamum. The last of the Attalids, Attalos III, being without heirs, bequeathed his kingdom to the Romans in the year 133 B.C.

During the great Roman peace in the first and second centuries A.D., the Pax Romana, the city spread out far beyond the walls that were erected under Eumenes II. The population grew to around 160,000. One of the earliest Christian communities of Asia Minor was formed in Pergamum. With the deterioration of

Roman influence and the threat, during the Byzantine Empire, of Arabian, then Seljuk and Ottoman attacks, the city gradually retreated back behind the walls of the mountain fortress. In the 14th century, the Ottomans conquered Pergamum, the ancient walls decayed and the city of Bergama was founded at the southern foot of the mountain.

In the year 1864, the German engineer Carl Humann noticed by accident some wonderful stone reliefs that were going to end up in calcium ovens as building material. He traced back their origin and in this way discovered the famous Altar of Zeus on the ancient acropolis. His findings can be seen today at the Pergamum Museum in Berlin. Under the guidance of Conze, Dorpfeld and Boehringer the excavations were continued, so that today one can get a good idea of the concept of urban development put into practice here. Not only the best possible effect for each individual building was desired, but also the harmonious integration of the building into the totality of the

town's panorama, considered a work of art. The reconstruction of the Trajaneum, as well as the excavation to the north of the Temple of Demeter by the German Archaeological Institute are still in progress; for these projects the newest findings of archaeological research are taken into account.

Driving through this pretty country town with its bright houses on the main street, the visitor comes, just past the prominent brick structure of the Red Basilica, to the road that leads to the acropolis. In a kind of giant S-curve, it winds up the mountain to the upper parking lot. After a short climb, one reaches the upper gate of the fortress, the Kings Gate, and the **upper part** of the city. To the left appears a large open space that used to be entered via a propylon and which was enclosed on the cliff side by a two-storied colonnade. On its west side towered the **Temple of Athena**. From the top story of the colonnade, one had access to the famous **library** with its 200,000 works – a result of the collecting mania of the Attalids – which was considered one of the most significant in all antiquity. Pliny reports that the Egyptians – not welcoming this competition for their library at Alexandria – halted the export of papyrus, thereby necessitating the development of goatskin as a writing material here. The invaluable collection of books was sent to Alexandria in 41 B.C. as a present from Mark Antony to Cleopatra. There it was destroyed in the course of a rebellion in A.D. 391.

On the right side of the path that ascends up the mountain were the **palaces** of the Pergamene leaders. Even today one can still find remnants of the beautiful floor mosaics from the palace of Eumenes II. Giant cisterns took care of the water supply. The water reached the city by way of a 45-kilometer-long water main that worked according to the principle of interconnecting pipes. To keep up with increasing water consumption during the Roman era, several aqueducts were built.

Through the northern wall the visitor arrives at the **Garden of the Queen**, named after a Temple of Faustina, the wife of Emperor Marcus Aurelius, which served in earlier times as an arsenal and depot. From here there is a beautiful view towards the east to Kestel Çayi, the antique Ketios, a tributary of the Bakir Çayi.

The path along the northwestern edge of the cliff leads back into the walled area and to the **Temple of Trajan**. This temple, built in honor of the emperors Trajan and Hadrian, rests on mighty foundations and is surrounded on three sides by colonnades. By utilizing fragments of the building that survived, the archaeologists who worked here have succeeded in conveying to visitors an idea of the former magnificence of this structure. The temple conforming to the Corinthian order (9:6 columns), was built of white marble and could be entered via a large outside staircase. The gleam of the facade that faces the valley could be seen from a great distance.

Across the **Athena Terrace**, the path goes down stairs leading to the **theater**. One of the steepest theaters of antiquity, it seated about 10,000 people. The view is imposing from the theater into the valley of Bergama Çayi, the ancient Selinus river, a further tributary of the Bakir Çayi. In front of this backdrop that was only obstructed by an easily removable stagehouse, plays were performed during Greek times. To the right of the stagehouse, a temple was built under Caracalla to the god of theater Dionysus, in which Caracella let himself be idolized as the new Dionysus.

If you leaves the theater halfway up on the left side, you will come across a narrow terrace to the **Pergamum altar**. Two stone pine trees planted by Carl Humann after he had finished his excavations show the way. The altar has been reconstructed in Berlin; only its foundations (36x34m) give an indication here of this building, unique in art history. The horseshoe-shaped altar, dedicated to Zeus, was created during the reign of Eumenes II in commemoration of the successful campaign against the Galatians. On a 120 meter long and 2.30 meter high frieze, the battle of the Pergamenes against the Galatians was depicted symbolically as the Olympians against the Giants. Plasticity, movement and depth of expression reached a high point with this work.

Beneath this stretches the **upper agora**, or marketplace, upon which the hut and grave of Carl Humann can be found. If one follows the path downhill (marked for most of the way by blue spots) one comes by way of the old road to the middle city. The less affluent people lived here. The meeting rooms, baths, stores, and kitchens laid bare by the excavations give helpful information about the living conditions of the population during Greek and Roman times. Further southeast, more recently, urban

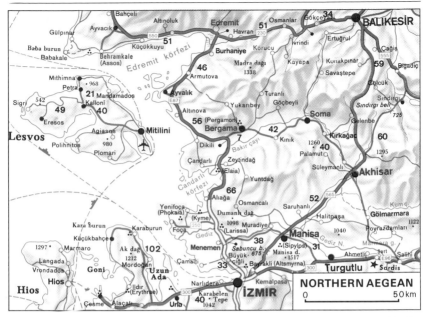

communities of the Byzantine Age were laid bare in layers, making it possible to trace the development of the city during the Middle Ages.

South of this, spread out across a large terrace, is the **Temple of Demeter**. Already built under Philetaerus, it is considered one of the oldest buildings of the city. It stood, strongly fortified, outside of the walls of the acropolis. The cult of the earth-mother Demeter, a mystery cult, stood in opposition to the cult of the Olympian gods, in that it promised, by way of cleansing rituals, a better life after death. From the spectator tiers, the initiated, among whom one could also find women and slaves, were allowed to witness the ritual sacrifices.

Southeast of this lies the **upper gymnasium**, the most impressive of three schools that were intended for different age groups. The upper gymnasium was meant to serve the bodily and spiritual training of adolescents above 15 years of age, the *neoi*, before they came of age and were to take over the duties of citi-

zens. Costly, marble-fitted, heated baths, an auditorium with 1000 seats and a roofed stadium were all a part of this complex. Beneath it lay the **middle gymnasium** for the *ephebes* (10 to 15 years); still lower was the **lower gymnasium** for the *paides* (6 to 9 years). Through a Hellenistic gate, which in Roman times connected the middle gymnasium with the lower gymnasium and was later integrated into the medieval defense wall, the visitor leaves the middle city and enters the lower agora. The **house of the consul Attalos**, above and to the right, shows the typical Pergamene peristyle house of a rich citizen, complete with an inner courtyard surrounded by columns and living quarters with friezes on the walls.

The **lower agora** was formerly bordered by a two-story colonnade that ran all the way around and along the back of which there were stores. A tablet with the police ordinance that was found, now in the Bergama museum, shows the strict rules concerning house and path construction, as well as the care of the foun-

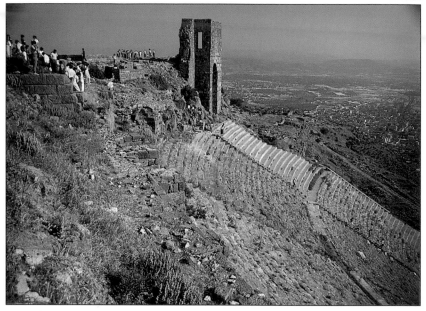

tains, cisterns and water pipes. The stone spheres on the agora are from the arsenal. Underneath the main road are still fragments of the main gate, an indication of how the city was expanding under Eumenes II.

Along the road or returning back through the excavation site, one reaches once again the upper parking lot. The most prominent building here is the red hall, **Kizil Avlu**. It was probably built during the reign of Emperor Hadrian (117-138) and served the Serapis cult, a mixture of Egyptian and Olympian cult forms for all merchants and soldiers who came together from all parts of the Mediterranean. With three naves and galleries, and covered in the lower wall area with marble plates, it is among the largest structures of the city. In Christian times it served as a church. One of the seven epistles of the Apostle John from the is-

land of Patmos was addressed to the community of Pergamum, the town where – according to Revelations – the throne of satan (the altar of Zeus) is. In the center of town on the right side of the street is the **archaeological museum** of Bergama, interesting because of its finds from the excavation sites on the fortress hill and the Asclepius sanctuary. These serve to round out a first impression of the antique city.

To reach the **Asclepion**, you can go from the city out towards the right along a narrow street up the hill, past military barracks. (No photos please!) From the parking lot you can follow the **Sacred Way** to the holy district of Asclepius. The street was bordered by colonnades, in whose stores devotions were sold to the visitors here. Through a **propylon**, the visitor entered the inner area. The Asclepion of Pergamum was considered in antiquity, along with those at Epidaurus and Kos, one of the most important temple precincts of the god Asclepius. A citizen of Pergamum, Aristarch, brought

Above: The great theater of Pergamum, today known as Bergama. Right: Browsing and buying in the busy streets of Bergama.

doctors here from Epidaurus after they had healed his broken leg. A kind of sanatorium was developed, in which by way of natural healing, warm and cold baths, mudpacks, diets, movement therapy, temple sleep with dream interpretation, and suggestion, patients were treated ambulantly.

In the second century A.D., the famous doctor Galen lived here. Later the personal physican of Emperor Marcus Aurelius who, next to Hippocrates, was the most significant physician of antiquity. Galen's achievement was that he compiled, for the first time, all antique medical, scientific knowledge into a unified, logically-sound system.

His numerous works were regarded up until modernity as absolute standards in the medical field. According to an inscription above the entrance, death could not enter the Asclepion. The fatally-ill and dying were banished from the area. A round stone in the forecourt with a snake drinking from a bowl is the symbol for the life-renewing and preserving forces of the god Asclepius.

The **round temple of Asclepius** was located to the left of the propylon. In the **Athena library** to the right of the propylon, the patients could educate themselves with spiritual and philosophical literature during the pauses in their treatments. The inner court was surrounded on three sides with a covered alley of columns where movement therapy was given on the clay floor. A small **theater** which is today host to classical theater pieces during the Bergama festival, also served as a distraction and edification for the patients. Bubbling in the middle of the square was the **holy spring**. An underground spring *(kryptoporticus)* leads to the southeast corner of the court, where healing sleep therapy took place in the **Temple of Telesphoros**. Sun terraces were located on the south side. Latrines with constant running water were located at the southwest corner.

The Sacred Way leads from the Asclepion complex through the **Viran Gate** to the city center. Halfway there you reach the great Roman **theater** and then the **stadium**. West of here is the **amphitheater**, which was built over a stream that flows to the Selinus River. The stream provided water for sea battles and water games in the amphitheater. East of the point where the modern road from Asclepion merges with the main street are three burial mounds or **tumuli** from Pergamene times.

Further to the south, in the direction of Izmir, streets branch off after the refinery town Aliaga and head towards the **Foça isthmus**. On the western part of the isthmus, at the northern entrance to the gulf, is the harbor city **Foça**, Phocaea in ancient times. On the way to it, there is a monumental tomb named Taskule which was carved completely from the surrounding stone. It is considered the most important relic of old Phocaea. Phocaea was the northernmost city of the twelve-city league which the Ionians formed

during the great Aegean migration at the beginning of the first millennium B.C. when they settled the west coast of Asia Minor. The Phocaeans were brave seafarers and went as far as the western Mediterranean Sea, where they founded cities such as Massalia, today Marseille (around 600 B.C.). The scenery here nowadays is dominated by the ruins of a medieval Genoese fortress.

In the northern part of the isthmus lies **Yenifoça**. It was founded by the Genoese to facilitate the production of alum, which is used as tannin and as a corrosive. Yenifoça is a small harbor city opened up by tourism, with beautiful, quiet **bathing inlets** nearby.

In the direction of Izmir, near **Menemen**, is the fork that leads to Manisa, in ancient times Magnesia ad Sipylus. Whoever prefers to take the inland route

Above: Pergamum in mist and rain seems a kind of psychotherapy center. Right: Windmills are still used to pump water in some parts of Turkey.

from Bergama through the charming landscape travels via Soma and Akhisar directly, or from Akhisar with a detour through Sindirgi, Simav, Usak, Kula and Sardes to Manisa. The detour leads through an area famous for its hot springs and nomadic carpet weaving.

Between Simav and Usak, the road forks toward Kutahya and goes past the famous temple of Zeus in Aezani. Kutahya, like Iznik, became famous because of its porcelain pottery work.

MANISA

At the foot of the Manisa Dagi lies picturesque **Manisa**, called Magnesia ad Sipylus in ancient times. Stretching in the north is the fertile basin *(ova)* of the Gediz River, called Hermus in antiquity, which is famous for its sultana grapes. Although it lies outside the gates of the urban center of Izmir, it has been able to maintain the character of a traditional Ottoman city. Its roots, however, go back even further. Nearby, in **Akpinar**, a Hit-

tite stone relief of an enthroned goddess with cylindrical headware was found, leading to the assumption that the area was within the Hittite empire's sphere of influence around 1400 B.C. In 190 B.C. the Romans defeated the Seleucid Antioch III at Magnesia with the help of Pergamum under Eumenes II. The Byzantine Emperor Johannes Dukas III retreated here after the Romans had taken Constantinople in 1204.

Manisa became Seljuk in 1313 and Ottoman in 1390. The Ottoman sultans Murat II and Murat III were particularly fond of Manisa and happily resided here. The young Ottoman crown princes were sent to Manisa, where they gathered experience for their future tasks as sultans by working as representatives. Worth seeing is the **Ulu Cami** which was built in the year 1366 by the Seljuks. In the front court, Byzantine columns and capitals support the surrounding arcade. The parallel prayer house is covered by one great dome supported by an octagon, and 19 smaller domes. The **Muradiye Camii**

of the 16th century shows Sinan's influence. In the mosque complex is a small **museum** with an ethnographic department worth seeing, along with interesting archaeological finds from the Manisa area. These include a marble shrine to Cybele from Sardis.

A special event in Manisa is the annual *mesir* festival which takes place in April. A specialty concocted in kettles from various spices and called *mesir macunu* is thrown to the crowd from minarets.

From the **Byzantine citadel** in the southern part of the city there is a beautiful view of the city and the plain. Also interesting in Manisa is a rock formation called **mourning Niobe** because of its shape, that of a human head. Niobe was the daughter of Tantalus. Both daughter and father had challenged the gods in their arrogance and were punished. Niobe was a mother of seven sons and seven daughters, and haughtily laughed at Leto because she had only two children, Apollo and Artemis. As punishment, she lost all 14 children and turned to stone from grief. The characters from both of the above legends originated in this region. The Tantalus castle is presumed to have been about 500 meters east of the Akpinar relief on the rock Yarik Kaya.

SARDIS

Following the Gediz valley further upstream, you will approach Sart, **Sardis** in ancient times, shortly before Salihili. Sardis was the capital city of the Lydian Empire and reached its high point in the period between the reign of King Gyges (around 685 B.C.) and that of Croesus (560-546 B.C.). The fabled riches of Croesus are based on Sardis' location on the Paktolos river, a tributary of the Hermus, that in ancient times carried gold. Under the acropolis the Lydian-Greek city developed, and in the north the Roman one.

In the year 546 B.C. Sardis was conquered by the Persians. Croesus interpreted the sly saying of the oracle at Delphi – "he who crosses the Halys will destroy a great empire" – absolutely incorrectly. Once he had crossed the central Anatolian Halys, known today as Kizilirmak, he was defeated by the Persian king Cyrus the Great. In Persian times the "street of kings" started in Sardis and led via Ankara to Susa.

The ruins of the **Temple of Artemis** that lie to the south of the village of Sart, tell of Sardis' stirring past. Built in the 6th B.C. century by Croesus and consecrated to the Anatolian mother- goddess Cybele, the complex was destroyed by the Greeks from Ephesus when they captured the city from the Persians in 499 B.C. and rebuilt it under Alexander the Great. The temple, separated in the middle by a dividing wall, was thought for a long time to be dedicated simultaneously to Artemis and Zeus. More probable, however, was that here, in addition to Artemis, the deified Roman empress Faustina was honored. The dividing wall was not added until the final phase of extensions under Antonius Pius (A.D. 138-161). Bilingual inscriptions in Lydian and Aramaean have made it possible for linguists to decipher the Lydian language as a Semitic one and pinpoint the origin of the Lydian people as being in the Assyrian region.

The excavations of the Roman city lie to south and north of the road that leads to Salihili, which here follows approximately the route of the old king's road which led to Susa. The findings are from the time of the reconstruction under Tiberius, after the city had been almost completely destroyed by a heavy earthquake in A.D. 17. A clear picture of the living conditions of the inhabitants of Sardis was obtained when the **Bronze House** was excavated and a Lydian house, with various instructive household objects was also found.

To the northeast of the village Sart, a **gymnasium** with bathing facilities from the 2nd century A.D. has been partially reconstructed. The monumental marble courtyard makes it possible to get an impression of the splendor of one of the gymnasiums built during the emperor's times. Also reconstructed is the south wing of the palace, an open square surrounded by colonnades, built for physical training, and a **synagogue** from the third century. The last is considered one of the most important remaining Jewish sacred buildings in Asia Minor, and still impressives one with its decorative mosaics. Already by the middle of the first century, probably due to the influence of the Apostle Paul, Christian communities began to form in the Gediz valley. Sardis and Philadelphia to the east, now known as Alasehir, were among the seven apocalyptical churches in Asia Minor to which from Patmos John addressed his open letters.

Right: Grape harvesters take a break on the rewards of their bountiful land.

Whoever climbs up onto the **acropolis** will be rewarded with a wonderful view of the valley. Around 10 kilometers to the northwest lies the city of the dead, the **necropolis**, with its numerous burial mounds. The highest one is supposed to be that of Alyattes, Croesus' father.

If you cross the mountain chain Boz Daglari to the south of Sardis on a winding sand road in the direction of Odemis, you will come to **Birgi**, a remote country town in which Ottoman time seems to have stood still. The town is characterized by its typical houses from the 18th and 19th centuries. An example of such a stately home is the **Cacir Oglu Konagi**. Above the ground floor, the panelled and artistically-painted upper floor rises up and juts out. Above that, there is the slightly slanted roof. On the inside, grouped around an open courtyard, are opened and closed rooms. While the utility rooms and the living quarters of the domestics were located on the ground floor, the actual living area of the family was confined to the upper floor.

Worth a visit is also the **Ulu Cami** from the 14th century, with building pieces "borrowed" from the nearby antique Hypapa. The splendid *minbar* is (just like the entrance door wing that was brought to Selimiye from Edirne) artistically carved out of wood.

The way to Izmir from Birgi passes through Odemis and Torbali. If you drive via Sardis or go from there directly to Izmir, an excursion to **Kemalpasa** must be recommended.

This town was called Nymphaeum in ancient times. Here the Byzantine emperor in exile during the rule of the Latins, Michael Paläologos, signed a history-making contract with the Genoese in 1261. It stipulated that the Genoese would receive special trading privileges in Izmir and Constantinople if they would help free Constantinople from the Latins and Venetians. This was the basis for the development of the Genoese trade monopoly along the coast of Asia Minor in the centuries to follow. Fragments of the Byzantine palace still exist.

EDIRNE
Accommodation
LUXURY: **Rüstempasa Caravanserail Hotel**, Iki Kapili Han Cad. 57, Tel: 181-12195.
MODERATE: **Balta**, Talat Pasa Asfalti 97, Tel: 181-15210. **Park**, Maarif Cad.7, Tel: 181-14610.
BUDGET: **Kervan**, Kadirhane Sok. 134, Tel: 181-11382/11167. **Sultan**, Talatpasa Bulv. 24, Tel: 181-11372/13333. **Fifi Turistik Tesisleri** (Motel), Demirkapi Mev., E-5 Üzeri, Tel: 181-11554. **Motel Londra Camping**, E-5 Karayolu, Kapikule/Edirne, Tel: 181-13711.

Tourist Information
Tourist Information, Talatpasa Asfalti 76/A, Tel: 181-15260/21490.

Access / Transportation
You can reach Edirne by bus from all points in Turkey, but most connections come from Istanbul. There are also trains from Istanbul and connections from Europe. Local transportation is by taxi, minibus and bus.

Grease Wrestling
A good time to visit Edirne is in early July when the annual *Kirkpinar Grease Wrestling* championships are held outside town in the hallowed field of Kirkpinar, where, according to legend, two great wrestlers vied for the grand prize all night and were found dead in the morning in a grim embrace. In addition to the prospective *pehlivan*, or professional wrestlers, the city also fills with gypsies from across the land. Conversely, this is not a time to visit for those who prefer peace and quiet.

BURSA
Accommodation
LUXURY: **Almira**, Ulubatli Hasan Bul., Tel: 24-153030. **Hotel Kervansaray Termal**, Çekirge, Tel: 24-353000. **Çelik Palas**, Çekirge, Tel: 24-353500. **Anatolia**, Çekirge Meyd., Tel: 24-367110. **Dilmen**, Murat Cad., Çekirge, Tel: 24-366114.
MODERATE: **Büyük Yildiz**, Uludag Cad. 6, Tel: 24-366600. **Termal Hotel Gönlüferah**, Murat Cad. 24, Tel: 24-362700. **Kent**, Atatürk Cad. 119, Tel: 24-218700. **Kirci**, Çekirge Cad. 21, Tel: 24-202000. *BUDGET:* **Diyar Oteli**, Çekirge Cad. 47, Tel: 24-209786. **Adapalas**, I. Murat Cad. 21, Tel: 24-333990. **Yat Oteli**, Hamamlar Cad. 31, Tel: 24-363112. **Artiç**, Atatürk Cad. 95, Tel: 24-219500. **Akçam**, Uludag Yolu Üzeri, Çekirge, Tel: 24-368303.

Restaurants
Bursa is famous for its *iskender kebab*, the creation of a local cook which has spread throughout the country. Many restaurants in town specialize in the plate of thinly-sliced *kebab*, served with tomato sauce, yoghurt, melted butter and *pide*-bread.
A good (the original!) place to start is **Kebabçi Iskender**, Tel: 24-211076, or **Kebapçi Iskender Iskenderoglu ve Ortaklari**, Tel: 41-214615, run by the sons of the original Iskender. **Altin Ceylan**, Kültürpark Içi Bursa, Tel: 24-209770. **Çiçek Izgara Lokantasi**, Belediye Cad. 15, Tel: 24-211288. **Cumurcul**, Kükürtlü Çecirge Cad., Tel: 24-353707. **Özkent**, Kültürpark Içi, Tel: 24-202021. **Sönmez**, Yükseller Mev.,Tel: 24-145460.

Festivals
An interesting time to visit Bursa is in July at the time of the annual *Bursa Festival*. Amid the dances and folklore events, step into the *Kozahan* to see the silk merchants at their trade.

Spas
Bursa is the most famous spa area of Turkey, with many establishments dating back to the Roman area. The hot mineral springs are called *Kaplicalar*, and most hotels have their own pools and facilities.
Yalova, on the coast between Bursa and Istanbul, and **Bolu**, between Istanbul und Ankara, are favorite places for "taking the waters". The region around **Kütahya**, **Kula** and the town of **Simav** boasts a mutitude of spas with different temperatures and mineral qualities to choose from, promising cures or relief from ailments ranging from gall stones to barrenness.
The **Eynal** thermal waters emerge on the surface at a boiling hot 97°C. Cooler are the baths at **Emet**, between Simav and Tavsanli on route 595, where the water emerges from the ground at temperatures of 45-50°C. Some 20 km from Simav down road 240 toward **Gediz**, a cluster of hot springs and related facilities line the road. High in minerals, these baths feature a yellow sulphur deposit much favored by those suffering from rheumatism, neuralgia and other nervous disorders.

Access / Transportation
In addition to the Istanbul–Bursa highway, the southern shore of the Sea of Marmara is connected to Istanbul via ferry boat service to Yalova, Mundanya and Erdek, from where taxis or buses take you to Bursa. There are flights to Bursa from Istanbul by Sönmez Airlines twice a day.

Tourist Information / Airport
Tourist Information Bursa, Ulu Camii Park 1, Tel: 24-212359/213368. **Bursa Sönmez Airport**, Ottoman Tur, Cernal Nadir Cad./Kizilay Pasaj, Tel: 24-222097.

ULUDAG
Accommodation

LUXURY: **Grand Yazici**, Delisim Bölgesi Uludag, Tel: 2418-1050. **Kervansaray Uludag**, Tel: 2418-1187. *MODERATE:* **Beceren**, Tel: 2418-1114. *BUDGET:* **Alkoçlar**, Tel: 2418-1130. **Büyük**, Tel: 2418-1216. **Dag Club Datça**, Tel: 2418-1020. **Ergün**, Oteller Bölgesi, Tel: 2418-1100. **Genç Yazici**, Oteller Bölgesi, Tel: 2418-1040. **Kar**, Tel: 2418-1121. **Ibo**, Oteller Bölgesi, Tel: 2418-1140. *HOTELS IN THE VICINITY:* **Atamer**, Hasanga Mevkii, Gemlik, Tel: 2511-4594. **Karaka Motel**, Gemlik, Tel: 251-84371. **Köksal**, Güzelyali, Mudanya, Tel: 257-42400. *CAMPING:* **Nur Camping**, Yalova Road, Tel: 2414-7453.

Restaurants

Bülent Garan Tesis, Mandira Mev., Uludag, Tel: 2418-1247. **Gümüsraket**, Eski Mudanya Yolu, Mudanya, Tel: 24-432057. **Denizati**, Iskele Mev. 1, Mudanya, Tel: 257-41056.

NORTHERN AEGEAN
Accommodation

AYVACIK/ASSOS: *MODERATE:* **Assos Eden Beach**, Kadirga Koyu, Behramkale, Tel: 081-13060. Reservation in Istanbul: 1-1406441. **Assos**, Ayavçik, Tel: 1969-1437. **Behram**, Assos, Behramkale, Tel: 081-12758.

BOZCAADA: *BUDGET:* **Koz**, Seref Sok., Tel: 1965-1189.

ÇANAKKALE: *MODERATE:* **Grand Truva Hotel**, Kayserili Ahmetpasa Cad., Yaliboyu, Tel: 196-11024. **Iris**, Tusan Cad., Güzelyani, Tel: 196-28100. **Mola Motel**, Güzelyali, Tel: 196-28022. **Tusan**, Güzelyali Köyü, Tel: 196-28210. *BUDGET:* **Anzac**, Saat Kulesi Mey., 8, Tel: 196-17777. **Güleç**, Cevatpasa Mah. Velibey Sok. 6, Tel: 196-12500.

GELIBOLU: *MODERATE:* **Boncuk**, Fener Ovasi Mev., Tel: 1891-1461.

Tourist Information / Festival

Çanakkale Tourist Information, Iskele Meydani 67, Tel: 196-15012. *Anzac Day Celebrations* take place on April 25.

Dobag

Ayvacik is the home of DOBAG (a natural dyes research project). This is where Harald Böhmer first realized his idea of using natural dyes for carpets, and aside from his house in Istanbul, this is the only outlet for these unique rugs in Turkey. The price is determined by the number of knots in each piece, and no bargaining is allowed. The fortunate traveler will chance on Böhmer himself and may even be invited to the village of Süleymanköy to witness the dying process in action.

GULF OF EDREMIT
Accommodation

AYVALIK: *LUXURY:* **Grand Hotel Temizel**, Sarimsakli, Tel: 663-42000. *MODERATE:* **Club Berk Hotel**, Sarimsakli, Tel: 663-40775. **Club Hotel Murat Reis**, Altinkum Mevkii, Balikesir, Tel: 663-41456. **Club Washington**, Tuzla Mevkii, Balikesir, Tel: 663-41779. **Aytas Motel**, Sarimsakli, Balikesir, Tel: 663-41257. *BUDGET:* **Billurcu**, Sarimsakli, Tel: 663-41189. **Büyük Berk**, Sarimsakli, Balikesir, Tel: 663-41045. **Soley**, Sarimsakli, Küçukkoy, Tel: 663-41415.

BERGAMA: *MODERATE:* **Asude**, Izmir Asfalti 93, Tel: 541-11669. **Berksoy Hotel**, Izmir Yolu Bergama, Tel: 541-12595. **Iskender**, Izmir Cad. Ilica Önü, Tel: 541-12123. *BUDGET:* **Efsane**, Izmir Cad. 86, Tel: 541-12936.

EDREMIT: *MODERATE:* **Chalet Chopin**, Cam Mah. 12, Altinoluk, Balikesir. Tel: 671-61044. *BUDGET:* **Arsiyan**, Akçay, Tel: 671-41033.

ERDEK: *BUDGET:* **Arteka**, Çugra Mevkii, Tel: 1989-2139. **Gül Plaj**, Kumlu Yali Cad. 78, Tel: 1989-1947. **Kirtay**, Tatlisu Köyü, Tel: 1978-1044. **Özgün**, Çugra Mevkii, Tel: 1989-4722. **Pinar**, Mangirci Mevkii, Tel: 1989-7024.

FOÇA: *MODERATE:* **Leon**, 1. Mersinaki, Tel: 5431-2961. **Foça Holiday Village** (Club Med.),Tel: 5431-1607. *BUDGET:* **Hanedan**, Sahil C., Büyükdeniz, Tel: 5431-1515. **Pension Bir**, Fevzipasa Mev., Tel: 5431-1108. **Pension Fokayus** , Sahil Cad., Tel: 5431-2420.

GÖNEN: *MODERATE:* **Yildiz Oteli**, Banyolar, Tel: 1985-1840.

MANISA: *MODERATE:* **Tütün**, Devlet Kara Yolu Üzeri 21, Akhisar, Tel: 558-15067.

Access / Transportation

Access to the northern Aegean and the Gulf of Edremit is limited to private vehicles and buses. The main bus terminals are at Çanakkale, Balikesir and Izmir, where one can pick up local buses or minibuses to various destinations. The closest airports are at Bursa and Izmir.

Tourist Information

Tourist Information Erdek: Hükümet Caddesi, Karsisi, Tel: 1989-1169. **Tourist Information Ayvalik:** Çamlik Caddesi Yat Limani, Karsisi, Tel: 663-12122.

Olive Oil

Turkey is one of the largest producers and exporters of olive oil products in the world. The best, virgin olive oil, is produced in and around Ayvalik. The Komili family is king here, although there are any number of small producers one can privately court.

THE AEGEAN COAST

IZMIR
ÇESME
EPHESUS
PAMUKKALE / MILETUS
BODRUM / MARMARIS
KAS

IZMIR

Whether approached from the north, east or south, the city of Izmir looks like a giant octopus, sprawling its arms over the surrounding hills into the mountainous regions beyond. From neighboring peaks, there is a spectacular view of the Gulf of Izmir. Little wonder that this port city has expanded so rapidly in recent decades, from a population of 400,000 in 1960 to over 2.5 million inhabitants today. The former name of **Smyrna** recalls a great but fateful history, throughout which this city endured the ravages of battles, earthquakes and fires. Yet the visitor must look carefully to find traces of the past among the modern facades of the city.

The oldest traces of settlements along the gulf date back to 3000 B.C. and are found upon a hill in Bayrakli on the northeast corner of the bay. Around 1000 B.C., Aeolian Greeks, pursued by Ionian Greeks, arrived here and established a colony, naming it after the myrrh growing abundantly in this area. Smyrna is

Preceding pages: The grandiose Roman theater of Ephesus is still used for productions today. Left: A horse and buggy in Izmir bringing a touch of nostalgia to the town's visitors.

said to be the birthplace of Homer, where he wrote the *Iliad* in the 8th century B.C. Alexander the Great had General Lysimachus erect a fortress on Mount Pagus along the southern bay.

Thus protected, Smyrna thrived in the valley below and continued to prosper greatly under later Roman influence. In A.D. 178 the town suffered a devastating earthquake, but it was restored to its former splendor by Emperor Marcus Aurelius. Over time, shipyards were built as Byzantine, Seljuk, Genoese and Ottoman merchants vied for access. Smyrna grew to be one of the most important centers of trade. In the late 19th century, the Gediz River, known in classical antiquity as the Hermus, threatened to cut off Smyrna's access to the open sea as it emptied large quantities of silt from the north into the bay. It was therefore diverted into the bay from the west.

At the end of World War I, Smyrna was occupied by the Greeks, who expected to be given the city after the ratification of the Treaty of Sèvres (1920). However, in 1922 Kemal Atatürk recovered the city during the last stages of his campaign for Turkish self-determination. In the process, Smyrna's northern quarters, home to most of its foreign population, went up in flames. It was later to rebuilt according to ideas that resulted from an urban development competition. Atatürk's Turkish Republic (1923) was determined to pattern new development on western planning models.

Nestled in the heart of modern Izmir is the lush **Kültürpark**. Here main roads converging onto a central marketplace create a starlike formation. Within the market halls, Turkey's largest trade fair takes place annually in summer, drawing exhibitors and buyers from the Middle and Near East. South of the Kültürpark lies **Basmane Station**. One of its first train routes led into the rich agricultural hinterlands of the Menderes River Valley. Tobacco, cotton, raisins, figs and olives continue to be the primary staples exported from Izmir's ports.

Approaching the northern tip of the city, one encounters the **Alsancak Quarter** jutting into the bay. Formerly a Greek and Armenian neighborhood, it is now the location of **Alsancak Station** and the **ferryboat harbor**. One of the few historical buildings dating earlier than 1922 now houses the **Atatürk Museum** along the coastal promenade. Others can be found in the parallel street, Cumhuriyet Bulvari: the **Selçuk Yasar Museum** housing contemporary Turkish art, the Mavi Bar and the Yengec Restaurant. Also located along the coastal promenade are the NATO headquarters for the southeast sector. The post office is on the Square of the Republic, Cumhuriyet Meydani, the larger hotels stretch along the border of the lively bazaar, and the banks are scattered along the southern end of Cumhuriyet Bulvari.

Next to the commercial and yacht harbor and the customs offices lies **Konak Square**, the heart of the city. The only vestiges of the Ottoman era are the Konak mosque and clock tower. The square is flanked on the north by the modern City Hall, on the east by shopping plazas, and on the south by the **bus station**, behind which stands "the ship" of the **Atatürk Cultural Center**. Along

the winding road to the south are the **Ethnological Museum**, the **Archaeological Museum**, displaying the famous statues of Poseidon and Demeter from the agora, and the medical clinic. Following Esrefpasa Caddesi you will arrive in the older sections of the city at the foot of the fortressed mountain. The **bazaar** contains examples of historic Osmanli architecture, such as the 18th century **Kizlaragasi-Han** and the **Hisar Camii**, built in 1597. To the east, under the tall columns of the **agora** and in the shops beyond, the treasures of the Orient and Occident traded hands in former times. The most beautiful site in Izmir is surely **Kadifekale**, the "Velvet Fortress" on Mount Pagus, which has a tea garden and a stunning panoramic view. Gazing to the west, you can view the peninsula of Çesme forming the southwestern border of the Gulf of Izmir.

ÇESME

Both natives and strangers alike agree that the Çesme Peninsula is a vacationer's paradise. The name Çesme means "spring," of which there are many, providing the peninsula with hot and cold water. The route from Izmir passes by the popular beach, **Inciralti**. To the south, the thermal springs **Agamemnun Kaplicalari** provide relief for rheumatoid and kidney ailments. Continuing westward along the main road, you will reach the magnesium-rich thermal springs of the village of **Urla**. Just north of Urla, excavations have brought to light numerous painted archaic terracotta sarcophagi and the ancient town of **Klazomenai**, home of the philosopher Anaxagorus (approx. 500 to 428 B.C.). Returning to the main road, the visitor comes upon the ruins of a Roman bridge near **Içmeler**. To the north, older Aegean villages can be found along the **Karaburun Peninsula**. The village of the same name offers a peaceful refuge, although a stronger tourist

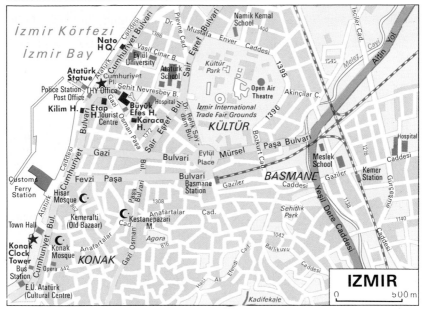

İzmir Körfezi
İzmir Bay

Nato HQ.

Atatürk Statue

Police Station
Post Office

Kilim H.

Custom
Ferry
Station

Town Hall

Konak Clock Tower
Bus Station

E.Ü. Atatürk
(Cultural Centre)

Cumhuriyet Bulvari

Vasıf Çınar B.
Eylül University

Atatürk School

THY Office
Şehit Nevresbey B.
Hospital

Etap
H.Tourist Centre

Büyük
Efes H.
Karaca
H.

Dr. Plevne Cad.
Mustafa
Şair Eşref Bulvari
Enver Caddesi

Namik Kemal
School

Kültür Park

Open Air Theatre
Akinçilar C.

İzmir International
Trade Fair Grounds
KÜLTÜR

Gazi

Bulvari

Fevzi Paşa

Hisar Mosque

Kemeralti
(Old Bazaar)

Kestanepazari
M.

Konak Mosque
KONAK

Gazi Osman Paşa Bul.
Şair Eşref Bul.

Eylül Place
Bulvari
Basmane
Station

Anafartalar Cad.

Agora

Anafartalar Cad.

Mürsel

Gaziler

Paşa Bulvari

BASMANE
Caddesi

Meslek
School

Sehitlik
Park

Ballikuyu

Efendi Cad.

Kadifekale

Bozkurt Cad.

Yeşil Dere Caddesi

Hospital

Kemer
Station

Caddesi

Caddesi

IZMIR

0   500 m

presence is detectable. Situated along the western side of the Karaburun Peninsula between Ildir and Balikliora is the ancient town of **Erythrai**. Scant remains of the city walls and a theater indicate its importance in the former Ionian League.

Çesme, a bather's paradise, awaits. Known in antiquity as Kysus, Çesme was a strategically important point along the water route between the Isle of Chios and Erythrai in a bay to the northeast. Two great sea battles took place here: in 190 B.C. the Romans, led by Scipio Africanus, conquered the Phoenician-Seleucid fleet, whose general was the famous Carthaginian Hannibal. In 1770, the Turkish fleet anchored here was completely destroyed by the czarist Russian fleet, contributing heavily to the decline of the Ottoman Empire. The 14th century **Genoese Fortress** is now a museum for Osmanli weaponry, as well as host to an annual music festival. A former 17th century caravanserai has been renovated as a modern luxury hotel. **Beaches** of fine white sand stretch to the east and west of Çesme along the turqoise waters of the Aegean Sea. Popular for its tourist accomodations, **Ilica** is named after its hot springs. They even bubble out of the sea bed, making year-round swimming possible. The coastal water is particularly shallow here, enabling one to walk far out. Certainly even the ancient Greeks favored these "Coasts of Light" as a divine place to linger and rest.

Continuing on towards Selçuk, the departure point for visiting ancient Ephesus, it is best to pass through Izmir. Those who wish to take a leisurely detour can branch off behind Urla towards **Seferihisar** in the south. From there a dirt road leads towards the bay of Sigacik, to ancient **Teos**, which also belonged to the Ionian League. Here dwelled the poet Anacreon (around 540 B.C.), known for his songs in praise of love and wine. Recent excavations have unearthed a small Dionysos shrine, the agora and an odeum. From Seferihisar, a modest road winds along the coast to the beaches at the mouth of the Derebogaz. Further in-

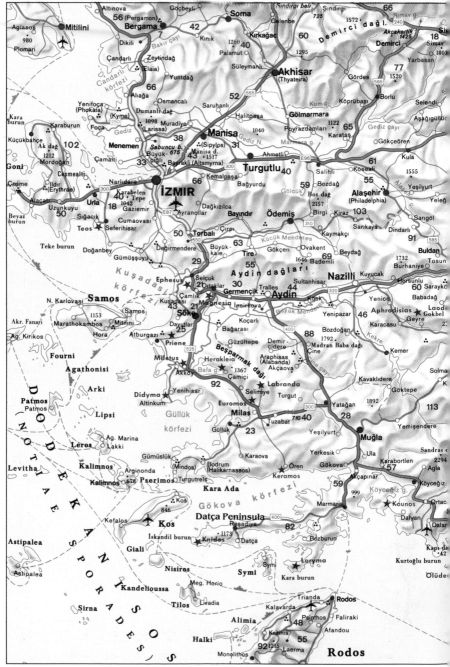

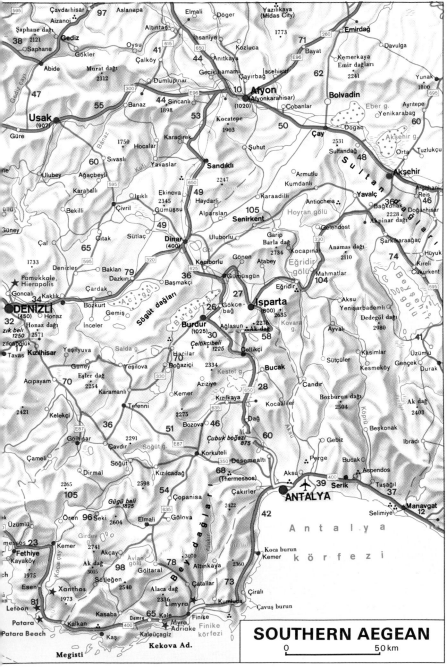

SOUTHERN AEGEAN

0   50 km

land lies **Kolophon**, rendered one of the most powerful cities in the Ionian League by its rich agricultural resources, horse-breeding, and the export of its famous pine resin. Following a war in 287 B.C. Lysimachus resettled the inhabitants in Ephesus. Portions of the fortification walls of **Kolophon** still stand. The ruins of a theater may be found in the former port of **Notion**, and **Claros**, a valley to the east, was home to an important cave oracle of Apollo. Selçuk is best reached via Yonca.

EPHESUS

A small town of about 20,000 inhabitants, modern Selçuk is situated next to and in parts of ancient Ephesus. It extends to the alluvium along the eastern border of the Küçük Menderes River, the ancient Caystros. Northwest of the heart of this region, upon the slope leading to

Above: The pleasant beaches and quiet sea of Çesme attract many visitors.

the citadel, lies the St. John basilica. From here one has a splendid view of the Caystros Valley below. Entering the basilica through the so-called Door of Persecution, you will see to the left a relief presenting in visual form the complicated history of Ephesus' colonization. Over the centuries Ephesus was relocated several times, as silt from the Caystros filled the former bay area. The matriarchal goddess cult also played a significant role in Ephesus' development far into the Christian era.

In the 2nd millennium B.C., native Carians settled at the foot of the citadel hill. They erected a shrine in honor of the great Anatolian mother goddess, Cybele. Ionian settlers arrived around 1000 B.C., led by Androcles. As the Greeks mingled with the native Carians, so also the cult of Artemis, Goddess of the Hunt, gradually merged with the cult of Cybele, to whom the very first temple was dedicated around 700 B.C. A pillar still stands on the southwest slope of the citadel, sole evidence of the many renovations the temple underwent over the next thousand years. The first construction to become famous was masterminded by the Cretan architect Chersiphron, and its magnificent interior was sponsored by the Lydian King Croesus. This temple was destroyed and rebuilt during a period of strife between Greece and Persia in the 5th century B.C. During this time the philosopher Heraclitus lived in Ephesus. His theory that everything is in perpetual flux foretold the dissolution of the popular perception of a static world order. After the crazed Herostratus set fire to the temple in 365 B.C., the wealthy and powerful citizens of Ephesus set about its reconstruction, commissioning the famous Deinocrates to build a temple that would surpass all others. In following centuries, the size and splendor of the shrine attracted pilgrims from all over Asia Minor, bringing unimaginable wealth to Ephesus and earning the temple its status among the Seven Wonders of the ancient world.

Over the years, the Caystros River continued to deposit silt along the coast, making it increasingly difficult to reach the ports and causing an epidemic of malaria along the inland marshes. Lysimachus therefore made plans for a new city about two kilometers further southwest, at the former necropolis. When the Ephesians refused to occupy the territory of their dead, he coerced them by cunningly arranging for the water mains to plug up. The new Ephesus was established between northerly Mount Pion (Panayir Dagi) and southerly Mount Koressos (Bülbül Dagi). Strong fortification walls ran along the two mountain ranges and the western front opened onto an easily accessible harbor. The shrine to Artemis was outside the city's perimeters. During the reign of Augustus Caesar (27 B.C.-A.D. 14), who declared Ephesus to be the capital of the Roman province Asia Minor, and during the reign of Emperor Hadrian (A.D. 117-138), the city flourished and experienced extensive growth and prosperity. This was the era of the *Pax Romana* and Ephesus, being situated at the end of the Anatolian trade route, profited from the unrestricted trade. The city's population expanded to over 200,000. The first major conflict between Christianity and the cult of Artemis arose in A.D. 56: passing through Ephesus on his second missionary campaign, the Apostle Paul preached "that gods shaped by human hands are no gods at all." The silversmiths had achieved their prosperity through the sale of miniature shrines for Artemis and saw their livelihood threatened by these teachings. Expressing their indignation in the theater, they nearly instigated a popular uprising.

Despite expensive dredging efforts, the new harbor was also succumbing to silt build-up. Ephesus suffered further setbacks when the Goths invaded in A.D. 263 and Constantinople became the new capital in 330. The girth of the city's ramparts was drawn inwards, new walls were built encompassing just the harbor area and excluding the lower agora. Despite the gradual decline of Ephesus, it was chosen in 431 as host city for the third Ecumenical Council, which came to a determination about the role that Mary, mother of Jesus, played in his incarnation. It was established that Mary was not only mother of Jesus but also mother of God. In this function, she was to assume the power and attraction of the pagan goddess, Artemis. Mary's presence in Ephesus can be traced back in history. Just beyond Mount Koressos stands the **House of Mary**, where it is said that Mary lived for many years with Jesus' favorite disciple John, and where she is alleged to have died.

By the beginning of the 6th century, Ephesus was just an unimportant town, yet the emperor Justinian chose to set an example for all Christianity in the former pagan metropolis. Thus, he had the Saint John basilica built over the shrine to Ar-

temis on the citadel hill. The groundplan is arranged in the shape of a cross and shelters the tomb of St. John, the evangelist whom God charged on Mount Patmos with the mission of guiding Christian followers in Asia Minor during the early years. Ephesus began to develop anew, this time around the hill of the basilica, fortified with walls and a citadel. The Turkish invasions began in the 11th century, and a small regional empire was established under the Aydinogullari dynasty, which built its primary mosque, the **Isa Bey Camii**, at the foot of the hill. The city was renamed after Hagios Theologos Ayasoluk. Only in 1914 did it accept the modern name, Selçuk.

The **Saint John basilica** was formerly topped by six domes. According to records, the tomb of St. John lies at the intersection of the arms of the cross-shaped

Above: Ephesus is one of the most complete excavation sites in the world. Right: The library of Celsus is patronized today by the literary and the plain interested.

floorplan. Inscribed on a plaque on the wall is his letter of address to parishioners in Ephesus. His identity and character still remain shrouded in a great deal of mystery because it has not been possible to prove whether John the Apostle, the favorite disciple of Jesus who accompanied Mary to Ephesus, is one and the same person as John the Evangelist, who composed this letter on Mount Patmos. The monograms of Justinian and Theodora are inscribed upon the corbelled capitals of the columns.

Below its massive retaining walls stand the remains of the **Isa Bey Camii**. Its construction in 1375 was sponsored by Emir Isa Bey from Aydin. Basically a simple structure, its lavishly decorated portal shows the influence of Seljuk architecture. The two domes above the *mihrab* hall are supported by four massive granite columns taken from the ancient thermal baths in the port of Ephesus. The road to the south leads to the ruins of the **Artemision**. Until the mid-19th century, its location was unknown,

since the ancient structures along the Caystros river plains were covered by a full meter of alluvial accumulation. In 1866, the Englishman Wood stumbled upon an inscription revealing the route of the processional road. Following this path, he discovered the temple. One of the famous pillars of Croesus' temple can now be viewed in the British Museum in London. Branching southward off the route to Kusadasi, a road leads to the Hellenistic and Roman ruins. The first sites on the left are the **Vedius Gymnasium** and the colossal **stadium**. Beyond the entrance and immediately to the right, a path leads to the basilica of the **Double Church**, also known as the Church of the Blessed Virgin, where the Ecumenical Council met in 431. In Roman times, the 260-meter-long building had been a *museion*, a place for literary and scientific study. The stone pine-lined main road leads right into the **Arcadiana**, paved with marble around 400 during the reign of Emperor Arcadius as a resplendent boulevard that was even lit up at night. At one time, the port was situated just west of the Arcadian Way, but the incredible quantities of Caystros silt deposited over the centuries have caused it to recede 8 km. The Byzantine wall of the city at that time encompassed only the Arcadiana, the theater, the stadium and the port. To the north of the Arcadiana were the **baths** and **gymnasium of the port**. Looming on the east side is the **theater**, which still packs a full house every summer during the Efes Festival. It can seat about 25,000 people and has excellent acoustics, despite deterioration of the stage area. What a predicament the Apostle Paul must have faced, as he was shouted down with the chant "Great is Artemis of the Ephesians!" during the uprising of the silversmiths.

Crossing the Marble Way, one reaches the **Library of Celsus**. Recent restoration on the eastern facade has recovered some of its former splendor. With its construction, consul Aquila wished to honor his dead father Celsus Polemaeanus, governor of the province of Asia. His tomb lies underneath the middle recess. The four statues to the left and right of the entranceway embody his virtues. The Celsus library was one of the three largest of the ancient world, smaller only than those at Alexandria and Pergamum. Its precious writings went up in flames when the Goths invaded in 263. From the forecourt, one passes through a gate donated by two former slaves, Mazeus and Mithridates, and onto the **lower agora**, the marketplace. The **Temple of Serapis** stands in the southwest corner. Across from the library, the **Curetes Way** leads uphill past the **Temple of Hadrian** on the left. The exaggerated ornamentation of the temple, like that of the library, is an expression of a cultural creativity that knew no limits during the reign of Hadrian. The frieze in the portico portrays the founding legend with Androcles and the wild boar joining a procession of the gods.

Built into the slope behind the temple are the **Baths of Scholastica**, once a huge, two-story bath complex with cold and hot water rooms, and a still-existent system for heating the floor with hot air. In the antechamber stands a statue of the wealthy Christian patroness, Scholastica, who sponsored the renovation of the baths around 400. Adjoining them to the west are the so-called **House of Pleasure** and the luxuriously furnished **latrine facilities**. Excavations of the **hillside dwellings** stretch along the southern side of the Curetes Way. In a roofed area set up somewhat like a museum, archaeologists have tried to reconstruct the lifestyle of the wealthier Ephesian citizens in Roman times, using copies of typical furnishings; the originals may be viewed in the Selçuk Museum. Excavations still continue at this time. Across from the street that leads back down to Curetes Way, stands the somewhat crudely recon-

structed **Fountain of Trajan**. In the middle recess is a huge statue of the emperor surrounded by gods and members of his family. This street, also known as Embolos, was formerly the main commercial strip. Shops were housed under a roofed colonnade, whose floor was covered with expensive mosaic work. Statues of wealthy citizens lined the street. Steps flanked by a statue of Hercules holding the pelt of the lion of Nemea lead to the upper passageway. To the left stands a monument, now converted to a fountain, which Memnius, a grandson of Sulla (138-78 B.C.), had built in honor of himself and his family. The **Temple of Domitianus** once stood across the way. The remnants of the emperor's statue were found in the supporting vault, which now houses the **Museum of Inscriptions**. The only decorative features left are a few caryatid maidens dancing in honor of Artemis. Further east, the "basement" of the upper agora houses former shoprooms and the **Nymphaeum**, a fountain in the tympanum upon which the Poliphem legend was once portrayed. Public fountains existed in abundance, sponsored by affluent citizens. They were fed by a sophisticated system of aqueducts, the Roman remains of which can still be viewed near the Selçuk train station. The municipal administrative buildings once surrounded the **upper agora** or state agora. Behind a columned hall with three aisles, built in honor of Augustus Caesar and his wife Livia, stood the **Prytaneum**, the town hall in which the sacred fires of the city were kept burning. The adjoining roofed odeum could seat an audience of about 2000 and was used primarily as an assembly room. Further to the east lie more bath ruins and the **East Gymnasium**, also termed Girl's Gymnasium, after the statues found there. The Magnesian Gate, eastern entranceway to the former city, stands just outside the museum area and to the right of the road leading to Selçuk.

Right: Who is watching who in the museum of Selçuk?

Following this road southward away from Selçuk, one comes upon the **House of Mary**. Catherine Emmerich, a stigmatized nun, was able to describe the church and its surroundings without having ever left Germany. In 1891, Lazarists began digging at the location described in her visions. The foundations of a church were indeed unearthed. Scientific analysis dates the oldest sections of the wall to the first century and written records support the claim that Mary may have spent several years in Ephesus and died here.

Back in the valley, a path branching left after the Magnesian Gate goes to the **Grotto of the Seven Sleepers**. Legend has it that seven young Christians fleeing the persecutions of Emperor Decius (250-253) were walled up, to awaken almost 200 years later when Christianity had become the state religion. Many Ephesians chose to be buried here, in the hopes of one day reawakening in similar fashion.

A visit to the small **Archaeological Museum** in Selçuk which boasts a rich collection of artifacts, is a fitting final treat. Special displays include the busts of Augustus Caesar and his wife Livia found on the upper agora, parts of the altar of Domitianus, the original frieze from the Temple of Hadrian, a fresco of Socrates taken from one of the homes on the slope, and a variety of domestic furnishings.

Not to be missed are the two **Statues of Artemis**, found in the Prytaneum. There are various interpretations of her many-breastedness. Recent research finds herein a male fertility symbol, linked with the consecration of bull testicles during sacrifices to the goddess. The Artemis statue then symbolizes fertility and the continuation of life, through the synthesis of male and female elements.

The road from Selçuk to Kusadasi travels southward and parallel to the coastline. Fruit orchards, shady stone pine forests and olive groves line the way. Since the mid-1980s, **Kusadasi** has undergone extensive growth and development. Huge modern hotel complexes with swimming pools (beaches are scarce here) have consumed the coast and spread into the olive groves. Still a tranquil harbor town just a few years ago, Kusadasi has now taken on the character of a bustling tourist center. It is the starting point for many longer cruises, as well as shorter boat tours along the coast and to Samos or Patmos. There is a large yacht harbor. An extensive commercial district has developed around the port. During cooler and calmer seasons one can still get a sense of the charm of this small town. In the 13th century, Genoese merchants established a port here called Scala Nova or Nea Ephesos, because the older port in Ephesus had silted up. In Osmanli times, it was renamed Kusadasi, Bird Island, after an island lying offshore to the southwest, **Güvercin Ada** (Pigeon Island). Lit up at night, the town decorates the Bay of Kusadasi like a jewel. An old 17th century caravanserai, now renovated as a hotel, dominates the village center. Within the courtyard, in the shade of palm trees, you can enjoy a glass of *raki* in style, surrounded by magnificent scenery.

The bathing cove at **Kadinlarplaj**, a small strip of sandy beach lined with vacation homes and hotels, lies in southern Kusadasi. Further south, several beautiful beaches remain almost deserted because they are difficult to reach. The island of Samos rises out of the sea only 1.7 km away from the tip of the peninsula created by the **Samsundagi Mountain Range** (1237m). This range has been declared a national park to protect the indigenous Mediterranean flora growing there. In ancient times it was called Mykale. The center of the Ionian League, the so-called Panionion, was located on its northern side. The islands along the western coast of Turkey were formed by the gradual sinking of the Aegean land plates and the rise in the water table after the ice ages. After winding through the idyllic Aegean landscape, the main road eventually turns from the coast towards the east, passing through **Söke**.

Nestled in the valley of the Büyük Menderes (Great Meander), this prospering rural town is surrounded by cotton plantations and has a growing textile industry. Before continuing south, it is worth the extra time to take a detour up the slopes of the Meander Valley through the scattered ruins of **Magnesia on Meander** (not to be confused with Magnesia on Sipylos). The infamous tyrant of Samos, Polycrates (whose demise became the basis for Friedrich Schiller's *The Ring of Polycrates*), was crucified here in 522 B.C. In 460 B.C. Themistocles, the military commander banished from Athens, became satrap of the area.

Aydin, known in ancient times as Tralleis, brought forth both the local Seljuk dynasty of the Aydinogullari and the architect of the Hagia Sophia, Anthemius. Fertile soil, abundant water and the mild climate have made this valley into a garden paradise and the regional center of fig and fruit plantations. Northwest of **Sultanhisar**, along the southern slope of Aydin Daglari, lies ancient **Nysa**, which flourished during the time of the Roman emperors. From here there is a beautiful view over the Meander plains, particularly pleasant to gaze upon while resting in the shade of an olive tree in the well-preserved theater. To the north of **Denizli** lies ancient **Laodiceia**. During Roman times it became one of the wealthiest cities in Asia Minor through its wool and cloth industry.

PAMUKKALE

Traveling northeast, the visitor can already glimpse from afar the white terraces of **Pamukkale**, whose name translates as "Cotton Fortress". This unique

landscape was created by 35° C hot springs, the calcium content of which precipitates as water, is forced out of the earth at high pressure and rapidly cools on the earth's surface. The terraces were carved out at a time when these slopes were a quarry for the construction of ancient Hierapolis further up. Through the ages, clumps of calcium carbonate have accumulated along the edges of the terraces, forming small basins in which the bubbling water collects. The natural landscape appears particularly rich in contrasts on clear summer afternoons. Looking upward, you will see the white stalactite formations of the basins glare brightly against the backdrop of deep blue sky, bordered by the pink blossoms of oleander thicket. The area has been preserved under environmental laws which prohibit development. During dry seasons, the white splendor of terraces nevertheless turns gray from street dust carried in by the visitors.

Founded by the people of Pergamum in 190 B.C. as a competitor to the Se-

leucid city of Laodiceia, **Hierapolis** became an important center for wool products in Roman times. Well-known for the healing properties of its thermal springs, it was also one of the most popular spas in the empire. At that time, the Holy Spring bubbled forth at the **Shrine of Apollo**, which was also the regional oracle. Now the wellspring has moved to the inner courtyard of a motel, where guests can relax in body temperature water, surrounded by ancient columns. Huge **thermal baths**, now housing the **Archaeological Museum**, and fountains were constructed around the shrine. Further up on the mountain stands the expansive **theater**, whose exquisite marble reliefs along the stage walls portray scenes from the legends surrounding Niobe, Artemis and Apollo. Even higher, northeast of the theater, the **Grave of Philipp** extends across a long terrace. Legend has it that he died here with his children as an early Christian martyr.

The Martyrium of St. Philipp was constructed in Hierapolis in the 5th century.

The octagonal building with small side rooms is accessible via a broad flight of steps. In earlier times it was the frequent goal of mass pilgrimages. Those who make the trip up to it are rewarded with a stunning view of the ancient city and the lower valley of Çürüksu, a rift valley created by the same volcanic activity which continues to bring forth the hot springs. Vast portions of the city still remain buried under dense layers of calcium carbonate, greatly hampering excavation work. Driving north along the terrace, parallel to the ancient **column-lined avenue**, you must pass through the city gates to reach one of the most extensive **necropolises** in all Asia Minor, including fine specimens of Hellenistic grave mounds, elegantly inscribed sarcophagi and Roman mausolea. Many

Above: The strange chalkstone terraces of Pamukkale, the "Cotton Fortress," dominate the Meander Valley. Right: Sculpture in Geyre, the former Aphrodisias, a center of a cult of Aphrodite.

older, convalescing spa guests spent their final years in Hierapolis and chose to be buried there.

Further north, in the village of **Karahayit**, the evaporating waters of the iron-rich thermae leave luminous red, ocher and brown deposits. The motels offer comfortable lodging for those who wish to extend their stay. The swimming pool of the *Tusan Motel*, for example, is a natural basin where one can swim laps against the spectacular backdrop of the Çürüksu valley and 2300–meter–high Akdag mountain range beyond. The considerable water consumption of the motels, where thermal waters flow even from the tap, has inevitably had an effect on the quantity of water bubbling forth from the sinter terraces.

Heading eastward, a well-constructed highway travels from Denizli past two inland saltwater seas, Açigöl and Budurgölü, towards Antalya. Southwest of **Denizli**, by the village of Geyre, lies ancient **Aphrodisias**, accessible via the Kazikbeli Pass and **Tava**. As a result of the American-sponsored excavations, since 1961 under the direction of Kenan Erim, Aphrodisias is now considered one of the most significant archaeological sites in Turkey. The Aphrodite cult originated in Mesopotamia and Cyprus, but flourished quite early in this 600 m-high fertile valley. Höyük, an artificial hill along the southern edge of the site, was created by various overlapping layers of settlements. The very deepest layers exposed date as far back as 3000 B.C. The economy of the region relied on the export of exquisitely colored, bluish-white marble found in the Akdag range in the northeast of the city. In the first century B.C. a sculpure school was founded here, probably by sculptors from Pergamum. Samples of their work were soon exported throughout the Roman Empire, and under the reign of Augustus Caesar, played an important role in the adornment of Rome. Buildings in Aphrodisias were designed on a grand scale and ornamented with precious marble. Highlights of a tour of the area should include the **theater**, which is located along the eastern side of the bronze age Höyük, the **Thermal Baths of Hadrian**, a small **odeum** and the **School of Sculpture**, where excavations unearthed splinters of marble and unfinished works. The magnificent **Temple of Aphrodite** was renovated as a church during the Byzantine era. An arch was built into the short side of the temple and surrounding columns were incorporated into the building as part of the nave and supports for the gallery. After being declared the seat of the bishopric, the city was renamed Stavropolis, city of crosses. The bishops were particularly anxious to wipe out the cult of Aphrodite because of prostitution activities at the Goddess' temple.

To the north looms the **stadium**, where sporting events and a sculpture competition took place. An architectural jewel, the newly-restored **Tetrapylon** serves as the magnificent eastern gateway to the

Temple of Aphrodite. Also worth visiting is the collection of beautiful marble works from the sculpture school displayed at the local **museum**. There, a monumental **statue of Aphrodite**, many-breasted and replete with fertility symbols, recalls sublime Artemis in Ephesus.

The way down into the Meander Valley passes through **Karacasu**. Approaching the town, you will see a restaurant on the right side of the bridge traversing the Dandalaz River. On a calm day one can savor delectable trout under the shady trees in the garden overlooking the running waters, perhaps serenaded by the Anatolian rhythms of a saz player. Back in the valley, a road south of Söke branches off into the delta of the Meander and towards Priene. Centuries of clearing the timber from the mountainous regions for use in the construction of houses and ships, as fuel for household stoves, and for the huge ovens in the thermal baths have barred the soil of any protective covering. Consequently, the downpour of winter rains has washed away much of

There are currently no clear indications of Ionian **Priene's** location, although it lies buried somewhere in the marshland of the Meander. One of the famous sons of this city was Bias (around 625-540 B.C.), counted among the Seven Wise Men of the ancient world, along with Thales and Solon. Under his leadership, the city experienced an enormous upswing. However, in the 4th century B.C., with the inevitable silting up of the bay, the inhabitants of Priene were forced to found a new city closer to the coast along the slopes of the Mykale mountain range. Alexander the Great even sponsored the construction of a temple to Athena there. The new city only had direct access to the sea via its somewhat remote port of Naulochos. Eventually this harbor began to clog up, and Priene once again fell into obscurity. Around the birth of Christ, the distance to the sea had stretched to 8 km; today it is 15 km.

The excavation site visible today is that of the second city. Visitors will find a basically uncomplicated Hellenistic city layout, considered an exemplary model of ancient settlements. It is laid out in checkerboard fashion, although following the contours of the slope. The **Temple of Athena** towered over the city along the **upper terrace**. It was designed by Pythius, who also created the Mausoleum in Halicarnassus, one of the Seven Wonders. The temple's classical measurements and ideal proportions set a standard for succeeding Ionian temples. The Greeks conceived of an architectural structure as more than just an arbitrary design of straight lines. It was an organic entity realized in stone and patterned after human proportions. Thus, a column had a head, the capital; a body with a belly, the shaft with its curves or entasis; and a foot, the base of the pillar. All these elements maintained specific ratios, as did the number and arrangement of columns and the measurement of the groundplan and façade of the building.

the thin layer of topsoil, leaving bare limestone landscapes in many areas. The topsoil carried away by these floods gets deposited in the valleys and along the coast. Slowed down by the heavy quantities of silt in the water, the rivers wind and meander until emptying into the marshland along the delta. In areas where water consumption and drainage have been carefully regulated, as along the middle Meander Valley, agriculture has flourished. As early as the 5th century B.C., Herodotus had already termed the Meander a "laborer", pushing the coastline further towards the sea by about 6 meters every year. In ancient times, the river flowed into the Gulf of Latmos, along whose shores such cities as Priene, Myos and Miletus developed. Now this gulf has completely disappeared, causing the decline of these cities.

Above: The ruins of the temple of Aphrodite in Aphrodisias. Right: Remains of the temple of Athena in Priene.

The entarsis of the pillars had to correspond with the curvature of the building itself. The entire construction thereby consisted of a series of lines and curves in precise ratio to one another. Along the carefully-nailed blocks of stone, the visitor can still see the holes chiseled out for the bronze clamps which held the blocks together. The drums, cylindrical stones laid one above the other to form a column, were bound together with bronze bolts; molten lead was then poured into the hollow column.

From the temple terrace one can see far out over the cotton fields of the Meander Valley. On the same terrace stands the theater, in which the Greeks performed sacrificial ceremonies in honor of the god Dionysos. During Roman times, it was customary for animal fights to take place in the orchestra, while the actors performed on the raised proscenium. The viewers were also seated on a raised area, and were protected from the action by massive fences or a wall. In Priene, the most honored guests had the seats closest to the orchestra. The theater was a place where humanity could interact with the gods who ruled over nature and determined the course of events. The performance was virtually a religious event.

A path leads up to the **Shrine of Demeter**, and further northeast, barely negotiable, well-worn steps continue to the former **acropolis** and a panoramic view. Spread along the **middle terrace** were public buildings such as the **Prytaneum**, **Bouleterion** and the **agora**. Lining the northeast side of the agora were the sacred halls, whose western façade is now exhibited in the Pergamum Museum in Berlin. Along the **lower terrace** a **stadium** and **gymnasium** have been unearthed. The **residential quarters** surrounded the inner city. Along a city block of 35 x 47 meters, four domiciles with individual courtyards could be found. In Hellenistic times, Priene had about 5000 inhabitants. The layout of the city was planned so that every citizen would be able to participate in public life and make use of the infrastructure.

MILETUS

One crosses the delta on a narrow road heading south towards Miletus. In late summer, brightly-clothed women can be seen harvesting cotton. The cotton plant belongs to the malvaceous family of herbs. When the ripening capsules, containing the white threads of seeds which we know as cotton, burst out of the fruit pods, harvest time has arrived. After the women pick the cotton by hand, tractors bring the full sacks to the receiving station of the cooperatives. Since not all cotton capsules ripen simultaneously, it is necessary to harvest the same crop several times to pick only the ripened, and therefore highest quality, cotton. A single harvesting by machine produces a lower quality cotton which brings a lower price. The relationship between wages and

Above: The donkey is a widespread means of transportation even in western Turkey.
Right: Recalling the splendor of days past in the amphitheater in Miletus.

market prices obviously plays an important role.

In antiquity, **Miletus** was located on the southern shore of the gulf of Latmos on a peninsula stretching northward. Today, it lies about 10 km from the sea! In former times, there were two large ports, the Port of the Theater to the southwest, and the Port of the Lions to the north. The most important inland products, such as textiles from the domestic wool industry and grain from the coast of the Black Sea, were shipped off from these ports. Miletus was mother city to 80 Milesian colonies along the Mediterranean and the Black Sea. Thales, a native of Miletus (625-545 B.C.), dwelled there during the golden age. Civic structures clustered around the ports.

The most impressive construction still standing is the **theater**, from where you can glimpse a hill which at one time was the Island of Lade. From here, one could have viewed the fierce sea battle in 494 B.C. in which the Persian fleet defeated the Ionian Greeks. After the city's reconstruction and again in Roman times, there were brief upward swings. Yet, Miletus never recovered its former luster and appeal. During Byzantine times, it was seat of the bishopric.

The medieval **fort** above the theater indicates that during the Crusades, Byzantines, Seljuks, Genoese and Venetians coveted access to this city.

The streets of ancient Miletus were laid out along strict right angles, according to the Hippodamic system. Hippodamos, who lived in Miletus in the 4th century, conceived this design and applied it to many city plans. Here he arranged for the streetways to open out onto the sea in the northwest, thereby letting cool sea breezes provide dwellers with relief from the humid climate.

From the rear of the theater one can see the **Port of Lions** and the city's center further south. Civic buildings line the **Avenue of Columns**. Noteworthy are the

remains of the **Port Memorial** and the **Delphinion**, the shrine to Apollo. The Avenue of Columns ended at the **agora**, which was entered via a famous gate which now can be viewed in the Pergamum Museum in Berlin.

To the west, the **Baths of Faustine** display the typical structure of a Roman bath: via the *apodyterium* (changing room) with private chambers along the sides, one entered the *frigidarium* (cold bath) before continuing on to the *tepidarium* (warm bath) and *laconicum*, a sweat room. Between these rooms lay the *caldarium* (hot bath).

In Roman times, a **Sacred Street** led from Miletus to the Milesian oracular city of **Didyma** (near Yenihisar), 20 km to the south. Recent excavations have revealed the course of its path past the pilgrim haven, Panormos. The final stretch of the way was flanked by reclining stone lions and by archaic statues probably representing the branchides, priests of the sanctuary. Upon arriving, the visitor is awestruck by the monumental size of the **Temple of Apollo**, the so-called Didymaion. It was considered among the most important and powerful oracles of antiquity, in direct competition with the oracle at Delphi. Lydian King Croesus compared the prophesies of the Didymian and Delphian oracles. He finally accepted the advice of the oracle at Delphi before his campaign against the Persians, but applied it in such a manner that he destroyed his own empire. The temple wielded considerable power as a data bank, information center and financial bureau. Correspondents were sent out on investigations throughout the known ancient world, and the data was then collected in extensive archives. Those who came seeking counsel were expected to bring a temple offering, the quality and quantity of which seemed to determine the breadth and generosity of the predictions and judgements. Even at that time, advice was recognized as a service with a price. However, the Didymaion functioned not only as an oracle and counseling service, but also as a deposit and

credit bank. Even Croesus placed his riches under the protection of the temple. The interest rate on credit was fairly reasonable when compared to the financial services of other large temples. As a result, the temple was able to accrue immense revenues.

Following the destruction of the first temple in 494 B.C. during the wars against the Persians at Lade, Alexander the Great planned a new temple to surpass in size and glory the Artemis temple in Ephesus. However, its design was so overly ambitious that it never reached completion. The business of the temple nonetheless continued uninterrupted throughout the various stages of construction, providing the necessary income to finance this enormous undertaking. The interior of the temple remained open, without a roof, throughout this time. But within its walls, a smaller temple over the sacred springs housed the

Above: The mighty temple of Apollo in Didyma, whose oracle rivaled that of Delphi.

oracle. Here mantic priestesses, in a trance state probably induced by drugs, provided divinely-inspired interpretations of information collected by priests.

In the mid 1980s, German archaeologists made a sensational discovery. Sunshine falling onto the inner walls at a certain angle brought to light etchings of the colossal floorplan and design of the temple. The interior wall had served as a giant drawing board for the architects and builders. From these sketches one can deduce how they had intended to incorporate the perfect proportions of an Ionian temple into the design of the Didymaion. It was a great boon for researchers that the temple remained unfinished, for the delicate traces of the etchings would have disappeared during final polishing of the stone. After such grandeur, the vacation resort of **Altinkum** south of Didyma is a fitting spot to relax on beaches of golden sand and sample the fare in one of the fish restaurants.

You must pass through Akköy to reach the Söke-Milas highway running eastward and **Lake Bafa**, the Gulf of Latmos until the 4th century B.C. Now an inland body of salt water with abundant fish, it remains connected with the Meander by only a small canal. The ridges bordering the southern shores of the lake consist of shale rock containing veins of marble. In ancient times, the marble was dislodged and transported by boat to both the Temple of Apollo in Didyma and the Temple of Artemis in Ephesus.

Along the lake's eastern shores, which are accessible only via a very poor road from **Mersinet**, the ruins of ancient **Herakleia** lie scattered. These vestiges of a bygone era extend over untamed romantic landscapes on the slopes of the Besparmak mountains, made of fissured granite and gneiss. The city of Herakleia blossomed in Hellenistic times while still located directly on the coast. Sites worth visiting include the well preserved **city walls**, constructed of squared blocks of gneiss, and also the **Temple of Endymion**. This local hero was the lover of Selene, Goddess of the Moon, who lulled him into an eternal slumber. In early Christian times, monks retreated to the solitude of the mountains and constructed fortified monasteries on the islands of Lake Bafa and on Latmos. The monastery of St. John was established in 1088. Local guides lead charming day trips to the ruins by boat and on foot. Worth stopping for on the way to Milâs are the olive groves of **Euromos**, which surround an almost completely unscathed Corinthian Temple of Zeus dating back to the Roman era. The fluting is probably missing from the pillars because the temple was never fully completed.

As capital city of the province, **Milâs** has a bustling atmosphere, particularly on Tuesdays when people from the region gather at the market. From the 13th until the 15th century, Milâs was the center of the Seljuk emirate of Mentese, which wielded regional influence. The **Ulu Cami** dates back to this period, having

been built in 1378 under Ahmet Gazi out of the plunder from many other ancient temples.

Modern Milâs is built over the remains of ancient Mylasa and lies at the center of the historical landscape of Caria. The Carians, an indigenous people, first made their mark in history as mercenaries of the Egyptian pharaoh in around 700 B.C. From about the 5th century B.C. onwards, Caria was a Persian satrapy. For a time it was a member of the powerful Greek Dekian League. In the fourth century B.C., it wisely sided with the Persian king. The province was thus assured considerable autonomy. Mausolus (377-353 B.C.) was the most famous member of the dynasty that reigned here. He moved his residence to Halicarnassus, but nevertheless supported the sumptuous development of Mylasa.

In the southeastern section of Milâs lies a mausoleum which the Turks named *Gümüskesen*. Made in Roman times, it is modeled after the famous mausoleum of Halicarnassus: Rising from the base of the burial chamber are pillars holding up a pyramid-shaped roof. A processional path leads from Mylasa to **Labranda**, to the Caria Temple of Zeus, in which the water of life was venerated. Today, the temple is also accessible via a gravel road which offers breathtaking views of the plains of Milâs.

From Milâs, a road heads westward towards Bodrum. You can take a detour to **Güllük** and travel by boat from there to **Iasos**, where vestiges of a rampart built by Mausolus still stand. Also worth seeing are the remains of a large Roman home with an inlaid mosaic floor.

BODRUM

From a distance, **Bodrum**, the ancient city of Halicarnassus, looks like a huge ancient theater imbedded in the terraces which surround Bodrum bay. The bay itself is actually divided into two smaller

ruled under Persian sovereignty, women enjoyed an unusual position of power as the wives of their brothers. Artemisia was one such woman: She distinguished herself at the Battle of Salamis under Xerxes in 480 B.C. The historian Herodotus (484-425 B.C.), one of the sons of Halicarnassus, described the conflict between Greeks and Persians in vivid detail in his "Chronicles of History," which also offer his view of the world at that time as he experienced it on his many travels.

In 387 B.C. the seat of the Carian throne was transferred from Mylasa to Halicarnassus. Reigning together with his sister and wife, Artemisia II, Mausolus had the city magnificently refurbished in the Hellenic style. While still alive, he also commissioned the construction of his famous burial ground, the **Mausoleum**.

Centuries later, after the mausoleum had been destroyed in an earthquake, the Knights of St. John, under the direction of the German knight Heinrich Schlegelholt incorporated ruins into the **Fortress of St. John** (15th century). Only the foundation of the original monument still remains undisturbed. The defense of the fortress was left to knights of diverse nationalities, each entrusted with a separate wing. Today it houses a museum, whose exhibits bring to life the city's history. Of particular interest is the exhibit about underwater archaeology, which contains significant shipwreck finds.

Those who seek restful solitude will find it along the peninsula to the west of Bodrum. The harbor town of **Turgutreis** takes its name from a Turkish admiral who was born here in the 16th century and died during the siege of Malta. Sunbathers, windsurfers and sailers will find everything their hearts desire here. Near Gümüslük, entry is currently prohibited to the public, since zealous excavation of **Myndos** is underway.

One of the most spectacular coastal landscapes in all of Turkey stretches be-

bodies by the peninsula where the Castle of St. Peter stands. White cubic houses lie nestled among gardens and vineyards. As a result of the protected coastal location, the climate is mild even in winter. Bodrum is a port of call for cruise ships and large ferries headed towards Rhodes, as well as for smaller ships destined for Kos and Knidos. It maintains an extensive yacht harbor. Today it is virtually run as a city-state in Turkey, its laws designed primarily to accomodate vacationers. Those searching for sun, surf, sailing and swimming will find ideal conditions here. Several cafés, restaurants, discotheques and nightclubs also provide opportunities for social mingling.

Bodrum, known until A.D. 1000 as Halicarnassus, has a few unique chapters in its history. It was founded by Dorian Greeks in about 1200 B.C., next to a native Carian settlement. At the time of the Persian occupation, when Carian princes

Above: The protected bay of Bodrum. Right: Friendly atmosphere at the bar.

tween Bodrum and Antalya. Mt. Taurus falls steeply into the Mediterranean here, having reached a height just east of Fethiye of over 3000 meters. Picturesque little villages grew up around the few small coves, which for a long time were almost only accessible by ship. Protected from the cold north winds, these warm waters offer a veritable oasis and are favored by vacationers. In the spring, you can swim in the sea while snow still covers the mountain tops, or go for a hike across the blossoming Aegean terrain. In summer, the lukewarm waters offer ideal conditions for snorkeling and investigating underwater treasures, or you can travel by boat from cove to cove, visiting quaint harbor towns. Exploring this paradise will certainly engage all of your senses! Among the smaller ancient ruins, many of which remain relatively undisturbed and are accessible only on foot, you will get a true sense of the *genius loci*, the spirit of the place.

The route from Bodrum to Marmaris traverses the graceful and charming landscape of the backcountry of Milâs and Mugla, through pine forests with occassional breathtaking glimpses down into the plains formed by rivers branching off from the Taurus. The unpaved road from Milâs to the village of **Ören** further south passes below the medieval **Beçin Fortress**. In Ören lies ancient **Keramos**, where one can view the remains of an **acropolis** upon which a **Temple of Zeus** once stood. **Mugla** was the preferred residence of the Emir of Mentese during the 15th century, the time of the construction of the **Ulu Cami**. To the south of Mugla, at the 775-meter-high Çiçeklibeli Pass, you can look far down onto the plains of **Gökova**, ancient Carian **Idyma**. From here, it is easy to travel by boat to idyllic island of **Kedreia**, ideally situated in the Keramian Gulf.

MARMARIS

In recent years, **Marmaris** has become a well-known vacation area because of its splendid location along a protected bay

with beautiful beaches and surrounded by stone pine forests. It is also conveniently close to Dalaman Airport in the east. For the island of Rhodes, ancient Physkos to the north of the present city was the most important bridgehead in all of Asia Minor. Today the heart of Marmaris is on the long peninsula, where wood-panelled houses cluster around a medieval **fort** in the older section of the town. Also located here are the yacht harbor and the jetty for ferries traveling to Rhodes. Pleasure boats destined for Datça and Knidos also stop here.

The up-and-coming vacation spot of **Datça** can be reached over land and sea. A road runs along the narrow peninsula on a dam, with splendid views of the sea to both sides. The road to the western point of **Knidos** is rather poor; it would be best to take a boat from Datça. First settled by Dorians, Knidos flourished during 600 B.C., basing its commerce on

Above: The harbor of Marmaris, one of the most popular vacation spots.

marine trade and pottery production. The medical school here became famous during the Hellenistic period as the arts and sciences flourished.

Sostratos, who built the world-famous lighthouse of Alexandria, was a native of Knidos. The most famous piece by the sculptor Praxiteles, a statue of Aphrodite, once stood in Knidos, but is now housed in the Paris Louvre. A small strip of land connected the western tip of the peninsula with Cape Triopion, where two **ports** conveniently opened to the north and south. The Hellenistic **city walls** stretching from the northern naval harbor to the **acropolis** are particularly well-preserved. Just north of the **theater**, an awkward path leads up to the acropolis, but the spectacular view on top certainly merits the climb.

To visit **Caunos** and the more isolated coves to the east, you can travel by boat from Marmaris and enjoy the coastal scenery. However, it is easier to reach Caunos via Dalyan, which lies south of **Lake Köycegiz** along a canal connecting the inland waters with the open sea. Amber trees, which grow only in southwestern Turkey, can be spotted along the shores of the Lake Köycegiz. These trees are valued in the local economy because the amber derivative, storax balsam, is an important ingredient for the perfume industry. Traveling by boat from **Dalyan** over the canal to Caunos, the visitor can already glimpse from afar the monumental facades of rock **tombs** (4th century B.C.) etched into the steep cliffs.

A short hike to the northwestern slope brings you to the former port city of Caunos, which once bordered the ancient kingdoms of Caria and Lycia. The Lycians, according to Herodotus, were probably a people who had migrated out of Crete in late Minoan times and mingled with indigenous inhabitants. Although they called themselves "Termiles", the Hittites used to refer to them as "Lukki"; which was the probable origin of the name Lycian. The Egyptian Tell-el-Amarna tablets list the Lukki among the "Tribes of the Sea," which threatened Egypt in the time of the Pharaohs. Lycian culture was a synthesis of Greek and Anatolian characteristics.

From any higher elevation you can view the marshland of the Dalya delta, cut off from the open sea by the **Iztuzu Peninsula**. Following much debate between the environmentalists and the representatives of tourist interests, the area is now an environmental preserve for the giant Caretta sea turtle which journeys here between May and August to bury its eggs about 1/2 meter below the sand. Trespassing on the nesting grounds is prohibited during this time so as not to disturb the shy turtles during their critical task. The baby turtles hatch after 2 months, dig their way to the surface and head towards the water.

The road from Dalyan to **Fethiye** via Dalaman travels through lovely stone pine forests. Fethiye, ancient Telmessos, developed into a modern port city since the destructive earthquakes in 1856 and 1957. Situated on the gulf of the same name, its tourist industry has thrived upon the abundance of isles and coves nearby. Now only the rock tombs stand as testimony to Fethiye's long history.

The **graves of Telmessos** constitute one of the most extensive necropoli along the southern coast. Their "architecture" offers clues about the building style of the Lycians, who lived in wooden houses with beams held together by pegs and pivot-sockets, and covered by a roof of straw and loam. While no such houses remain today, apparently the dead were afforded more permanent shelter in the form of stone tombs modeled after their wooden homes.

The **Tomb of Amyntas** in Telmessos, on the other hand, is in Greek style with the façade of an Ionian temple. A Lycian tomb near the museum downtown stands as testimony to their permanency. Although the ancient tombstone has slipped slightly, the tomb itself survived virtually unscathed the earthquake which demolished almost the entire city. Looming above this is a **fortress** built by crusaders from Rhodes.

South of Fethiye lies the bather's paradise of **Ölüdeniz**, the Turkish **Dead Sea**. It is formed by a peninsula which extends into a lagoon, with white sand beaches. This type of landscape has become a symbol for beach tourism on Turkey's southern coast. Fortunately, this particular area was established as a national park in 1978, just in time to prevent coastal development. Along the stretch of road to Fethiye, one can take a charming walk from the village of Hisarönü to the abandoned town, **Kayaköy**. In Ottoman times the Turkish population became an increasingly small minority as Greeks immigrated here from the Aegean islands. In 1922, after Atatürks War of Independence, the 20,000 Greeks living here were forced to move to Rhodes. Since then, most of the approximately 1200 houses have remained unoccupied. Although plans are underway to transform this into a vacation town, the atmosphere of abandonment and dilapidation still lingers.

The highway through the backcountry heads into the valley of **Xanthos**. This was once the heart of Lycia; its greatest cities were centered here. Turn off the road at the modern village of Kemer to visit the ruins of **Tlos**, one such city. The earliest writings that identify it describe its participation in the battle led by the Carian satrap Pixodares, brother of Mausolus, against Caunos in the 4th century B.C. Ruins of the city are clustered around the **hill of the acropolis**, the northern face of which is hollowed out by yet more rock tombs.

The most interesting of them, the Bellerophon tomb, lies at the foot of the rock precipice. It portrays the Corinthian hero Bellerophon fighting the fire-breathing monster, Chimera. This is presumably the tomb of one of the rulers of Tlos, whose dynasty descended from Bellerophon. The acropolis is crowned by a **fortress** from which a local despot, Kanli (the bloody) Ali Aga, ruled over the city in the 19th century. From here, the view into Xanthos valley is spectacular.

Along the eastern side of the acropolis is the actual **municipal sector** of the town. Most of the ruins, such as the stadium, baths and theater, date back to the Roman era, when the patronage of wealthy Lycian citizens financed much of the town's expansion. From Tlos you can hike to the Akdag.

Another Lycian metropolis, **Pinara** (meaning "sound"), extends across the other side of the Xanthos Valley. In order to find your way more easily among the extensive ruins, it may be helpful to hire a guide down in Esen before making the ascent. At the far northeast corner of the

Right: The quiet beach of Ölüdeniz, the so-called "Dead Sea."

city lies a beautifully-situated Lykian **theater**. The **necropolis** to the far west rewards visitors with a stunning overview of the landscape as far as the Akdag mountains.

The road southward into Xanthos Valley leads right into **Xanthos**, capital of the Lycian Empire and center of the Lycian League of 20 cities. Lycia established one of the earliest republican governments known to the world; it was ruled by public representatives and a president. But by the 7th century B.C., the Lycians had fallen under the sovereignty of the Lydians and Persians. Herodotus described the proud Lycians' efforts to liberate themselves from the Persians in 454 B.C.: As the Persian general Harpagos was trying to occupy the city, the men – realizing that the situation was hopeless – brought their wives, children and slaves into the fortress and set fire to them, only to die themselves in the desperate battle that ensued.

The Lycians did not regain their independence until the 5th century. It was during this time period, between the 6th and 4th century, that they developed their characteristic tombs, which do not seem to be derived from either Oriental or Greek culture. These columned tombs shelter an urn which is placed on a tall rock pillar. The intention was for the remains of the dead to rest higher, so that the Harpies could more easily carry their souls to heaven.

The reliefs on the **Monument of the Harpies** (south of the Roman **agora**, built during Xanthos' second golden age under Roman rule) portray two women sitting and three men standing, all being honored by their relatives as their souls are carried off to heaven by these winged creatures. Next door is also a columned tomb, but of a house-like design with a gabled roof. Other tomb variations can be found with flat roofs. South of the Roman **theater** stands the **Monument of the Nereids**, which still maintains the façade

of an Ionian temple, but whose other adornments may now be viewed in the British Museum in London.

The sacred center of the empire, **Letoon**, lay south of Xanthos. The three **temples** here are dedicated to Apollo, Artemis and their mother Leto. Leto fled to Letoon with her twin children when she was forced to leave Delos.

A trilingual stone inscription offers a key for deciphering the Lycian language. The alphabet resembles that of the Greeks, but the construction of words appears to distinguish Lycian as a unique Indo-European language. According to one theory, Lykian is related to Luwian, a language spoken in western Asia Minor before the arrival of the Hittites.

This clashes with the belief, held by Homer and Herodotus, that the Lycians originated from the island of Crete. In any case, with the decline of the Lycian Empire, Greek dialects became more prevalent.

Patara (Kelemis) was a popular port during the Roman era; today it lies further south at the delta of the Xanthos River. The Apostle Paul stopped here on his way from Ephesus to Tyros. Saint Nicholas is alleged to have been born here, as was Apollo, the God of Light. Remains such as the **triumphal arch** and the **theater** project out of the sand dunes along a beautiful long stretch of beach. Like Iztuzu Beach, this is protected as a nesting ground for sea turtles. Therefore, sun umbrellas cannot be driven into the sand and the beach is off limits at night.

Kalkan, formerly the Greek town Kalamaki, would still feel like a Greek island were it not for the silhouette of a Turkish minaret. Only a few years ago, time seemed to stand still in this picturesque town, but tourism has caught up with it, although in tasteful form. The untamed wilderness of the coast here is captivating. Fresh water bubbles out of the ocean floor, channeled through the underground network of hollow cavities caused by chalk formation. Lovely **Kapitas Beach** stretches to the east of Kalkan and can be reached either by flights of

stairs from the street or by boat. The popular Turkuvaz or Mavi Magara, the **Blue Grotto**, opens onto the eastern side of the beach.

KAS

The up-and-coming port town of **Kas** lies on a small bay nestled into the mountains not far from the southern point of Lycia. Just outside the bay is the easternmost of the Greek islands, Kastellorizon, called Meis Adasi by the Turks. As is the case in so many parts of the Lycian coast, a small, sleepy fishing village has been transformed into a lively vacation center. Just above the modern port, known to antiquity as Antiphellos, lies the older colony of **Phellos**.

In Hellenistic times, the port town of Antiphellos gradually came to dominate its mother colony of Phellos, until the latter faded into obscurity. In addition to the

Above: House façades with a Greek flair in Kalkan. Right: A Lycian tomb near Demre.

Lycian tombs, the view of the bay from the theater is well worth seeing. The sea and the mountains are equally appealing to visitors of this coast. Those who hike the 1800-meter-high **Asas Dag** or make the longer trek up to the 3024-meter-high Sallanmaz Tepesi, the tallest peak in the **Ak Daglari**, will have a magnificent view of the coastline.

As a special treat, you can take a boat trip to the lovely island of **Kekova**. The branched bay between island and mainland has offered a safe anchoring ground to ships throughout the ages. Along its northwest shores, there are countless underwater ruins which are a veritable paradise for snorklers. Across from the island near the mainland village of **Kaleüçagiz** lies ancient **Teimiussa** ("place of the three outlets," referring to its location). Interesting are the necropolis and ancient **Simena**, modern Kale, certainly one of the quaintest towns in all Lycia. Simena can only be reached by boat or along footpaths. The ruins are interspersed among houses standing beneath the pewter-capped walls and turrets of the medieval city. Since ancient times, the coast has continued to gradually sink into the sea, creating a surreal scenery of partially-submerged sarcophagi and other ruins. Divers may be disappointed: As much of this is an archaeological zone, access is restricted.

East of Kas in the valley of **Demre**, the role of agriculture along the Demre River is quite visible. Tomatoes, eggplants and other vegetables grow in the greenhouses, while further south near ancient **Andriake**, Roman wheat granaries from Hadrian's time still loom over the landscape. It is likely that Andriake and Patara were the only trade cities using this type of silo to store grain for Rome and the legions stationed here in the East. Situated at the mouth of the Andrakos river, Andriake was the port for Myra. In A.D. 61, the ship that brought the Apostle Paul to Rome for his last visit anchored

here to wait for better winds. The strong current of the river prevented the silting up of the port until the Byzantine era.

Myra already achieved fame in the Lycian era. Countless Lycian **cliff tombs** of an unprecedented variety of styles and with rich pictorial messages make Myra's wall of tombs one of the most impressive in all of Lycia.

On the front relief of one of the stone houses of the dead, relatives share in a final parting meal while the deceased rests on a stone table. To the left of this image, the dead man is shown with his weapons, indicating that he probably died heroically in battle. Below the cliffs, the tiers of a **Roman theater** still exist.

The **Church of St. Nicholas** dates back to the 11th century; his tomb, an early Christian sarcophagus, lies in the southern nave. The worship of St. Nicholas is actually connected with two different historical figures: Abbot Nicholas of Sion (a monastery near Myra), who later became bishop of Pinara in Lycia and died in 564; and Nicholas of

Myra, who allegedly was imprisoned by order of Diocletian. The latter was also a bishop – indeed, one of the greatest of the fourth century, who participated in the Council of Nicaea in A.D. 325. He is believed to have died on December 6th in 350. Merchants from Bari robbed most of his bones in 1087, although some are now held by the museum in Antalya. San Nicola in Bari has become the most important shrine to Nicholas in the western world. However, the veneration of this saint is even more pronounced in the Greek Orthodox and, particularly, the Russian Orthodox Church. He is the patron saint of sailors, merchants, students and children. The custom of offering gifts to children on St. Nicholas Day stems back to an old legend, according to which the bishop tossed three sacks of gold into the house of an impoverished noble man so that his three daughters might have dowries to marry with. Thus, the saint is pictured in some portrayals as a bishop holding a book upon which three golden marbles rest.

IZMIR
Accommodation
LUXURY: **Grand Efes Hotel**, Gaziosmanpasa Bul. 1, Tel: 51-144300. **Grand Hotel Plaza**, Sakarya Cad. 156, Teleferik, Tel: 51-592269. **Pullman Etap**, Cumhuriyet Bul. 138, Tel: 51-194090. *MODERATE:* **Anba**, Cumhuriyet Bul. 124, Tel: 51-144380. **Atlantis**, Gazi Bulvari 128, Basmane, Tel: 51-135548. **Hisar**, Fevzipasa Bul. 153, Tel: 51-145400. **Izmir Palace**, Vasif Çinar Bul. 2, Alsancak, Tel: 51-215583. **Karaca**, 1379 Sok. 55, Alsancak, Tel:51-191940. **Kilim**, Kazim Dirik Cad. 1, Tel: 51-145340. **Sinada**, Mürselpasa Bul. 2, Basmane, Tel: 51-195252. **Yumukoglu**, Sair Esref Bul. Çankaya, Tel: 51-136565. *BUDGET:* **Billur**, Anafartalar Cad. 783, Tel: 51-139732. **Kabaçam**, 1364 Sok. 2, Tel: 51-123353. **Kaya**, Gaziosmanpasa Bul. 45, Çankaya, Tel: 51-139771. **Saysen Gar**, Eylül Mey. 787, Basmane, Tel: 51-254545. **Zeybek**, Fevzi Pasa Bul. 1368 Sok. 5, Basmane, Tel: 51-197511.
Restaurants
Park, Kültürpark, Tel: 51-193590. **Crystal**, Kibris Sehitleri Cad. 70, 51-211320. **Deuxmegots**, Atatürk Cad., 148, Tel: 51-148686. **Denizkizi**, Hüseyin Ögütcen Cad. 29, Tel: 51-592758. **Mer-San**, Mustafa Kemal Cad. 112, Tel: 51-394460. **Smyrna**, Mithatpasa Cad. 888, Tel: 51-245290. **Palet**, Yali Cad. 294, Tel: 51-118436. **Yangeç**, Cumhuriyet Bul. 236, Tel: 51-217364. **Yeni Kordelya**, Atatürk Cad. 148/A, Tel: 51-148686.
Museums
Archaeological Museum and **Atatürk Museum**, Bahribaba Park, closed Mon, Tel: 51-148324.
Tourist Information / Other
Tourist Information, Gaziosmanpasa Bulvari 1, Büyük Efes Oteli Alti, Tel: 51-142147. **Turkish-American Association**, Sehit Nevret Bey Bul. 23, Tel: 51-215206. **Port Authority**, Yeni Liman, Alsançak, Tel: 51-210077/94.
The *Izmir International Trade Fair* takes place from August 26–September 10.

ÇESME
Accommodation
LUXURY: **Boyalik Beach**, Boyalik, Tel: 549-27081. *MODERATE:* **Çesme Marin**, Hürriyet Cad. 10, Tel: 549-27579. **Club Cardia**, Çiftlikköy, 549-21110. **Delimar**, Izmir Cad. 154, Ilica, Tel: 549-34300. **Hora**, Izmir Cad. PTT Yani 150, Ilica, Tel: 549-30452. **Inkim**, Izmir Cad. Ilica, Tel: 549-333900. **Kanuni Kervansaray**, Kale Yani, Tel: 549-27177. **Z Hotel**, PTT Arkasi, Ilica, Tel: 549-33900.

Restaurants
Dalyan, Dalyan Köyü, Tel: 549-47045. **Imren**, Inkilap Cad. 6, Tel: 549-26635. **Körfez**, Yalicad. 12, Tel: 549-26718. **Sahil**, Cumhuriyet Meydani, Tel: 549-26646.
Tourist Information
Tourist Information, Iskele Meydani 6, Tel: 549-6653.

KUSADASI / AYDIN
Accommodation
LUXURY: **Akdale**, Bayraklidede Mev., Tel: 636-13640. **Batihan**, Ilica Mev., Tel: 636-31423. **Fantasia**, Yavansu Mev. 134, Tel: 636-18600. **I Tusan**, 31 Ler Plaji Mev., Tel: 636-14495. *MODERATE:* **Club Caravanserail**, Atatürk Bul. 1, Tel: 636-14115. **Hotel Club Akdeniz**, Karaova Mev., Tel: 636-16971. **Kusadasi Holiday Village** (Club Med.), Arslanburnu Mev., Tel: 636-11135. **Surtel**, Atatürk Bul. 20, Tel: 636-20606. **Talat**, Camiatik Mah. Kanarya Sok. 8, Tel: 636-13461.
BUDGET: **Aydin**, Inönü Bul. 14, Tel: 636-14034. **Eke**, Birlik Yapi Sitesi, Tel: 636-13616. **Ölmez**, Kemerönü Mev., Tel: 636-14780. **Turkad**, Kadinlar Denizi, Tel: 636-11405.
Tourist Information
Tourist Information, Liman Cad., Iskele Meydani, Tel: 636-11103.

SELÇUK / EPHESUS
Accommodation
LUXURY: **Hitit**, Atatürk Cad. 2, Tel: 5451-1007. *MODERATE:* **Kalehan**, Atatürk Cad. 9, Tel: 5451-1154. *BUDGET:* **Ak Hotel**, Kusadasi Cad. 14, Tel: 5451-2161.
Restaurants
Efes, Efes Harabeleri, Tel: 5451-2291. **Hitit Restaurant**, in the Hotel Hitit. **Yeni Hitit**, Atatürk Cad., Tel: 5451-1920. **Yandim Cavus**, Sarapçikuyu Mev., Tel: 5451-1223.
Tourist Information / Festival
Tourist Information, Atatürk Mah., opposite the Efes Museum, Tel: 5451-1328. The *Ephesus Festival* takes place in Mid-June.

DENIZLI / PAMUKKALE
Accommodation
DENIZLI: *MODERATE:* **Altuntur**, Kaymakçi Cad. 1, Tel: 621-51057. **Aygören**, Cumhuriyet Cad. 26, Tel: 621-31017. **Palaz**, Kayalik Cad. 10, Tel: 621-30587. *BUDGET:* **Arar**, Delikli Çinar Mev. 9, Tel: 621-37195. **Laodikya**, Otogar Arkasi, Tel: 621-51513.
PAMUKKALE: *LUXURY:* **Ergür**, Karahayit, Tel: 6228-4170. **Hierapolis Merit Inter-**

national, Tel: 6228-4116. *MODERATE:* **Kur-Tur Motel**, Karahayit Köyü, Tel: 6228-4117. **Polat**, Karahayit Köyü, Tel: 6228-4111. **Tusan**, Edenizli, Tel: 6218-1010.

Tourist Information
Tourist Information Denizli, Atatürk Cad., Ufuk Apt. 8/4, Delikliçinar-Denizli, Tel: 621-43971. **Pamukkale Information**, Tel: 6281-1077.

BODRUM
Accommodation
LUXURY: **Boydas**, Yalikavak, Tilkicik Koyu, Mugla, Tel: 6144-1299. *MODERATE:* **Bodrum Maya**, Gerence Sokak 49, Tel: 6141-4741. **Flora**, P.K. 250 Gümbet, Tel: 6141-8200. **Ece**, Gölköy, Tel: 6147-7387. *BUDGET:* **Babana**, Yali Mev., Tel: 6147-7198. **Toloman**, Bitez Yalisi, Tel: 6143-4241. **Melisa**, Eskiçesme Mev. Gümbet, Tel: 6141-1044. *HOLIDAY VILLAGES:* **Club Monakus**, Yalikavak, Tel: 6144-1392. **T.M.T. Holiday Village**, Akçabük, Tel: 6141-1232.

Restaurants
Aktur, Bitez Kabakum, Tel: 6141-1030. **Amphora**, Neyzen Tevfik Cad. 164, Tel: 6141-2368. **Günsü Tur-Tes**, Cumhuriyet Cad. 98, Tel: 6141-2631. **Han**, Kale Cad. 29, Tel: 6141-1615. **Masa**, Cumhuriyet Cad., Tel: 6141-1702.

Tourist Information / Other
Tourist Information: Iskele Meydani, Tel: 6141-1092. **Port Authority Bodrum**, Iskele Meydani, Tel: 6141-1021. **Ildiz Carpets**, Pilavtepe/Milas, Tel: 6141-2846.

MARMARIS
Accommodation
LUXURY: **Altinyunus Marmaris**, Pamuçak Mev., Tel: 612-13617. **Grand Azur**, Kenan Evren Bul., Tel: 612-17020. **Munamar**, Içmeler, Tel: 6125-1360. **Marti La Perla**, Içmeler, Tel: 6125-1388. *MODERATE:* **Armar**, Yunus Nadi Cad., Tel: 612 15463. **Blue Rainbow**, Içmeler, Tel: 6125-1248. **Atlantik**, Içmeler, Tel: 6125-1001. **Nergis**, Kemal Elgin Bul., Tel: 612-15130. *BUDGET:* **Flamingo**, Siteler Mah. 23, Tel: 612-14000. **Marmaris**, Atatürk Cad. 54, Tel: 612-11308. **Yat**, Adaagzi, Tel: 612-16608.

Restaurants
A Restaurant, Haci Imam Sok., Tel: 612-14299. **Bamboo**, Atatürk Cad., Tel: 612-11339. **Club House**, Orhaniye Köyü, Tel: 612-11423. **Tilla**, Atatürk Cad., Tel: 612-11088.

Tourist Information
Tourist Information, Iskele Meydani 39, Tel: 612-1035.

DALYAN / DATÇA
Accommodation / Restaurant
DALYAN: *MODERATE:* **Antik Hotel**, Tel: 6116-1136. *BUDGET:* **Binlik**, Sulungur Cad. 16, Tel: 6145-1148.
DATÇA: *MODERATE:* **Ayditur Motel**, Karakesir Mev., Tel: 6145-1102. **Mare**, Iskele Mah., Tel: 6145-1211. *BUDGET:* **Dorya**, Tel: 6145-1614. **Lindos Pension**, Tel: 6145-1174. **Tropicana**, Iskele Mah., Tel: 6145-1930.
HOLIDAY VILLAGES: **Club Datça Holiday Village**, Iskele Mah., Tel: 6145-1170. **Knidos Holiday Village**, Tel: 6145-1105.
RESTAURANT: **Vido 2 Restaurant**, Emecik Köyü Çiftlik Mev., Tel: 6145-1165.

Tourist Information
Tourist Information, Belediye Binasi Iskele Mah., Tel: 6154-1163.

FETHIYE
Accommodation
LUXURY: **Aries Club**, Çalis Mev., Tel: 615-31100. **Pirlanta**, Karagözler Mev., Tel: 615-14959. *MODERATE:* **Likya**, Yat Limani Yani, Tel: 615-12233. *BUDGET:* **Seketur**, Çalis Plajlari, Tel: 615-31060. **Gülgöz**, Çalis Mev., Tel: 612-31204. **Moonlight**, Kesik Kapi Mev. **Pinara**, Bes Kaza Sok., Tel: 615-11874.
HOLIDAY VILLAGES: **Ölüdeniz Holiday Village**, Tel: 6156-6020. **Robinson Club Lykia**, Ölüdeniz, Kidirak Mev., Tel: 6156-6214.
CAMPING: **Deniz Camping**, Hisar Önü Köyü, Tel: 615-11598.

Tourist Information
Tourist Information, Iskele Mey. 1, Tel: 6151-11527.

KALKAN / PATARA
Accommodation
LUXURY: **Patara Prince**, Patara, Tel: 3215-1338. *MODERATE:* **Grida Apart Hotel**, Köy içi-Kalkan, Tel: 3215-1434. **Pirat**, Kalkan Marinasi, Tel: 3215-1178. *BUDGET:* **Kalkan Han Pension**, Köyiçi, Tel: 3215-1151.

KAS
Accommodation
MODERATE: **Club Hotel Phellos**, Dogruyol Sok., Tel: 3226-1953. **Ekici**, Hükümet Konagi Yani, Tel: 3226-1417.
BUDGET: **Mimosa**, Elmali Cad., Tel: 3226-1272. **Puya Pension**, Meltem Sok. 16, Tel: 3226-1080. **Toros**, Çarsi Içi, Tel: 3226-1923.

Tourist Information
Tourist Information, Cumhuriyet Meydani 5, Tel: 3226-1238.

THE MEDITERRANEAN

ANTALYA
KEMER
SIDE
MANAVGAT
ALANYA
ANTAKYA
SAMANDAG

ANTALYA

Boasting over 250 days of sun every year and accessed by a modern international airport, there is little argument that Antalya is the most beautiful and colorful city along Turkey's southern shore. Proximity to the antique cities of Lycia, Pisidia and Pamphylia, not to mention Antalya's own abundance of historical and cultural riches, opens yet another dimension for visitors. These include everyone from adventure travelers and package tourists to yachtsmen and motorcyclists.

Although it is possible to see the city's sights within a day, you should stay a little longer and view everything at leisure. Hotels and *pansiyons* abound in every price range and can be found almost anywhere in Antalya: Along the main boulevards, within the romantic old quarter of Kaleiçi, dotting Konyaalti Beach to the southwest and all along Lara Beach to the east.

Known in antiquity as Attaleia, the city was founded in 158 B.C. by Attalus II, King of Pergamum, although it reached its zenith under the Romans. Unhappily, most of what they built has long since

Preceding pages: Idyllic scenes in the old harbor of Antalya in southern Turkey.

vanished: Aside from a few sections of the original inner and outer city walls the most impressive material legacy of the antique period is the **Hadrian Gate**, commemorating the emperor's visit to the city in A.D. 130.

Most of Antalya's other prominent historic structures are a syncretic mix of elements from before and after that period. The base of the sturdy **Hidirlik Kulesi,** the Seljuk Turkish lighthouse overlooking the harbor, was once the tomb of a high-ranking Roman; the nearby **Kesik Minare** ("Truncated Minaret") itself may be Turkish, but the adjacent 16th-century mosque was converted from a 6th-century church originally dedicated to the Virgin Mary, and built on the foundations of a small Roman temple.

The city's oldest Seljuk Turkish monument and most prominent landmark is the **Yivli Minare** ("Fluted Minaret") which stands in a quiet garden a mere stone's throw from Antalya's lively hub at **Kale Kapisi Meydani** (Castle Gate Square). No trace of the gate referred to remains: City planners, more concerned with traffic problems than history, tore it down in 1940. The minaret is decorated with hundreds of tiny turquoise tiles set into the red brickwork. Access to the *serifiye,* or balcony used to call the faithful to prayer, is not allowed, although it is possible to visit the adjacent **Alaattin Mosque**. Once again, the mosque reflects a cultural syncretism: Used as a Byzantine basilica, the six cupolas rest on arches supported by columns dating to the Roman era. Standing within the same complex are a Seljuk *medrese* with only parts of its outer walls still surviving and a dervish monastery, which now houses a gallery for fine arts. Two Seljuk *türbe* can be found behind the mosque. The smooth, white masonry of the smaller, octagonal tomb is particularly beautiful in its simplicity, and incorporates a number of ornaments of Roman origin.

In most ancient cities, the **citadel** is set on an appropriately bleak peak or crag, where lookouts might espy the approaching enemy. How strange that Antalya's citadel is found beneath the modern town in **Kaleiçi** ("inside the castle"), the maze of narrow, twisting lanes that make up Antalya's quaint old town. Those of a military cast of mind will inwardly shudder as they watch kids hurl down innocuous paper airplanes on the unwary from the tea garden on the heights above.

Today, Kaleiçi is the largest typical Ottoman quarter in Turkey. More than 700 houses are still standing in the area, which has now been declared an historical zone. Most of the late 19th-century buildings are made of a complex combination of timber, wattle and stone built around courtyards decorated with orange, fig and palm trees. The upper stories jut out over the narrow lanes of the quarter, and wooden laths crisscross the ornate bay windows, providing additional privacy for the inhabitants. Throughout summer the bewitching scent of jasmine lingers in the air while fruit and vegetable merchants push their heavily-laden carts, extolling the virtues of their wares as they move along the narrow lanes.

The houses vary greatly in terms of repair. Restoration is not cheap, and most of the original house owners are not in the financial position to afford it. Investors from Istanbul, Ankara and elsewhere are now stepping in with capital and turning many of the old houses into *pansiyons*, restaurants or new outlets for carpets and leather ware. One particularly nice restoration is the **Sultan Pansiyon** in Merdivenli Sokak. Check in, or at least stop by for a look at the before-and-after photographs of the house and to have a chat with the proud owner. For those interested in a bit more luxury, try the beautifully restored **Turban Adalya Oteli**, located just off the main square in the old area of the harbor. The building used to be a bank branch office a hundred years ago, but has been converted into a hotel favored by lovers and newlyweds.

All streets invariably lead down to Antalya's **Eski Limani**, or Old Harbor, where souvenir shops, trendy bars, tea gardens and outdoor restaurants line the cobblestone wharf. Vendors with their bright blue push-carts sell an assorted array of delicious, freshly-roasted nuts to the promenading crowds, while young boatswains coax tourists and locals aboard their excursion skiffs for a half-hour jaunt along Antalya's cliffs. The marina is also the departure point for a number of longer seafaring expeditions.

Antalya's pleasant **Karaalioglu Park** runs the length of the cliffs east of the marina. Decorated with exotic flowers, flame trees and gently swaying date palms, the park is a favorite place for local families and tourists alike. A fantastic view unfolds across Antalya Bay towards the misty Bey Dagi Mountains to the west. Cotton-candy stalls and colorfully dressed *Maras* – Ice cream vendors – add to the on-going carnival atmosphere. Arguably the best of the lot are the meandering fresh juice merchants with their mandarins, oranges or lemons rolling by on a blue cart: A glass of freshly-squeezed juice is a refreshing way to quench your thirst.

Antalya's commercial heart throbs at **Kale Kapisi Square**, the noisiest street

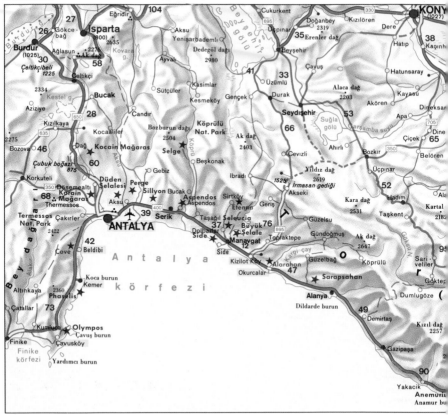

corner in the city. Honking horns, police whistles and the wail of the muezzin blend into a unique cacophony that takes a little getting used to. So does the traffic: Cars and fleets of minibuses fly past, seemingly oblivious to traffic lights. Foreign pedestrians should take lessons from the local teaboys who can be seen expertly diving between bumpers without ever spilling a drop from their trays. The knots of shoeshine boys are equally adept and will dodge cars and trucks across the square to find and convince you that your shoes need a little polish – even if they are in fact made out of canvas!

On the far side of the square along **Cumhuriyet Caddesi** is the city's small but lively covered **bazaar**. The shops specialize in everything from jewelry to handmade kitchen utensils. Here in the bazaar, a humble watch repairman ekes out a living next to a showcase window glittering with gold, while the sweet and spicy odor of a confectionary lingers in the air, only slightly tainted by the smell of fresh hides from the saddle maker's stall next door. Down yet another side street there are a few small textile workshops, where local women feed raw cotton into the rotating cylinders of antique gins that somehow resemble the blades of a lawn mower. The cotton emerges clean and soft out of one side, while the seeds and other impurities pile up in a dark corner of the shop. For those who prefer viewing items of even greater antiquity, a

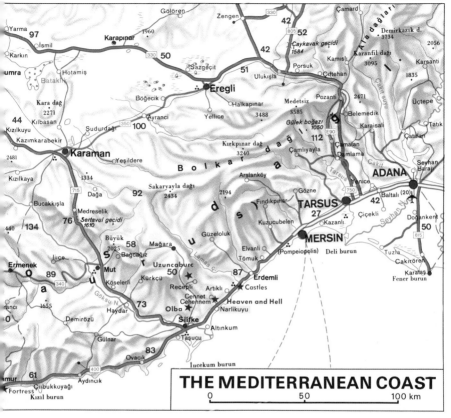

trip to the local **Archaeological Museum** is suggested. Located on Kenan Evren Bulvari on the way out to Konyaalti beach west of town, the large modern complex houses a wealth of exhibits from regional digs, all displayed in chronological order and ranging from prehistoric material removed from the Karain Cave to interesting artifacts dating from the Ottoman period.

Especially striking is the assembly of marble statues depicting Greco-Roman deities and emperors. Hadrian enjoys the lion's share of attention in stone. The collection of beautifully-ornate sarcophagi and a large well-preserved mosaic set into the museum's floor are also worth seeing, as is the collection of exquisite

opalescent glass vases, bowls and bottles dating back to Hellenistic times. Note the separate room devoted to Greek icons as well as several bones which once supposedly belonged to St. Nicholas. Clay and bronze figurines, as well as smaller objects of daily life dating from the fourth millennium B.C. are displayed in other showcases. The extensive and colorful ethnographic collection concentrates on the interior of Ottoman houses, costumes and antique carpets of the Antalya region. Also interesting are the fascinating exhibits of the *Yörük* (nomadic tribes), with goat hair tents and all articles of daily use on display. Taken altogether, the collection renders a comprehensive impression of Antalya's rich historic past.

Perge and Aspendos

The rich Pamphylian plain was a natural site for the development of classical civilization and the Antalya area is a literal treasure-trove of antique sites. Some destinations are but a few minutes out of town in the fecund Pamphylian plain, while others require a little more effort.

Perge, only 13 kilometers to the east of Antalya down the E-24 and two kilometers north of the farm town of **Aksu**, is the most accessible. The site renders a fine impression of the wealth and splendor of the ancient world.

The city allegedly dates back to the aftermath of the Trojan War, but is first mentioned in the annals of Alexander. Like most of the cities of Asia Minor, Perge saw its greatest prosperity under the Romans, and most of the city's impressive ruins – with the exception of the

Above: In the great theater of Aspendos.
Right: Fragments of an ancient column in Perge.

Seleucid-built city walls and defensive towers – date from this period.

The first structure seen when approaching the site is the third-century **theater** which held 15,000 spectators in its day. Scenes from Greek mythology are carved into the white marble of the orchestra pit. The stage itself lies in a jumble – a fine quarry for locals, whose labor in splitting the ancient blocks apart has been greatly aided by earthquakes.

Across the road is the city's **stadium**, which has been spared the fate of the theater and remains one of the best-preserved structures of its kind in Turkey. 12,000 spectators used to fill the stands for the chariot races and gladiator contests once held here. The crowds apparently were not so different from the sports spectators today. The vaulted chambers alongside the stadium served as "refreshment stands": The wall inscriptions state the name and trade of the respective proprietors.

After paying the nominal admission charge to the site, enter Perge through the massive **city gate** and proceed along the **colonnaded street** leading to the **nymphaeum** and the **acropolis**. The impressive Roman **bath complex** stands to the left just inside the city walls. Built in the 2nd century A.D. and reconstructed in the fourth, its five chambers give an insight into the Roman genius for civil engineering and the system of water supply, temperature regulation and floor heating.

The city's main thoroughfare, some 20 meters wide and 300 meters long, is lined with gigantic columns. Deep grooves show where iron wheels cut into the massive slabs of soft stone. Traces of the many commercial shops which once lined the street stand to either side, and several segments of fine mosaics still adorn the sidewalks. Note, too, the **water canal** running from the acropolis down the center of the street: The drinking and waste-water system of the city would be the envy of many a Turkish town.

South of the main street is the fourth-century **agora**, where restoration is presently underway. The series of columns surrounding the market suggest that it was once covered, and fragmentary mosaics set into the floors of many of the shops underline the fact that this was no flea market, but a luxury shopping center. A huge marble slab in one shop on the north side of the *agora* is simply but effectively decorated with a hook and carving knife – it was the local delicatessen store.

Back at the entrance, note the tomb of **Plancia Magna**, priestess of Artemis and benevolent patron of Perge, who contributed a number of statues and public buildings to grace the city in the 2nd century A.D. Most of these statues (and other "pergalia") are now displayed in the Antalya museum. Many of these were defaced by over-zealous Christians: A biblical reference notes that St. Paul and Barnabas preached here in A.D. 46, resulting in the predictable destruction of the statues and symbols of pagan idolatry.

An interesting side trip for old stone buffs is the journey to ancient **Sillyon**, the least visited of the major Pamphylian sites. Take a left turn off the E-24 between Aksu and Serik, and follow the dusty road inland to the small village of **Yanköy**, nested into the western flank of the acropolis. Founded by Greek settlers around 1000 B.C., the city was besieged by Alexander but managed to hold out, thanks to its sheltered location and excellent defenses. These now lie scattered beneath the acropolis, conquered by earthquakes and mudslides. During the course of your trudge uphill, note the handsome **gymnasium** and the **stadium.** Only the walls of the former still stand, while the latter is put to good use today as a vegetable patch. The uphill path winds past the remains of the city's ramparts and two terraced bastions before ending on top of the vast **acropolis**. A pleasant breeze takes the worst out of the sweltering summer heat, and the vista over the cotton fields towards the blue Taurus mountains is breathtaking.

Most of the antique structures are located around the southeastern part of the mound, including a number of cisterns half buried among the thistles and rubble of ancient walls along the edge of the precipice. Note the **theater** and **odeum** – only a couple of rows of seats stay pinned in place, the rest tumbled downhill in a mudslide 20 years ago.

Other remains on the acropolis include a few small temples, a ruined **fortress,** a **Byzantine tower** and a small **Seljuk mosque**, suggesting that Sillyon was still inhabited during the 13th century.

Just 50 kilometers east of Antalya lies the Pamphylian city of **Aspendos**. Take a left turn off the coastal highway to Belkis, and then drive five kilometers further into the inland.

The origins of the city are uncertain. Legend has it that the city was founded

Above: The ancient theater of Aspendos is still used for athletic events and cultural festivals. Right: A shepherdess near Antalya spins yarn using a simple spinning "wheel."

by the Greek seer Mopsos around 1000 B.C. Whether by him or another, Aspendos soon became one of the major cities along the south coast of Asia Minor, linked to the sea by the River Eurymedon (today Köpr Çayi) which was navigable up to Aspendos at the time. The city was taken by Alexander along with other costal cities in Asia Minor. Then came Ptolemaic, Seleucid and Roman rule. Under the latter, Aspendos enjoyed its greatest prosperity.

The most notable Roman edifice in Aspendos today is the magnificent **theater**, constructed during the reign of Marcus Aurelius. Set into the city's **acropolis**, it has survived the ensuing 2000 years nearly unscathed, only touched up a bit by the Seljuks who used it as a caravanserai for a long time.

They took the liberty of decorating the orchestra façade with exquisite turquoise tiles which are now on display in the Antalya museum along with the various classical statues that once graced the marble niches. The theater is still used as

the venue for sports and artistic perform-ances such as the annual Mediterranean Song Contest. Strangely the first image conjured up by the austere façade is that of a high-security prison.

The **agora, nymphaeum**, and a small **temple** are on the acropolis; other ruins of note include the **Roman baths** and a **gymnasium** standing by the road leading to Belkis. To the north, the impressive re-mains of a colossal **aqueduct** traverse a small valley. The city's water supply came from the hills and passed through two gigantic hydraulic towers, which are still standing.

Termessos

Back in Antalya, head north along the Burdur highway, turn left on the Antalya-Korkuteli road and take another left at the yellow signpost into **Termessos National Park**. Then start driving up and up, and when the road ends, start walk-ing: The ruins of the old Pisidian city of **Termessos** lie in the misty peaks above

and are still a half-hour's walk from the big parking lot.

Although nobody knows exactly when the city was founded, it is generally as-sumed that Termessos existed as far back as the 7th century B.C. Famous for raid-ing the Pamphylian cities of the plain, the remote location and impregnable de-fenses of the city led its many enemies to call it "the hawk's nest." Even Alexander the Great found it inconvenient to lay siege and avoided it as he moved on to bigger things further east.

The city fathers picked their allies well: During the long Mithric wars of late antiquity, Termessos sided with Rome, and was granted the status of an inde-pendent city as a result. Left to its own devices, the city flourished in the 2nd and 3nd centuries A.D., and most of the ruins seen today date from this period. A great earthquake in A.D. 567 destroyed Ter-messos completely, and the site was henceforth abandoned to the hawks, wild goats and other mountain creatures that still grace the area.

The first major edifice you'll find during your climb up the **King's Road** is the monumental **gymnasium**, now almost entirely overgrown with creeping ivy. More accessible is the great **theater** which seated some 4000 spectators in its day. Perched on the edge of a sheer cliff dropping a few hundred meters, the panoramic view of the distant coastal plain from the remaining seats is magnificent and alone worth the trip. Ibex and other mountain animals can be spotted on quieter days as they roam the rocky crags and peaks of the surrounding mountains.

Just behind the theater lies the city's paved **agora** where five enormous connecting **cisterns** are set deep into the ground – a fascinating example of ancient underground engineering which allowed the citizens of the city to endure many protracted sieges. Watch your step, though: The cisterns are wide open.

Close by stands the **odeum**, its outer walls still relatively well preserved, although the halls within are buried under a pile of rubble. Next door are the remains of **three temples**, one of them dedicated to Artemis.

The city's **necropolis** lies on a steep hill to the southwest with a wealth of sarcophagi scattered among trees and tangled shrubs. Most of these tombs lie toppled over and broken, their lids slid off to the sides – the sure mark of the grave robber, ancient or modern.

Back to the Beach

The real reason most people come to Antalya is not for the ancient remains, but for sea, sand and sun. The favorite intramuros stretch is **Lara Plaj**, a beach to the east of the city. The coastal road runs along the cliffs, and is served by regular *dolmus* from the bus station (Dogu Garases) in the east part of Ali Çetinkaya

Right: A water skier taking a break from the action off the beach of Konyaalti.

Caddesi. The action starts long before the beach itself, however: Smaller hotels offer access to the turquoise waters beneath the cliffs via long sea-stairs. A freshwater spring surges up from the sea bed off the rocks around **Otel Blue**, creating a chilling 15°C water temperature in some places; the springs also serve as a freshwater supply for the hotel swimming pool.

Further along the cliffs is the **Gençlik Parki**, a pleasant place to watch the **Lower Düden waterfall** plunging some 40 meters into the sea. The spectacle is even more impressive in winter, when the river carries more water.

Shortly after the waterfall, the cliffside road descends to the Lara Plaj and the sea. Accommodation can be found here in every price range, starting with **Huzur Lara Camping**, directly on the beach. The facilities include a parking lot, shops, restaurants and windsurfing facilities, but no shade. Scores of *pansiyons* and mid-range hotels offer the prospective lodger more comfort, while the five-star **Sera Club Hotel** tops the range with several restaurants, a casino, night club, tennis courts, aquatic sports facilities and the amenities of a helicopter landing pad.

West of the city lies **Konyaalti Beach**, once relatively quiet, but now dominated by the Steigenberger Hotel. The Ramada hotel chain is now building its own residences here as well. A right turn just past the new international harbor and free trade zone leads up to **Tünektepe cliff**, where a revolving restaurant and small hotel offer a superb view of Antalya Bay.

The cotton-growing plains of the Pamphylian flats soon make way for a dramatic change in landscape, with stone pine-covered mountains introducing the rugged and craggy domain of ancient Lycia. Some 25 kilometers along the way, a yellow sign points to **Akyalar Magaras**, a small mesolithic cave that requires a flashlight to view the prehistoric

drawings within. Other artifacts from the cave are on display in Antalya's museum.

A turnoff just after the second tunnel leads onto a lower stretch of the old Kemer-Antalya route which runs along the coast to **Beldibi.** Still classified as a village, the settlement has become a sprawling assembly of small hotels, *pansiyons*, outdoor restaurants, camp sites, holiday camps and new five star resort complexes. Drop in at the charming **Güvris Restaurant**, set on the shoreline and surrounded by lemon and stone pine trees. Run by a Dutchman named Sjirk and his Turkish wife Jale, the restaurant is very popular and tables must be booked well in advance. Sjirk's locally famous *nouvelle cuisine* is worth the wait.

KEMER

Less than an hour southwest of Antalya lies **Kemer**, a former fishing village which has been targeted for more tourist development than any other area in Turkey. One can well understand why.

Snuggled beneath the ruggedly beautiful, stone pine-covered slopes of the Bey Dagi range, the stretches of beach punctuated by secluded coves have become a favorite place to set up holiday villages and resorts like Club Med and Club Robinson, as well as lesser known enterprises like the Art Hotel, Palmiye and Club Salima.

The spillover from the package tour crowd has clearly affected the town itself. The main streets of Kemer, when not covered with piles of cement and building wires, are lined with shops hawking carpets, jewelry, gold and leather suits. Several small bars, cafés and restaurants offer a break from shopping, or relief from the gluttony associated with holiday-village menu fare.

One unusual eatery is **Pis Mustafa** ("Filthy Mustafa's"), an open-air fish restaurant near the middle of town. The place is tough to find since Mustafa and his wife seem to relocate their restaurant every year: It was last seen on Liman Caddesi near the harbor.

More bars, restaurants and Kemer's most popular discos are within the **Ayisigi Complex**, better known as Moonlight Bay – the social focal point in town. Evenings can be lively when wandering *saz* players come out to entertain the assembled crowd in nearby **Yörük Park**.

During the day Moonlight Bay is open to everyone. The complex has a swimming pool, 24-hour tennis courts and a variety of watersports equipment. This is the only public beach for miles around, as the grand hotels have more or less monopolized the entire coastline.

Kemer's modern **marina**, close to the **Tourist Information Office**, offers a wide range of facilities for the yachtsman, as well as numerous bars, restaurants and shops. Nearby is the **fishermen's harbor**. Although still in use today, most boats are used to ferry tourists to the Lycian city of **Phaselis**. However, travel by car gets you there faster.

Famous for the winter visit of Alexander the Great in 333 B.C. Phaselis, the ancient town, lies in a pine forest 12 kilometers south of Kemer. Founded by Greek settlers from Rhodes in 690 B.C., it quickly became a prosperous city. During the following centuries it came under Persian, Ptolemaic, Seleucid and then Roman rule, finally losing its role as the most important port on the Pamphylian shores to the flourishing city of Attaleia (Antalya).

Most of the extant urban structures to be seen today date from the late Republican period of Rome. Other elements date from the Byzantine period, when the city served as a bishopric. Like much of the rest of the coast, earthquakes, Arab incursions and general political instability led to its desertion by the 10th century.

Today, this site is overgrown with shrubbery. The more impressive ruins are

Right: There are two ways of using the Mediterranean winds. Far right: Sorting sardines from minnows.

around the **colonnaded street** which connects the northern and southern harbors. The numerous inscriptions on pavement slabs and column bases will interest those visitors with a knowledge of Latin. Remains of the city's **aqueduct** which brought water from freshwater springs to the north run along the perimeter of the site, with some sections in good repair. Near the south port and west of the column-lined street are three **agoras** indicating the city's former commercial importance. The **monumental gate** commemorates Hadrian's visit in A.D. 129.

The **city baths** offer a glimpse of how the Romans heated their steamy vaults. A series of waist-high terracotta pillars once supported thick slabs of marble flooring which were heated from below by a series of pipes. The floor is now mostly destroyed, and only a few broken tiles remain to give an indication of the formerly elegant interior.

A hike up the city's **acropolis** (nearly inaccessible due to brambles and undergrowth) leads to a small theater. Much of the seating is still intact although the stage building itself is in ruins.

Dozens of sarcophagi with smashed lids lie scattered around the **necropolis** north of Phaselis. Some tombs can be seen along the shore, with a few almost in the shallow water of the bay. One interesting tomb is beneath a tree near the parking lot, the last resting place of a wealthy citizen. Ornate and adorned with carved lions, a life-sized but headless figure rests on its tilted lid.

After an archaeological expedition, a plunge into the clear waters of one of the three bays will be a must. But watch out for the scores of treacherous sea urchins. These seemingly immobile creatures do have the nasty habit of cropping up wherever you put your foot down. If you get pricked, resist the urge to pick the spines out with a needle or knife; apply only olive oil and let them work their own way out of your skin.

The road leads southwest from Phaselis through rugged country into Lycia proper. Access to the sea is limited until one reaches **Kumluca** and **Finike** on the far side of Cape Gelidonya.

At the top of the land dominating the cape, take a left and descend through a series of hairpin turns to the village of Çavusköy, also known as **Adrasan**. Five kilometers before the village, a yellow sign directs you right through a boulder-strewn creek to the site of **Olympos** – once one of the wealthiest cities on the coast, but now a tumble of blocks and columns which are completely overgrown with semi-tropical vegetation.

Looming over the ancient site is **Mount Phoenix** where a natural gas system has preserved a perennial flame on top of the mountain. The ancients believed this to be the final resting place of the Chimera, the fire-breathing beast with the head of a lion, the body of a goat and the tail of a snake, which was killed by the hero Bellerophon with the aid of the winged horse Pegasus.

Two kilometers beyond Çavusköy are two small beach *pansiyons* owned by the brothers "Ford" and Mahmut. The former named himself after the Detroit car firm for unknown reasons. Equally mysterious is the fact that the two brothers have not been on speaking terms for the past decade. The cape also affords some pleasant snorkeling, and from time to time guests can enjoy inexpensive lobster brought in by local fishermen.

SIDE

Discos and bars crowd ancient walls and columns, and long, lonely stretches of beach have been usurped by prodigious hotel complexes. Native fishermen have become millionaire land developers or barmen earning tips in five foreign languages.

Yes, Side has changed. Those who remember the quaint little fishing village of the past had better think twice before returning to find paradise lost. Side has become one of Turkey's major tourist centers and is packed with all the delights and detritus of the trade like nowhere else in the country.

But paradise is what you make of it. If Side is no longer the quiet retreat it used to be, it continues to attract travelers and tourists from across the spectrum. It serves as the starting point for excursions to such ancient Pamphylian cities as Perge and Aspendos along the coastal plain, as well as to more remote sites in the Taurus mountains like Selge and Seleucia. It is this mixture of the strikingly modern next to the incredibly antique that makes Side unique – as if you were visiting an on-going party in an open museum.

History in the Harbor

The ancients obviously knew a good beach when they saw one, although the people who picked Side were probably more interested in landing their boats than lying on the miles of fine-grained sand. Settled by Aeolian colonists in the 7th century B.C., Side's early history remains obscure. It was not until the arrival of Alexander the Great that the local fishermen were abruptly jolted into the greater scheme of things.

Being part of the world in the post-Alexandrian period meant participation in the conflict between his heirs, the Ptolemites of Egypt and the Seleucids of Syria. Despite the rocky political fortunes of the day, the town became an important cultural and academic center. It even attracted the last great Seleucid ruler, Antiochus VII Sidetus, who spent a substantial part of his youth here.

Centralized order in the eastern Mediterranean collapsed with the Seleucid demise and local Cilician chieftains filled

Right: The well-preserved great amphitheater of Side dates back to the time of the Romans.

the void of authority. Side was soon given over to the profitable trade in human beings, and its docks were lined with hundreds of slave ships plying the waters to the island of Delos, which was at this time the central market for galley slaves and gladiators.

But local autonomy was short lived. In the 1st century A.C., the distant Romans included Side and the other coastal cities in their new Asian domains. Conquest, however, was not particularly onerous, and being part of *Pax Romana* had its advantages. Public structures such as the aqueducts, theater, baths, agora and temples suggest that the people at Side fared well.

The tranquility did not last long. A series of devastating earthquakes in the first century A.D. leveled much of the town. This may have abetted the proselytizing efforts of early Christian missionaries like the Apostle Paul, whose claim that "the end is nigh" might have seemed wholly believable given the circumstances. The early converts' zeal is evident in the local museum, where countless statues of Hermes and other pagan deities had their noses chopped off or were decapitated.

During the Byzantine era, the city served as a bishopric, but the security afforded by the Romans was gone. More earthquakes, as well as incursions by Arabs in the 7th and 8th centuries left the city destroyed. By the 10th century, the site was abandoned and once fine buildings buried and forgotten beneath sand dunes and tangled shrubbery.

Ruins among the Billboards

The incoming road winds past a landscape dotted with relics of the Roman and Byzantine periods. Most notable of these is the 2nd-century Roman **aqueduct**, which was part of an intricate water supply system that tapped into the nearby Melas (Manavgat) River.

Beyond the main gate, a colonnaded street leads past the **Roman baths** to the museum. Opposite from it lies the huge **agora** where fragments of broken columns and marble reliefs are neatly laid out. Labeled and numbered for future restoration, they are overshadowed by the monumental **theater** which still stands in reasonable repair, although the orchestra pit lies in a jumble of carved stones and marble. Seating some 20,000 spectators in its day, its rows of seats are still the scene of convivial action at sunset, when locals and strangers alike gather to enjoy the spectacular view.

Between the agora and the theater lie the remains of Side's **public latrines**, dating back some 2000 years. Their smell indicates they must still be in use today.

The second, smaller city gate stands right next to the theater where the road takes a sharp turn. Visitors with their own cars are advised to be cautious when negotiating the entrance since locals on minibikes and motorcycles often attempt to make a simultaneous squeeze-through at high speed. The **bus terminal** is just inside the city walls. Cars should be left at the parking lot next to the terminal; the village simply gets too crowded in summer to maneuver.

The **Old Town** consists of scores of shops, small hotels, and fast-food stalls packed between marble slabs, columns and other fragments of the past. Carpet and leather shops dominate the commercial scene.

Make your way down the clogged main artery of the town to the **old fishing harbor** located at the tip of the peninsula and the partially-restored **Temples of Apollo and Athena**.

The tiny cove is protected by a wall of rocks from winter storms, but has recently been dredged to accommodate the fishing boats even if precious little fishing goes on these days. Locals have discovered that it is far more lucrative to market excursions for tourists than cast the lowly net. The standard trip is a four-hour jaunt along the coast and up the Manavgat River.

Quayside Fisheries

Happily, Side's harbor has its fair share of excellent eateries where one can sample a variety of fresh fish and seafood. Most of the better restaurants are found on the western side of the peninsula. They range in price and style from intimate tables set under authentic fishing nets to fancy establishments.

Amiable, unpretentious and with a 20-year reputation behind it is the **Aphrodite Restaurant**, located on the western edge of the harbor. Giant prawns served with lemon wedges and a tasty garlic dip are a bit pricey but can be recommended, as can the shrimp casserole with tomato sauce, topped with melted cheese. Those who prefer fish should select one at the display counter. It will be weighed and then grilled *(izgara)* or fried *(tava)*. In any case you should taste it.

Above: Coffee is virtually a synonym of Turkey, but tea is also available. Right: Fast and healthy food on the waterfront.

Bars and Pubs

Half a dozen outdoor bars line the path which leads past the Temple of Apollo left (east) of the harbor. The **Café-Bar Dioniyos** (nicknamed the "Intel Bar" due to the consciousness level of its clientele) offers a pleasant and low-key ambience. Haydn concertos and Bach are the featured items on the musical menu. Next door is the charming **Apollonik Kafeterya** of old-timer Dietmar Friese. A German sculptor and restorer turned land developer who settled in Side 30 years ago, Friese is one of the few foreigners who can truly claim to have known Side as it once was. Most of the restoration of the Temple of Apollo is his work, and the four double rooms at Apollonik Pension next door, which shares a wall with a Byzantine basilica, used to be the only place people in the know would stay. Another favorite drinking establishment in the vicinity is the **Odeon Bar**, set in a lovely garden down a street near the temple. The western shore of the peninsula is where

the louder action is. About halfway down the main street, which leads to the harbor, a narrow side street cuts across to the old town square where much of Side's nightlife is concentrated. The **Ambience Restaurant-Bar** serves good Turkish cuisine at reasonable prices and has tables on the waterfront. Its discotheque is presently the trendiest around. A few meters away is the **Denizati Discotheque**. Those who really crave the big beat should visit one of the neighboring five-star hotels, like the **Asteria** to the west or the **Meridien** to the east.

In addition to having the loudest sound systems, the luxury hotels also tend to have the best stretches of beach and a whole range of aquatic facilities which are usually free-of-charge for guests. A notable exception is the **Turtel Hotel** which has grown from ten beach bungalows to its present size of 1000 beds, but still charges a fee for windsurfing. The nearby **Özcan Riding School** supplies horses for those who wish to explore Side by this leisurely mode of transportation.

Rollicking on the River

Those who are tired of frying on the beach, might enjoy a trip up the **Manavgat River** on one of the fishing boats which service the Side harbor. Be prepared for a "hands-on" experience, as the captain may need some help maneuvering through the sand bars at the delta.

Once on the river, the apparently innocuous fleet of fishing boats divides itself into opposing armadas of Roman "galleys". In the place of Greek fire, the ammunition employed is buckets of ice-cold river water. Beware: Neither man, woman, beast nor baby is spared in the water fights which continue all the way to the **Küçük Selale**, or "Small Waterfall". The falls are pretty limited and consist of just a few rocks hidden beneath the surface of the water, effectively terminating further upstream exploration for deep-keel boats.

The shady and cool outdoor **Küçük Selale Restaurant** serves grilled or fried trout for boat and bus visitors. The return

journey by boat promises another series of water fights.

MANAVGAT

If you are a tourist-weary trooper who wants to be based close to Side but is less than eager to spend every minute there, a good alternative is **Manavgat**, a surprisingly pleasant market town some four kilometers to the east. Situated on Highway 24 and divided by the Manavgat River, the town is affectionately mispronounced "Man of God" by its admirers and offers food and lodging at about half the price than Side does. The ambience is more Turkish, the pace slower, the smiles warmer and the service friendlier.

A good choice of accommodation is the relatively new **Otel Kervan**. Its 15 simple but spacious, clean and bright

Above: Rugs come in all shapes, sizes and prices in Turkey. Right: This grandiose waterfall, named Büyük Selale, is one of nature's wonders in the area of Manavgat.

double rooms (replete with complimentary disposable razor) overlook the river.

Monday is the day to be here, when Manavgat turns into Tractorville. Merchants and wandering traders all gather at the market to sell their wares and meet old friends. A couple of blocks east of the river, the market is a great place to replace lost or torn underwear and socks. Rope, twine, cheap metal forks, knives, spoons and hand-worked tin buckets can be haggled over as well. Locally produced crafts are rare: Bogus Lacoste shirts seem to guarantee more turnover than knitted hats.

Manavgat's more conventional commercial activities are centered along Lise Caddesi and Fevzipasa Caddesi. These streets are lined with countless shops, family-run restaurants and cafés catering for the locals. Aimed at the tourist overspill from Side are a few carpet and leather shops along Antalya Caddesi. One of them, the **Sultan,** advertises itself with an old, rusting VW "beetle" hoisted in the air, sprayed by a constant jet of

water. What this has to do with leather coats and skirts is anybody's guess. More interesting is the inconspicuous **quilting workshop** of Hüseyin Solmaz, tucked away in Kordon Caddesi: The incredibly bright, colorful display of satins inside needs no advertising.

Although Manavgat's market is a great attraction, it is the ice-cold waters of the turquoise **Manavgat River** that bring most travelers to the town. Standing on the old German bridge (a steel structure dating back to 1937 and no longer used for motor traffic) be sure to look out for the sign "Boot Toors", a linguistic concoction of English, German and Turkish meaning "Boat Tours". The folks from Side may cackle as they splash, but the last laugh is on them: They have paid about ten times as much for the same wet trip up the river and have two hours to go before they return to Side to get dry again. You, meanwhile, are already sitting at the **Develi Restaurant** beneath the eastern side of the bridge, enjoying the best Gaziantep-style food in the country,

and at very reasonable prices. Try the *humus* and the *İçliköfte* for starters.

Seleucia

Some ten kilometers north of Manavgat is the **Büyük Selale**, or "Big Waterfall". Those with their own transportation can simply take a right-hand turn at the roundabout at the end of Antalya Caddesi on the edge of town and follow the well-posted road signs. *Dolmuses* are also available from the bus station. Admission to the park is expensive, and allows one access to an unpretentious restaurant with outdoor tables set among trout-filled ponds, all shadowed by the foliage of large mulberry trees.

About 13 kilometers north of Manavgat and just past the Büyük Selale are the ruins of Pamphylian **Seleucia**. A cross-country vehicle would be nice, but is not necessary to negotiate the track. The irony is that the road to the site follows the course of a Roman road which seems, in patches, to be in better shape than the

contemporary one. The site dates back to early Hellenistic times, taking its name from the ubiquitous and egocentric Seleucus I, one of Alexander's friends and founder of the Seleucid dynasty in the early 4th century B.C. The number of ancient towns named after this emperor seems only rivaled by the large number of main streets named after the first president of Turkey.

Just how integral Seleucia was to the Seleucid Empire is hard to say. With its capital in Antioch, the dynasty was primarily interested in Syria and parts east, although pretensions once included most of what is today Asian Turkey. Eventually, the Seleucids made the mistake of rebelling against Rome and were forced to withdraw from Anatolia. Border posts like Seleucia were soon populated by Roman veterans and their wives and

Above: The Romans had the know-how to build such bridges, here over the Köprü Çayi near Beskonak. Right: Healing waters and a chance to trade information.

children. Family bliss came to an abrupt end in A.D. 178 when one of the many large earthquakes turned the city upside down. Not even the Roman corps of engineers could deal with the destruction, and the garrison town soon became overgrown with bushes and trees.

Ruins of the **city walls** and other edifices lie scattered throughout the forested area and await further exploration by visitor and archaeologist alike. Impressive as well are the **agora** and the surrounding arcade of shops beside the semi-circular **council house.**

Those who trust Roman work after 2000 years of neglect can climb up onto the windowledges of erstwhile shops for a splendid view of Side and the coast. Nearby are the remains of a basement with a hint of mosaic on the floor. The building that once stood here has long since disappeared – transformed, no doubt, into the walls of a village house in the valley below. The northern face of the city is set on a gorge overlooking the Manavgat River with some 200 meters' sheer drop. This may once have been a garrison town, but today the legions have been replaced by lizards, and the beat of the military drum by the monotonous but musical rap-tap of a brace of woodpeckers, beating out a rhythm over the gentle rustling of the trees.

Back on the main road to Manavgat, take a left and follow the river back into the hinterland. The road winds along the river through hilly countryside dotted with stone pines, passing sections of the **Roman aqueduct** which once brought fresh water to Side. Beyond is the newly constructed **Lower Kepez Dam** which ensures regular water supplies for the villages and fields of the Manavgat plain, as well as preventing spring flooding. A dirt road leads to the dam around the reservoir. Only a few houses in villages like Karavaca Köyü were left above the manmade flood waters and now sit on a tiny sliver of high ground. Spared by the ris-

ing lake around them, they are crumbling into dust and mud.

Selge

Other journeys into the neighboring mountains are a bit more arduous, requiring a taste for travel that goes beyond walking from the beach to the bar. One such site is the ancient Pisidian city of **Selge**, known today as Zerk.

Take the turnoff into the **Köprülük Kanyon Milli Park** (Bridge Canyon National Park) at the yellow sign directing you to the village of Tasagil about 10 kilometers west of Side. Leaving the village, take a left turn and follow the good tarmac road through forested hills into the fertile valley of the Köprü Irmagi. **Beskonak** ("five houses") is a logging town perched high on the cliffs above a gorge. Where the deep, blue waters of the river cut through the rock some 30 meters below, the canyon is spanned by a **Roman Bridge**. Despite two or three missing guardrail stones, the Roman

bridge is as solid today as when it was built some 2000 years ago.

Above the bridge, the bumpy serpentine track continues up the mountain, skirting massive cliffs on one side and plunging into depths on the other. For those with the courage to look back over what their driver has just negotiated, each turn on the road presents a new breathtaking vista – an emerald sea of tree tops, amazingly regular rock formations bearing a resemblance to Aztec sculpture, distant waterfalls plunging into deep ravines and the snow-capped mountain peaks of the Taurus towering regally to the north and east. After all this, the paltry remains of Selge can be a bit disappointing, but the wild ride alone is worth it.

Once inhabited by more than 20,000 people, Selge is now represented by the poor and tiny settlement of **Zerk**. As you enter the village, a swarm of begging children, some with a remarkable command of foreign languages, will instantly surround you. Be armed with sufficient quantities of candy, small change or

The remains of two **temples**, assumed to have been dedicated to the deities Zeus and Artemis, sit on the largest of the three hills that used to comprise the ancient city. Nearby is the impressive **cistern** which used to get most of its water supply from an **aqueduct** to the northwest. On a hill to the east is the city's paved **agora**, surrounded by the foundations of other market buildings.

On the way back, you can stop and dine in Beskonak's only restaurant, the **Kanyon.** Fresh trout is the featured item on the menu. The connoisseur should be warned, however, that while the beer and Coke are refreshingly cold here, the fish are pool trout, and do not come from the whitewater down below where their wild, speckled brethren are fished with jigger and fly.

Etenna

For those who delight in nothing more than getting to where few have gone and fewer will follow, **Etenna** will beckon. Despite poor access roads, the trip is definitely worth the effort. Take the north-bound road at the Manavgat roundabout and turn off to the towards the villages of **Sarilar** and **Dolbazlar**. It is easy to miss, so look out for the white sign with village names. The real problem arises with the exit from Dolbazlar. As you enter the village you'll drive past the square; at the end of the square take a left turn – it may not look too promising, but it leads to a fork with the right-hand road heading to Sirtköy and Etenna.

From here on, the road turns into a dusty, tractor-chewed dirt track which strains shock absorber and passenger patience. The cotton fields soon give way to hilly, stone pine forests dotted with bee hives and giant heather.

colorful Turkish to drive them away, as the little beggars are rather insistent. Village women will try to sell their carved wooden spoons and other tourist items to you, since a small but steady flow of outside visitors provides extra income for the families in this isolated spot. This is a very distant echo of the favored occupation of their warlike, independent predecessors. The material evidence of civilization, however shattered, is far more impressive than the contemporary community: Countless blocks of cut stone lie in a jumble everywhere, some of them carved simply, others adorned with more complex reliefs. Throughout the extensive site nothing has been excavated, save in the standard, casual manner of acquiring pre-cut stone for one's home. The **theater**, still standing on the edge of the village, has remarkably been spared more vandalism, and is now the best-preserved structure to be seen.

Above: Spelunkers practicing their hobby.
Right: Separating the wheat from the chaff.

Unused to motor traffic, shepherds stare and goats scramble into the forest when cars pass; the rather nasty dogs of the region will take up the challenge and

chase anything with four wheels on it. Try barking back at them; nothing else seems to work.

After two more tempting left turns (eschew them, and go straight), the forest thins and gives way to tangled undergrowth, harsh rock and, eventually, small terraced fields with far too many stones in them to allow for much productivity. Finally **Sirtköy** appears, its stone-and-timber houses left unplastered and unpretentious. The ladies of the village squat in their yards in front of huge plastic tubs filled with the week's laundry. Goats and chickens wander about freely throughout street and yard, while young children follow the stranger's car as if it were a peculiar new toy.

Ask one of the older kids to guide you to **Etenna** ("Etenna, *lütfen"*) and the obliging youngster will lead you on a steep twenty-minute hike to the site, located on a hill northeast of the village. Founded by Greek colonists at the turn of the first millennium, the history of the city remains obscure save for a reference to

8000 of its young men who volunteered to fight fiercely for the Seleucid pretender Achaeus attempted to depose his nephew, Antiochus III, but was defeated and crucified in the skin of an ass.

No excavations have been effected on the site as of yet, so it is anybody's guess as to what the less obvious buildings mightt once have been. Like almost everywhere along the coast, an earthquake wreaked havoc here and most buildings toppled over, leaving chaotic piles of lichen-covered blocks and an occasional broken column or festooned slab, as well as plenty of rubble. Etenna apparently never had a theater or a stadium, but your dexterous guide will be quick to take you to a number of half-hidden reservoirs and **cisterns**, as well as to fragments of the ancient **city wall**.

The **necropolis**, on the much cooler, shadier and steeper northern side of the mountain, contains plenty of tombs, furnished with simple bunk-like resting places that have stone head rests. Downhill towards the village are the remains of

a **basilica** and a church where the local women pick fresh bay leaves for their tasty rustic cuisine.

ALANYA

Back on the main coastal highway and three kilometers past the Konya turnoff is **Kizilot Köy**, notable primarily for the fact that its residents are black: Their ancestors were brought from Egypt and the Sudan to work the extensive cotton fields of the area. Although the coastal highway runs along the seashore, the region is surprisingly undeveloped, with deserted, clean and sandy beaches, as well as lush banana groves growing on the inland side of the highway. The locals claim that the conditions here are ideal for spearfishing: Huge flat rocks beneath the surface provide feeding grounds for fish.

Above: The Red Tower on the Seljuk dock in Alanya. Right: Street vendors of "simit," a pleasant snack, pose for posterity.

Luckily, not all the architecture along the coast is still under construction. The area around Alanya, like Antalya and Side, boasts an interesting mix of late Roman and crusader buildings, as well as Seljuk Turkish structures. Some of the best examples of the last are the **Alarahan caravanserai** and the impressive **Alarakale fortress**, located some nine kilometers inland from the town of **Okurçarlar.** Intended to be an Armenian crusader fortress on the coast, it fell to the Seljuk Sultan Keykubat when he conquered this area from Alanya. The fortress contains the ruins of a palace, a crumbling mosque and a *hamam*, as well as the remnants of servants' quarters. A partially collapsed tunnel leads from Alarakale to Alarahan. Yet another Seljuk caravanserai, the **Serapsahan**, built by Sultan Keyhusrev (son of Keykubat I), is located 15 kilometers outside Alanya on the banks of the cool Serapsa River. Unfortunately, it cannot be visited.

The most impressive Seljuk-period structure along the coast, however, is in

Alanya itself: The immense fortress that crowns the promontory and dominates the town, 800-meters above the sparkling sea. Although primarily a Seljuk town, Alanya's history is much older. Known as Choracesion in antiquity, it served as the base of operations of one Diodotus, a local lord regarded as a pirate by the Romans. They reduced his fortress to rubble in 67 B.C.

Renamed Kalanaris during the Byzantine period, the city served as a bishopric, but only reassumed strategic importance when a series of Armenian dynasties came to power during the Crusades. They fortified the city's defenses but were tricked into surrender by Keykubat in 1222. Legend tells that the Seljuk sultan enlisted the services of hundreds of goats with candles tied to their horns during his nocturnal attack, giving the appearance of having far more soldiers than he did. The ruse worked and "Alayie" – as the city was renamed – became the winter residence of the Seljuk court. The city was subsequently taken by the Karamids in the early 14th century, and then by the Ottomans in the year 1471.

Below the inner defense walls stands the elegant **Süleymaniye Camii**, a 16th-century mosque dedicated to Süleyman the Magnificent, erected on the foundations of an earlier mosque built by Sultan Keykubat. To the left lie the remnants of an old **bedesten** and beyond, standing on the cliff's edge, are the **lighthouse** and the remains of a **hamam** – a strange juxtaposition of architecture. Inside the massive gateway are the ruins of the imperial residence and, along the north wall, restored Seljuk-period barracks with a flight of stairs made of red brick. Legend tells that these were used by Cleopatra when she descended to the sea for her morning dip.

A few traces of Byzantine frescos are visible on the crumbling walls within a small 16th-century chapel, dedicated to **St. George**. A fortress would be in-

complete without cisterns, and Alanya has several. The largest one, just left of the gate, made it possible to withstand long sieges.

Peeking over the top of the crenellated west wall, you can see a **Seljuk-period mint** and a **Byzantine church** clinging to a spit of craggy rock that extends out from the headland. The view from the platform, fixed high into the cliff at the northwest corner of the castle, can only be described as stupendous. Prisoners who were condemned to death were once hurled from this point, or pardoned if they succeeded in throwing a stone over the bulge of the precipice out into the sea. Visitors attempt the same feat today, mostly in vain.

To get a taste of old Alanya, try walking back down on or alongside the walls, which often serve as part of an old house. A good buy here are the silk scarfs made by local women.

Sultan Keykubat also left his mark on Alanya's bustling fishing harbor. Sheltered at the foot of the headland, the harbor is dominated by the massive **Kizil Kule**, or "Red Tower", which protected the sultan's warships and dockyards. A fine example of medieval military architecture, the tower has now been restored and houses an ethnological exhibition on the ground floor.

Although the harbor of Alanya has lost its strategic importance, it is still one of the liveliest areas in town. Scores of colorful fishing boats are tied up along the pier where fishermen sit and mend their nets while juice vendors, street sellers and quayside restaurants cater to the tastes of locals and visitors alike. The **Merakli Inegöl Köftecisi** serves up the best food in town, while the **Sato Restaurant** specializes in seafood at reasonable prices. A number of *pansiyons* and a couple of hotels are found in the vicinity of the harbor. A good choice is the pleasant **Kaptan Otel** which even has its own swimming pool. If you don't mind sharing your breakfast with an oversized family of cats, **Pansiyon Weisse Villa** is the place.

Alanya has its castles in the air and its grottos by the sea. **Lover's Grotto, Pirate's Cave** and the **Phosphorescent Cave**, where pebbles shine up mysteriously bright blue from the sea bed, are usually included in a one-hour package tour on small craft available at the harbor. Before getting to **Cleopatra Beach** on the other side of the promontory, boats pass beneath the cape and are usually bombarded by rocks and stones thrown from the platform above. Like the condemned men before them, none of the rock throwers are able to launch their missiles over the distance.

On the west side of the peninsula near Cleopatra Beach is the **Damlatas Cave**, which takes its name from the water dripping off its stalactites and stalagmites. Dating back some 20,000 years, the

Right: Woodsmen still ply their exhausting trade by hand in the hinterlands of Alanya.

warm and humid belly of the cave is still a favorite spa for those with asthma or other respiratory ailments. Nearby is the local museum, of limited interest for most. The visitor knows by this time what the reader does not: Alanya, although enjoying its share of historical riches, is primarily a tourist town.

New hotels, apartment blocks and construction sites line the main streets, and the long, fine stretches of beach to either side of the town are now filled with the most recent conquerors of the coast – the 40,000 Europeans who come to claim Alanya as their summer home. Most of the hotels in the middle and upper price range are tied up with larger tour-operators, but there are less expensive *pansiyons* tucked into the side streets.

A stroll down Damlatas Caddesi will take you to the old town, where sidewalk eateries tempt you with good and inexpensive food while carpet merchants and jewelers try to get you to buy their pricier wares. Although most of the restaurants tend to serve the same basic food, there are some happy exceptions. Try the **Manti Evi** off Yayla Yolu north of Atatürk Caddesi. The house speciality (the only one) is minced meat wrapped in pasta and topped with a tasty yoghurt and garlic sauce, expertly cooked up by the wife of Alanya's museum director. Regular patrons remove their shoes before entering the premises and settling down on their knees for the meal.

Spices, cotton and tomatoes can be found in the noisy babble of Alanya's **Friday Market** located just north off the junction of Atatürk Caddesi and Keykubat Caddesi. A friendly and colorful affair where rustics from the mountains sell their produce and stock up on a week's supply of groceries at the same time, the market is also a favorite gathering place for tourists stricken with *shutterbugitis* – that strange but seldom fatal disease that forces grown men and women into the most contorted positions imaginable

while looking through a 35 mm lens for that one perfect peasant picture. Regarded as harmless by the natives, the shutterbuggers have become an integral part of the market in Alanya.

In addition to the bus station, inconveniently located some three kilometers out of town, Alanya also boasts a *dolmus* terminal near the center of town which serves the shorter runs to Manavgat, **Akseki** and **Gündogmus**, a little town an hour's drive into the mountains northwest of town.

Another pleasant journey is to head along the **Dimçay River** into the Taurus Mountains. A dirt track starting out at the river mouth seven kilometers east of town leads through a wooded area and over several rickety timber bridges dangling dangerously above the icy waters of the Dimçay. The attractive **Serdar Restaurant,** a 20-minute drive upstream, is a favorite spot with the locals and serves a selection of grilled meats. For trout, you'll have to continue four kilometers further to the **Dogan Toros Restaurant**.

Whether the drive was worth it or not is up to the palate: The trout are all the fish-farm variety here.

Into the Taurus

Some 13 kilometers west of Alanya, a signposted road off the highway continues another 20 kilometers up to the pleasant village of **Güzelbagi** ("Beautiful Vineyard") which sits on a small plateau. Approaching the town, note the old stone houses fixed into the rock above tiny terraced fields where donkeys still pull the plow through the dark soil. Honey bees thrive here, far removed from the generous use of insecticides on the cotton plantations of the coastal plains. Antique beehives – meter-long, hollowed-out tree trunks sealed at both ends, except for a small hole allowing passage of the drones – are rarely seen nowadays, having been replaced by the familiar blue and white wooden hives manufactured by some anonymous urban entrepreneur. The flavor, happily, remains the same in both.

157

An abundance of wild mountain flowers and herbs lends a unique taste to the honey, available practically at every bend in the road.

After Güzelbagi, a small but well preserved Roman bridge takes you across the **Alara Çayi**, its blue waters flowing rapidly through a rocky gorge ten meters below. The left fork after the bridge will lead you through the picturesque village of Umutlu before arriving at **Gündogmus**. Located high in the mountains, the town is the largest settlement (and possibly the only one with a credit union) in the mountain area between Alanya and Akseki – also accessible from the Konya road just outside of Manavgat. About seven kilometers along the Akseki road, a waterfall plunges from a height of some 15 meters straight into a little lake, good enough for a quick dip if you can tolerate the chilly waters.

Above: The fortress complex of Anamur means business. Right: A proud broom maker in Silifke.

Eastern Mediterranean

The coastal road east takes a dramatic turn after the town of **Gazipasa**, climbing through terraced banana and citrus plantations into the stone pine-covered mountains. Here, pinned between steep cliffs and the sea, the highway offers thrilling vistas of waves crashing against the rocky shore far below.

The first major town along this wild coast is **Anamur**, about 130 kilometers east of Alanya. Before entering the town, a right turn leads to the remains of vast **Anemurium,** literally a cemetery city dating back to the days of the Phoenicians who once populated the coast.

Anamur itself is not a destination. Located a few kilometers from the sea, all it offers are a few *pansiyons* and shops, although there is a nice stretch of beach with several hotels, bungalows and, recently, local holiday villa construction. Environmentalists involved with the cause of the giant loggerhead sea turtles which frequent the beach at night to lay thcir eggs, are now fighting to get the beach declared a preservation area like Dalyan and Patara.

Down the road from the main beach is **Anamur Castle,** one of the best preserved crusader forts along the coast. It has its own small stretches of beach, accessible to either side of the walls or through breaches in them. Within there is a mosque built after the knights were finally driven away.

The coastal road once again takes off into the clouds as it winds its way east past more fortresses of mixed pedigree and in various states of repair. Eventually it descends to the Cilician plain outside the port village of **Tasucu.** There are several good hotels to the west of town with their own pools (or pools created in the rocks), as well as the pleasant Inter Hotel beach resort, set along a sandy cove even further west (about ten kilometers) along the road just traveled. Those who wish to visit the **Turkish Republic of Northern Cyprus** can take hydrofoils across to Girne (Kyrenia) from here as well; it is about a three-hour trip.

Inland from Tasucu and next to the Göksu River is the pleasant town of **Silifke,** the Turkified version of Seleucia ad Calycdanum – yet another of the cities built by and named after the first Seleucid king. Little remains of the Hellenistic site, as invaders and later settlers have destroyed or built on the foundations of the original city. There is, however, a nice Ottoman-period bridge in the middle of town and a worthwhile museum housing artifacts from the archaeological sites in the surrounding mountains, as well as paraphernalia dating back to the Christian era. Just outside of town, back along the Tasucu road, are the ruins of the **Aya Tekla**, a nunnery dedicated to St. Thecla, one of the Apostle Paul's converts who died for her faith.

Dominating the city and the road leading along the Göksu river into the Taurus Mountains are the remains of a **castle**.

One can assume that the foundations date back to the first defensive settlement in the area, but most of the blocks extant are from the late Byzantine period when Silifke was a critical stronghold keeping the Arabs from entering the central Anatolian plateau. A curious memorial here marks the site where the Holy Roman Emperor Frederick Barbarossa drowned in 1190 on his way to free Jerusalem from the Muslims.

A mandatory excursion from Silifke takes you north into the mountains to the Hellenistic-Roman site of Olbia/Diocaesarea, today known as **Uzuncaburç.** A good asphalt road winds 27 kilometers through the villages of Demircili, Imamli and Kiragigi where there are several interesting **Roman tombs**, but nothing to compare with the Roman buildings associated with the holy city of **Olbia.**

The site, first settled by the Hittites but developed under the Seleucids as a holy city, is situated in and around the town of Uzuncaburç (which can quaintly be translated as "rather tall tower"). It consists of a **theater, nymphaeum, gymnasium**, a **temple** dedicated to Tyche, the Roman goddess of fate, and a monumental **city gate**, as well as a **necropolis**. The primary structure, however, is the **Temple of Zeus Olbius**. This temple was first built in 295 B.C. by Seleucus Nicator and consists of 30 Corinthian columns which are still standing, with some of the friezes still in place. It was converted to a basilica in the 5th century of the Christian era.

A sharp left turn downhill along a bad gravel road just at the end of the village brings one to **Ura,** another ancient Hittite site in the mountains with Hellenic and Roman overlays. Do not expect too much, especially after having seen Olbia, as time and weather have largely reduced whatever structures once stood at Ura to a few boulders in the general rubble, covered in brambles and weeds.

From Ura, a gravel road slowly descends towards the coast east of Silifke via another necropolis overlooking a rugged canyon, known locally as **Tekkadinköy** ("Single Woman Village"). Another bad road leads to the peculiar **Mausoleum of Priapus** some ten kilometers below the necropolis. Standing alone in the brambles, the signature of the mausoleum is the god Priapus with his oversized organ extended on the right side of the structure to remind all comers that the local gentleman buried within was a very big man indeed.

An easier way to visit the mausoleum is to return to Silifke and take the coastal road east to **Susanoglu,** a coastal village with pretensions of becoming a tourist town. Plunge into town and try to find the single road leading into the hills behind it; there are no signs to guide you, and quite a few cul de sacs to frustrate all but the most diligent. Once on the dirt road behind the town, drive on for about 15

kilometers until a small green sign indicates a right turn down an even worse gravel path. At the end is the said mausoleum; the Tekkadinköy necropolis is about five kilometers further along the main road.

East of Susanoglu, the road winds along the increasingly craggy shoreline which has only a very limited share of tourist development. The incongruously large **Club Scandinavia** sits at the top of a tiny beach and is far too expensive for what limited services it offers; a better bet is a small, nameless camping ground with several bungalows five kilometers down the road.

Ten kilometers further on (and now 20 kilometers east of Silifke) is **Narlikuyu,** or "Pomegranate Bay", where a dozen fish restaurants surround a freshwater harbor and serve some of the best sea bass to be found along the coast. At the head of the village is a small museum dedicated to the **Three Graces**, a floor mosaic from a long-since vanished Roman house depicting the voluptuous forms of Zeus' daughters.

Just outside the village, a good tarmac road leads left off the main highway to the two peculiar geological formations known as the **Caves of Heaven and Hell**. The latter, *Cehennem Deresi,* is a huge, fenced-off hole in the ground and is inaccessible unless you have a rope ladder, while the former, *Cennet Deresi,* has been a place of pilgrimage since the earliest times. A long stairway heads down from the road to the remains of a **Byzantine chapel** at the entrance to the cavern. The pious were once inclined to take mud baths in the **Typhon's Grotto**; the modern visitor has a hard enough time negotiating the slippery stairs down to it. A note of caution: Resist the urge to run back up the stairs since a too rapid ascent can result in what seems to be a case of the bends. Just above and to the left of Heaven (next to the refreshment stands) is the **third cavern**, which might as well

Right: The mighty Kizkalesi outside Mersin belies the meaning of its name – the "Maiden's Castle".

be called "Purgatory", but isn't. After paying a modest admission fee, one descends down a spiral staircase into a stalagmite-filled cave with trails leading in all directions. Not surprisingly, it is not a popular place among claustrophobics.

Maiden's Castle

Several kilometers down the coastal road, a vast beach framed by two medieval castles (one on shore and one off) presents itself. This is **Kizkalesi**, a tourist village taking its name from the offshore castle where, legend has it, the daughter of a king was sequestered away after a seer predicted that she would die of a snake bite. It will surprise no one to hear that the lovely lady met her maker when her lover sent her a basket of grapes at the bottom of which was a snake ....

The village has evolved over the years from a quiet, idyllic hideaway to a full-service resort town with any number of small *pansiyons*, restaurants, bars and even a couple of pool halls. Recently, a few larger establishments, such as the **Club Barbarossa**, have opened their doors to foreign travelers who want a few of the extras, and to Turkish, middle-class vacationers from the nearby cities of Mersin and Adana.

Mersin, located about 50 kilometers further east, is a major port and a city tipped for rapid growth and development. Although pleasant enough for the inhabitants, it does not offer much to the traveler aside from boasting Turkey's tallest building (the Hilton Hotel) and being the ferry station link to Famagusta (Gazi Magosa) in northern Cyprus. Another 25 kilometers east is Tarsus, the hometown of the Apostle Paul and the place where Mark Antony first set eyes on, and then fell hopelessly in love with, Cleopatra. Despite the historic associations, it is not a particularly interesting town and most of the extant ruins, such as **St. Paul's Arch**, are later accretions from the period of the Crusades.

From Tarsus, one can link up with the northbound E-5 motorway for a drive to

the **Cilician Gates,** a half natural, half man-made pass through the Taurus Mountains connecting Cilicia to the Central Anatolian plateau. The alternative is to push on down the coast to the sprawling city of **Adana**, which is often described as Turkey's "biggest village". This is perhaps a little unfair because Adana, with a population of over one million in the hub of the fertile Çukurova plain, does indeed have all the attributes of a city, including its own airport, university and numerous hotels catering to agro-businessmen in town to bid on cotton and citrus futures.

Its sons have also left their mark on the national economy and the arts: Sakip Sabanci, whose family logo *SA* graces a dozen factories in town, is arguably the richest man in Turkey, while author Yasar Kemal *(Memed My Hawk)* is a perennial candidate for the Noble Prize for Literature. The city was also the primary back-

Above: Antakya, once a major town, now a Sleeping Beauty of sorts.

drop for the work of film maker Yilmaz Güney. Otherwise, there is little to detain the stranger in Adana save a visit to the excellent **Ethnography Museum**, a walk over the **Tas Köprü**, a second-century Roman bridge spanning the Seyhan River, and a meal in one of the city's many restaurants specializing in *Adana kebab* – the spicy hamburger that is cooked on a spit, to which the city has given its name.

ANTAKYA

The Cilician plain stretches out east and northeast of Adana and is studded with castles and fortresses. In their present state, most of these date from the period of the Crusades although many, if not all, have histories far older than a mere thousand years. The first of these is the **Yilan Kalesi**, or "Snake Castle", just south of the E-5 highway about 30 kilometers east of Adana. Strategically located on a long bend of the Seyhan River, the castle with its crenellated tur-

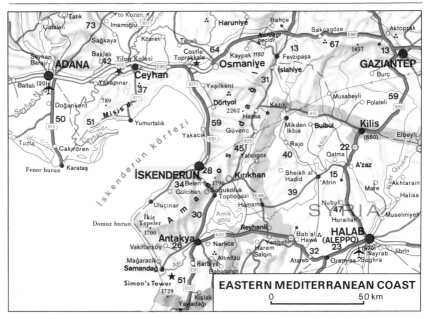

EASTERN MEDITERRANEAN COAST
0   50 km

rets is still in good shape. A little beyond the Yilan Kalesi turnoff, a paved road leads 30 kilometers north from the E-5 to **Kozan**, where a castle by the same name broods over the town on a cliff. Further down the E-5 at the Iskenderun/Gaziantep intersection looms another worthy addition to medieval military planning – the **Toprakkale**, or "Earthen Castle", which was used as a base for the Byzantine conquest of the old Roman province of Syria and its capital Antioch from the Arabs in the 10th century.

Take the southern fork of the road signposted for **Iskenderun,** a major port town dominated by a huge, Soviet-built aluminium factory and known for its excellent seafood – especially giant prawns. Although founded by Alexander the Great, the city looks like a fairly recent creation. Most buildings date from the post-World War I period when the town served as the administrative capital of Alexandretta, one of several mini-states set up by the French in Syria as part of their mandate. Paris only relinquished

control of the province in 1939, when a plebiscite was held to determine whether the population wanted to be associated with Turkey or with the newly-created state of Syria. The latter still includes the province on its own national maps.

Despite voting for inclusion in Turkey, there is no question that the people's ethnic and cultural differences distinguish the Hatay province from the rest of the country. Arabic remains the language of the streets, and Arabian culinary specialties such as *humus* and *tabouli* (chickpea and mint salad) remain standard fare in restaurants and homes.

An additional curiosity is the high proportion of Alevites among the Muslim population. This sect is a 16th-century off-shoot of Iranian Shiism, with a healthy mixture of heretical Christian and possibly even pre-Christian belief thrown in for good measure. Unlike mainstream Sunni Muslims, who are essentially followers of the "democratic" succession of leadership from the Prophet Mohammed through the Four Pious Caliphs, the

Alevites and their Shiite cousins believe in the "royal" or family line of succession of leadership from the Prophet to his son-in-law Ali.

But unlike the Shiites of Iran, the Alevites of Turkey have developed a number of decidedly non-Islamic habits and are reviled by true believers as heretics. They are subjected to incredibly vicious rumors ranging from the popular belief that members of the sect procreate in wild orgies, to the generally held notion that they refuse to wash. One peculiar result of this heap of abuse piled on the Alevites by religious fundamentalists is that they as a group have become the most secular people in the country. In this region, however, one can still find traces of Alevi tradition. Long, white-bearded *dedes,* who act as traveling wisemen, can be found at many of the hilltop and mountaintop shrines (the Alevites

Above: Hot peppers are part and parcel of Turkish gastronomy. Right: He is proud of being a Turk.

shun mosques), passing on Alevi lore to the youth.

The road south towards the Syrian frontier passes by several more crusader castles and the resort town of **Sogukoluk** before passing over a lesser mountain range and descending to the Orantes River valley. At the head of the valley is the town of **Antakya,** now the sleepy capital of the Hatay province, but at one time a city that rivaled even the glories of Rome. It was founded in 300 B.C. by the Seleucus Nicator as capital of the eastern Mediterranean kingdom that he carved from Alexander's empire.

Controlling a vast empire that, at its height, stretched from the Red Sea to India and from the Persian Gulf to the Russian steppes, Seleucus and his descendants bedecked the city with theaters, baths, gymnasia and even a large stadium to host rival Olympic games. Eventually, the dynasty was obliged to submit to the mastery of Rome, although Antioch as a city remained important as a place of late pagan and then early Christian thought. Wars, earthquakes and the vicissitudes of time, however, have now so reduced the city that it is difficult for the contemporary visitor to imagine the sway it once held in the greater scheme of the world.

Still, the city is worth a visit for a number of reasons. High on the list is a minor pilgrimage to the **Grotto of St. Peter**, where the Apostle allegedly established the first Christian church. Officially recognized by the Vatican as a shrine, it is likely that the cave was "discovered" by the crusaders during their occupation of Antioch in the 11th and 12th centuries, when the city was the capital of one of the four crusader kingdoms in the Middle East. Most of what remains of the **citadel** also dates from this period.

The main reason to visit, however, is to take advantage of the opportunity to admire what is arguably the best collection of late Roman mosaics anywhere in the Middle East, and possibly the world. Nicely displayed at the local **Mosaic Museum,** the bits of colored stone depict scenes and characters from mythology which once adorned the walls and floors of Roman villas at the resort of Daphne outside of town.

Some favorites are the *Happy Hunchback*, a deformed gentleman with a huge, erect penis and exquisite representations of Oceanus and Thetis.

Six kilometers south of town on the road to Syria lies **Harbiye**, a popular resort and picnic area built above the ancient **Grove of Daphne.** As part of their plan to assume both secular and sacred dominance over their rivals, the Seleucids built a temple and oracle complex here dedicated to Apollo, which remained in use until the 4th century. In his efforts to restore the old gods, the Byzantine emperor Julian the Apostate had the bones of several early bishops removed from the site; the next day outraged Christians burned the complex to the ground.

SAMANDAG

After the Christian restoration upon Julian's death, Antioch became a center not only of Christian theology, but also of asceticism dedicated to the discovery of God through intense self-sacrifice and bizarre meditation. The most famous of the spiritual acrobats was the 5th-century St. Simeon, who devoted his life to sitting naked on top of a pillar just east of Antakya. Sadly, it is located in the no-man's land between Turkey and Syria, thus inaccessible to modern visitors.

Simeon's example inspired others, including a sixth- century devotee also named Simeon who climbed onto his own pillar at the age of seven to spend his life in meditation and prayer. Word spread, and soon a monastery complex developed around his pillar on **Simeon's Mountain**, or Samandag.

Take the road to the town of Samandag (off the main intersection which flanks the museum) and look out for the yellow sign after about 20 kilometers. Turn left

and follow the increasingly bumby track leading to a white-domed Alevi shrine on the opposite hill.

From here, head north, and with any luck you will find a poorly-marked path leading to the monastery complex. If you feel lost, simply climb to the top of the rise, get your bearings, and proceed from there. It it is about a four-kilometer hike, but well worth the effort.

More accessible are several Muslim shrines in the area, including the **Shrine to Hizir** on the beachfront of Samandag. According to Koranic tradition, Moses met the obscure Muslim saint and asked to follow him in order to learn from the wise man. Hizir agreed on the condition that Moses did not question anything he did, despite the fact that Hizir's deeds – sinking a fishing boat, killing a child and preventing a poor, elderly couple from discovering a fortune in gold – seemed perfectly inexplicable and possibly evil.

Above: Detail of a mosaic in the museum of Antakya. Right: An Alevitic "dede."

When Moses finally demanded that Hizir give an account for his strange actions, the saint calmly showed Moses that every seemingly bad deed was a means of preventing even greater evil in the future. The two parted company at a location about half way up the neighboring **Musa Dagi,** or Moses Mountains. Here Hizir planted his staff, which subsequently took root and grew into the massive **holy tree** in today's **Hizirbeyköy.**

To get there, take the uphill road in the middle of **Magaracik**, a village just north of town of Samandag. Another curiosity here is the sole Armenian village left in the Hatay, **Vakiflarköy.** A simple church services for the remaining community of about 200.

Sadly, the traveler will have noticed by now that although Samandag seems to promise some nice beaches – the dark sandy shoreline extends for miles in either direction – they are badly marred by garbage thrown from passing ships.

But for those intent on taking the plunge, the most organized beach scene in the area can be found a few kilometers beyond Magaracik.

Nearby are the ruins of **Seleucia Piera,** the first, short-lived capital city of the Seleucid dynasty, which continued to serve as Antioch's port after Seleucus Nicator changed his mind and moved on. There are extensive ruins of a **necropolis** here, with the lower slopes of Musa Dagi riddled with tombs dating from both the pre-Christian and post-Christian eras. Noteworthy, too, is the impressive **diversion canal** dug into the mountain during the reign of Vespasian in order to prevent the silting up of the harbor area. The scheme was ultimately a failure, judging by the vast, fecund lowland that eventually will merge with the once pleasant, but now plastic-bag-plagued beach.

A new coastal road promises to connect Samandag directly to Iskenderun in the future, but at present it is best to return to Antakya and go on from there.

ANTALYA
Accommodation
LUXURY: **Antalya Dedeman**, Lara Yolu, Tel: 31-217910. **Club Sera**, Lara Yolu, Tel: 31-231170. **Falez**, Konyaalti- Falez Mev., Tel: 31-185000. **Kislahan**, Kazim Ölzap Cad. 55, Tel: 31-183870. **Ofo Antalya**, Lara, Tel: 31-231000. **Sheraton Voyager**, Yil Bul., Tel: 31-182182. *MODERATE:* **Altes Hotel**, Demircikara Mev., Tel: 31-232505. **Antares**, Lara Cad., Tel: 31-232244. **Isinda**, Altikum Mev., Tel: 31-290444. **Kozan**, Gençlik Mh., Tel: 31-126817. **Merve**, Cumhuriyet Cad., Tel: 31-187800. **Princess**, Lara Yolu, Tel: 31-233070. **Tigris**, Çaglayan Mh., Tel: 31-233332. *BUDGET:* **Aras**, Hüsnü Karakas Cad., Tel: 31-118695. **Kivrak**, Kazim Özalp Cad., Tel: 31-121893. **Orsa**, Tinaztepe Cad. 7, Tel: 31-181094. **Yalçin**, Hüsnü Karakas Cad., Tel: 31-118932. **Yayla**, Ali Çetinkaya Cad. 12, Tel: 31-111913. *CAMPING:* Three camping sites: **Bambus**, **Kanyaalti** and **Lara**.

Restaurants
Ahtapot Balik, Yat Liman Kaleiçi, Tel: 31-110900. **Dezincinin Kösesi**, Kaleiçi, Tel: 31-175329. **Hisar**, Kaleiçi Tophane Mev., Tel: 31-115281. **Kral Sofrasi**, Kaleiçi, Tel: 31-112198. **Yelken 2**, Eski Devlet Hast, Tel: 31-118489. **Yörükoglu**, Park İçi, Tel: 31-3250.

Museum
Archaeological Museum, Konyaalti Cad., Tel: 31-114528. Closed Mon.

Tourist Information / Other
Tourist Information: Cumhuriyet Cad. 91, Tel: 31-11747. **Port Authority**, Iskele Meydani, Tel: 23676. *Akdeniz- Akdeniz*, pop song contest held each fall (changing dates). The *Golden Palm Film Festival* also takes place each autumn to declare the winners of the Turkish "Oscar".

Caves
The Taurus Mountains are a spelunker's dream, with pot holes and caverns awaiting to be explored by professional speleologist and amateur alike. The most famous cave is the **Karain Magarasi**, where palaeolithic artifacts have been found. Located 27 km north of Antalya along the Burdur highway, the cave is lit and open to everyone. 20 km further along the Burdur road is the cave **Kocain Magarasi**. Take the turnoff marked Eksili and ask for the direction to the cave in the villages of Gevis, Bahçce, Camili or Ahirtas. The cave, an hour's walk away, is 600 m long and as high as 60 m in some places. The lower level is reserved for trained spelunkers with equipment. **Informations:** Pamfilya Travel Agency, 30 Agustos Cad. 57, Antalya, Tel: 31-1214015.

KEMER
Accommodation
LUXURY: **Iberotel Art**, Kiziltepe Mev., Tel: 3214-2611. **Phaselis Princess**, Tekirova, Tel: 3185-4070. **Ramada Renaissance**, Beldibi, Tel: 3212-3255. **Nona**, Deniz Cad., Tel: 3214-3170. **Pegasus Princess**, Deniz Cad., Tel: 3214-2285. **Sultan Saray**, Güynük, Tel: 3185-1480. *MODERATE:* **Bonn**, Deniz Cad., Tel: 3214-3191. **Dragos**, Deniz Cad., Tel: 3214-2489. **Gürkay Beltas**, Beldibi, Tel: 3184-8189. **Korient**, Iskele Cad., Tel: 3214-2130. **Olimpos**, Tel: 3214-1280. **Roman Plaza**, Deniz Cad., Tel: 3214-3900. **Sport**, Beldibi, Tel: 3184-8001. *BUDGET:* **Adonis**, Karayer Mev., Tel: 3214-2841. **Ambassador**, Liman Cad. 10, Tel: 3214-2626. **Roman Beach**, Deniz Cad. 33, Tel: 3214-3315. **Seker**, Atatürk Cad. 1, Tel: 3214-1325. **Murat**, Tel: 3214-1152. *HOLIDAY VILLAGES:* **Club Alda**, Beldibi, Tel: 3184-8151. **Club Aldiana Milta**, Tel: 3214-2232. **Club Marco Polo**, Çamyuva, Tel: 3184-6336. **Club Med Kemer**, Tel: 3214-1009. **Club Med Palmiye**, Tel: 3214-2890. **Club Salima Kemer**, Kiziltepe Mev., Tel: 3214-1521. **Robinson Club Çamyuva**, Tel: 3184-6383. *CAMPING:* **Erman Camping**, Beldibi, Tel: 3214-1112. **Erdemli Kervansaray Kizkalesi Mokamp**, Beldibi, **Turban Kiziltepe Camping**, Beldibi.

Restaurants
Günübirlik Tur-Tes, Tel: 3214-3250. **Mavi Akdeniz**, Tel: 3214-1219. **Pub Mandalina**, Liman Cad. 112, Tel: 3214-2172. **Yörük**, Tel: 3214-1777.

Tourist Information
Tourist Information, Belediye Binasi 10, Tel: 3214-1536.

SIDE / MANAVGAT
Accommodation
LUXURY: **Asteria**, Tel: 323-31830. **Cesars Hotel und Casino**, Kumköy, Tel: 321-32480. **Grand Prestige**, Titreyengöl, Tel: 3211-6600. **Iberotel Side**, Sorgun Mev., Tel: 3211-4715. **Novotel Turquoise**, Sorgun Mev., Tel: 3211-4722. **Saray Regency**, Titreyengöl Mev., Tel: 3211-6500. *MODERATE:* **Bella**, Bingesik Mev., Tel: 321-31816. **Cennet**, Tel: 321-31167. **Defne**, Selimiye Köyü, Tel: 321-31880. **Side Büyük**, Bingesik Mev., Tel: 321-31992. **Sirma Apartments**, Tel: 3211-2220. **Sol Kamelya**, Çolakli Köyü, Tel: 3244-1200. *BUDGET:* **Turtel Konak**, Selimiye Köyü, Tel: 3211-2225. **Hanimeli Pension**, Tel: 321-31789.

Mavi Su Pension, Tel: 3211-2219. **Taner Pension**, Tel: 321-31778. **Yat Pension**, Tel: 321-31465. *HOLIDAY VILLAGES:* **Eha Holiday Village**, Titreyengöl Mev., Tel: 3211-4710. **Robinson Club Pamfilya**, Acisu Mev., 3211-4700. **Sidelya Holiday Village**, Çolakli Köyü, Tel: 3211-4258. **Turttel Side Holiday Village**, Selimiye Köyü, Tel: 3211-2225. *CAMPING:* Two camping sites: **Kamelya, Mikro**.

Restaurants

Ayisigi, Çami Cad., Tel: 321-31400. **Bademalti**, Liman Cad., Tel: 321-31403. **China**, Liman Cad. 93, Tel: 321-31717. **Kalamar**, Liman Cad., Tel: 321-33364. **Sarapsi Han**, Liman Cad., Tel: 321-32826.

Tourist Information

Side/Manavgat Tourist Information, Tel: 321-31265.

ALANYA
Accommodation

LUXURY: **Serapsu**, Könakli Köyü, Tel: 323-51476. **Ananas**, Cikcilli Köyü, Tel: 323-19110. **Atlantur**, Dimçayi Mev., Tel: 323-14416. **Hamdullah Pasa**, Tel: 3235-1520. **Obaköy Banana**, Göl Mev., Tel: 323-17425. **Syedra Princess**, Mahmutlar Mev., Tel: 3175-1060.

MODERATE: **Alaaddin**, Atatürk Cad., Tel: 323-11048. **Anilgan**, Keykubat Cad., Tel: 323-21977. **Banana**, Cikcilli Köyü, Tel: 323-11548. **Blue Sky Bayirli**, Iskele Cad. 66, Tel: 323-16487. **Titan**, Kargicak Mev., Tel: 323-11063. *BUDGET:* **Alangün**, Atatürk Cad. 212, Tel: 323-13840. **Balik**, Dinek Mev., Tel: 323-12349. **Carina**, Güzelyali Cad., Tel: 323-17701. **Develi**, Bebek Sok., Tel: 323-17177. **Gallion**, Atatürk Cad. 123, Tel: 323-14392. **Özel**, Müftüler Cad. 35, Tel: 323-12220.

HOLIDAY VILLAGE: **Club Aquarius**, Konakli Mev., Tel: 323-11296. *CAMPING:* **BP Mocamp**, Okurcala Köyü (21 km east of Alanya in the direction of Gazipasa), Tel: 323-11488.

Restaurants

Inci, Gazipasa Cad., Tel: 323-11519. **Meram**, Gazipasa Cad., Tel: 323-13375. **Tamara**, Saray Mev., Tel: 313-13905. **Yönet**, Gazipasa Cad., Tel: 323-11223.

Tourist Information

Tourist Information, Carsi Mahalesi Kalearkasi Cad., Tel: 323-11240.

ANAMUR
Accommodation

BUDGET: **Anahan**, Tahsin Soylu Cad. 19, Tel: 7571-3511. **Dragon**, Iskele Mev., Tel: 7571-4140. **Karan**, Bozdogan Köyü, Tel: 7571-1027.

SILIFKE
Accommodation

LUXURY: **Altinorfoz Merit International**, Susanoglu, Içel, Tel: 7596-1211. *MODERATE:* **Club Barbarossa**, Kizkalesi Mev., Içel, Tel: 7584-1089. **Kilikya**, Içel, Tel: 7584-1117. **Tastur**, Tasucu, Tel: 7593-1045.

MERSIN
Accommodation

LUXURY: **Mersin Hilton**, A. Menderes Bul., Tel: 741-65000. **Gondol**, Gazi Mustafa Kemal Bul. 20, Tel: 741-71500.

MODERATE: **Club Soli**, Girit Mev., Tel: 7588-1630. **Nobel**, Istiklal Cad., Tel: 741-13023. *BUDGET:* **Damlaca**, Fasih Kayabali Cad. 6, Tel: 741-26034. **Ezgi**, Yeni Otogar Yani, Tel: 741-12014. **Hosta**, Fasih Kayabali Cad. 4, Tel: 741-14760.

Tourist Information

Tourist Information, Ismet Inönü Bul., Liman Girisi, Tel: 741-11265.

ADANA
Accommodation

LUXURY: **Adana Büyük Sürmeli**, Özler Cad., Tel: 71-123600. **Adana Sürmeli**, Inönü Cad. 151, Tel: 71-117321. **Inci Oteli**, Kurtulus Cad. 40, Tel: 71-158234. **Seyhan**, Resatbey Mah. Turhan, Tel: 71-175810. **Zaimoglu**, Özler Cad. 72, Tel: 71-113401.

BUDGET: **Hosta**, Bakim Yurdu Cad. 3, Tel: 71-123700.

Restaurants

Daylan, Atatürk Cad. 89, Tel: 71-129289. **Nihat**, Sivil Hava Mey., Tel: 71-127797. **Topaslar**, Alpu Köyü Mev., Pozanti, Tel: 71-361238.

Tourist Information

Tourist Information, Atatürk Cad. 13, Tel: 71-111323.

ANTAKYA / HARBIYE ISKENDERUN
Accommodation

ANTAKYA: *LUXURY:* **Büyük Antakya**, Atatürk Cad. 8, Tel: 891-35860. *BUDGET:* **Alpaydin**, Sehit Pamir Cad. 48, Tel: 881-18169. **HARBIYE:** *MODERATE:* **Detay**, Defne Cad., Tel: 8983-1054. *BUDGET:* **Çaglayan**, Örgen Cad., Tel: 8983-1011.

ISKENDERUN: *MODERATE:* **Arsuz**, Uluçinar, Tel: 8837-1444. **Cabir**, Ulucami Cad. 16, Hatay, Tel: 891-23391. *BUDGET:* **Bahadirli**, Prf. M. Aksoy Cad. 31, Hatay, Tel: 881-12923. **Güney Palas**, Temmuz Cad. 17, Tel: 881-11020. **Kavakli Pension**, Tel: 881-14606.

CENTRAL ANATOLIA

**ANKARA
BOGAZKALE
CAPPADOCIA
KONYA**

ANKARA

For most Turks, Ankara is a proud monument to the vision and dauntless energy of Atatürk, who transformed it from Angora, a sleepy Anatolian town of a few thousand known mainly for its sheep, into the capital of the modern, secular Turkish Republic. Today, the administrative and diplomatic center of Turkey is a city of 3,000,000 with wide European-style boulevards, university buildings, and planned parks. In contrast are the slum houses that sprawl across the hillsides on the edge of the city. These are called *gecekondu* – literally "rising up in a night"– because they are sometimes constructed in a single night. They are a useful reminder that Ankara, however it strives to be a European metropolis, is located in the heart of Anatolia. The city has remained somewhat provincial, and is overshadowed by Istanbul's cosmopolitan atmosphere.

The principal city thoroughfare is, not surprisingly, **Atatürk Bulvari**. It runs from the diplomatic and wealthy residential neighborhoods of **Çankaya** and **Gazi Osman Pasa** in the south to the heart of the old city in **Ulus**, which can trace its

Preceding pages: The rock towers give the landscape of Cappadocia a bizarre touch.

origins back to the Hittites in the second millennium B.C.

Located in the region of **Ulus** are most of the city's museums and historical sites. Principal among these is the **Museum of Anatolian Civilization**, situated directly beneath the walls of the imposing **citadel** in what was once the horse market. The museum itself is housed in two Ottoman buildings. The **Mahmut Pasa Bedesten**, a large ten-domed hall resting on four columns, was originally a bazaar warehouse which stored *tiftik,* the long, soft hair of the Angora goat. Trade in wool still remains an important source of income for local residents. The warehouse was constructed in the late 15th century by the grand vizier to Sultan Mehmet the Conqueror. The store rooms and administrative offices of the museum are in the **Kursunlu Han,** which was built a few years after the warehouse.

Inside the spacious museum, widely regarded as one of the most important in the world, are exhibits dating back to the Palaeolithic and Neolithic ages. Some of the artifacts excavated from one of the oldest human settlements in the world, at **Çatal Hüyük**, dating from 7500 B.C., are displayed. These include rare sculptures of the Mother Goddess, whose image has been found in the entire Mediterranean area. Equally impressive are the gold and bronze ornaments excavated from the Bronze Age and Hittite centers in Anatolia. If you want to avoid harassment from freelance museum guides offering to take you around, tape-recorded alternatives are available for a small fee from the reception desk. The museum is closed on Mondays. The outer walls of the citadel are just uphill from the museum. These were built in the 9th century by the Byzantine emperor Michael II. The earlier inner walls date from the 7th century. Flying from the ramparts are countless clothes lines – the first hint of the busy community within.

Take any one of the tiny streets that run through the picturesque crush of typical and colorful Anatolian peasant houses inside the walls of the castle and you will eventually reach one of the two fortified towers. The view from the top stretches across the city. On the way back, it is worth stopping at the **Turkish Museum of Handicrafts**, in a tastefully restored Ottoman house. It doubles as an Ottoman coffee shop and, upstairs, as a small *pansiyon*. If the citadel were a few kilometers outside Ankara, it would probably be a major tourist attraction. Instead, hidden in the city, few people visit it.

Turn right when you reach **Saraçlar Sokak**, which runs past the outer walls of the castle. You will eventually reach **Samanpazari**, a sprawling and confusing network of bazaars and shops, which is worth visiting. Especially attractive, for the pocket as well, is the copper market, or **Bakircilar Çarsisi**, at the top of the district. Every conceivable copper item is on sale – or can easily be made to order.

Within walking distance of the citadel is the **Haci Bayram Camii**, the city's most important mosque. It was built by the mystic Haci Bayram Veli, who founded the order of Bayramiye Dervishes in Ankara during the 15th century. To the side of the mosque is his *türbe*. The mosque stands next to the **Temple of Augustus,** originally built by the Phrygians to worship the Anatolian goddess of fertility before Roman occupation. Note the *Res Gestae* inscription in Latin and Greek carved into the remains of the temple walls. It details the state of the Roman Empire at the end of Augustus' 50-year reign, when all the gates of the empire were open and peace seemed to be on the verge of prevailing everywhere, at once, and for all eternity .... Augustus' evaluation of his empire did not succeed him, as proven by the sad state of the Roman ruins in the city. Note, for example, the lone **Column of Julian** in a square just off **Ulus Meydani** which is now a hectic and noisy *dolmus* terminal. The column was built to mark the visit of Emperor Julian the Apostate to Ankara in the 4th century. On top nest several storks; below, the pedestal has become a WC for the *dolmus* drivers. On nearby Çankiri Caddesi are the paltry remains of a **Roman bath** which dates to the 3rd century A.D.

Ulus is important to the modern Turk as the site of the first parliament building in the history of the Turkish Republic. Today it serves as the **Museum of the War of Independence.** Supported by numerous photographs of the war and members of that first parliament, the exhibits document the history of the war from Atatürk's landing at Samsun to the establishment of the Republic. The original assembly room has been kept exactly as it was.

Close by is the **Museum of the Turkish Republic** in the second, temporary home of the Grand National Assembly. The parliament met here until 1961.

Traveling to the south from Ulus along Atatürk Bulvari, you will pass the **State Opera House** which was founded by Atatürk. He was obsessive in encouraging the performance of Western music, in place of that inspired by Islam, in the Republic. He also established the Presidential Symphony Orchestra. Like many of

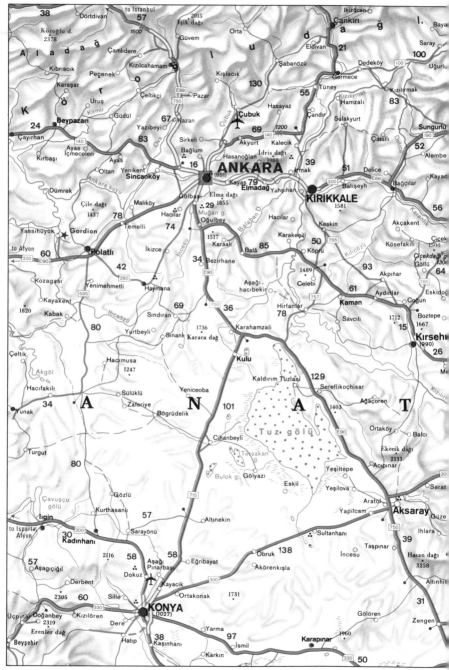

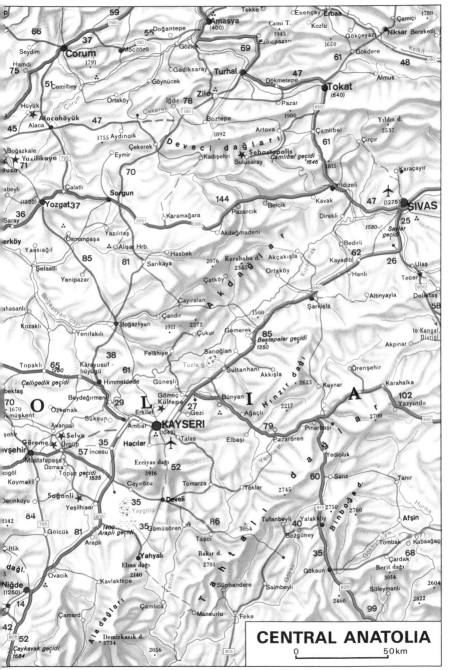

CENTRAL ANATOLIA

0   50km

the institutions dating to the mid-1930s, the national conservatory of music was founded with the help of exiles from Hitler's Germany: The refugees included such names as Carl Ebert and Paul Hindemith, who taught at the conservatory here.

Further south is the **Ethnographic Museum** with its impressive collection of Seljuk and Ottoman folk arts and handicrafts. For 15 years after his death in 1938, Atatürk was buried in the entrance hall. In 1953, his body was moved to the much more impressive **Anit Kabir** in the Maltepe district of the city. The mausoleum is surrounded by dozens of gardens and took nine years to build. The main entrance is along the **Lion Road** lined with 24 Hittite carved stone lions. To the right of the entrance is the **Tower of Independence**, and to the left the **Tower of Freedom.** In front of both are a series of statues which symbolize the

Above: The museum dedicated to Kemal Atatürk, the father of modern Turkey.

Turkish nation. Atatürk is buried directly under a marble sarcophagus in the **Hall of Honor**, on the outside of which is a relief portraying all the battles he successfully fought. In the courtyard outside the mausoleum, Ismet Inönü, the second president of the Republic and a close friend of Atatürk, is buried in an austere tomb. On the left side of the courtyard is the **Atatürk Museum** which hosts a variety of Atatürk memorabilia including medals, swords and even one of his dinner suits. Next to the museum is the **library** where over 3000 books which he read and annotated are collected. Some of his official cars are on view in a hall directly opposite the museum.

Kemal Atatürk's **Private Residence** in Çankaya, next to where the current president lives, has been converted into a museum with a diligence revealing the popular reverence in which he is held. By the foot of his bed plastercasts taken of his hands and face after his death are displayed and, altering nothing, his billiard table has been preserved intact. In the

Atatürk Orman Çiftligi Park on the northwestern fringe of the city is an exact replica of the house in which he was born in 1881 in Salonika, which now is a part of Greece.

Out of Ankara

There are several day trips to be made from Ankara for those who choose to use the city as their base (or are resident there). The first choice is usually a visit to **Gordium** (Yassihöyük), the ancient capital of the Phrygian empire, located about 100 kilometers west of Ankara just about 20 km past the town of Polatli.

The Phrygians once dominated much of western Anatolia and grew wealthy to the point where their greatest king, the famous Midas, became associated with the legend of the "golden touch". It was also here that Alexander solved the riddle of the Gordion Knot by the simple expedient of hacking the knot through with his sword. Several large burial mounds are all that remain of the city.

Another favorite outing for Ankarites in need of respite is about an hour northwest along the main Istanbul road at the town of **Kizilcahamami**. This town doesn't look like much, but there are lovely trout-filled lakes in the pine forests behind it, as well as a popular spa from which the town takes it name. Several other alpine resorts are in the vicinity of **Bolu**, about another hour down the road. These include a restored **Ottoman spa** complex just outside town on the way to the popular ski resort of **Kartalkaya**, and the woods around **Abant Lake**, about an hour north of Bolu on the Istanbul road. To the northeast is the **Yedi Göller National Park** nestling in the lesser Black Sea mountain range. The "seven lakes" in question are really just large ponds, but the scenery is beautiful. From here, roads lead north to the mining town of **Zonguldak**, which is quite literally built upon (and now sinking into) the mine shafts. To the west and east, respectively, are the western Black Sea resort towns of **Akçakoca** and **Amasra.**

An alternative route to the western Black Sea is via **Çankiri**, where there is the 16th-century **Ulu Cami** built by Sadik Kalfa for Süleyman the Magnificent, and **Kastamonu,** dominated by an 11th-century fortress. Nearby is the colorful town of **Safranbolu,** known for its checkerboard houses. On the intensely populated coast itself are the pleasant towns of **Inebolu** and **Sinop**, the latter boasting a castle originating in the time of the Pontic Kings and a huge radar base dating from the Cold War.

BOGAZKALE

Some 200 kilometers northeast of Ankara on the Samsun road is **Bogazkale**, the starting point for a tour of what remains of one of the most illustrious but least-known ancient Anatolian civilizations, the Hittites. Theirs was an empire that, during its peak in the 13th century B.C., rivaled those of Egypt and Babylon; one which left nothing comparable to the pyramids for posterity, but which achieved an extraordinary level of political and social sophistication.

This is evident from even the most cursory inspection of their imperial capital, **Hattusas**, today a three-kilometer drive from the village of Bogazkale. Hattusas is a city which housed 15,000 people in an area of 202 hectares, once surrounded by six kilometers of 10-meter-high stone walls. For 600 years it was one of the most important population centers in the ancient world. It was a city of wealthy homeowners, with primitive sewers and water pipelines, expensive jewelry and copper bathtubs.

Today, 3000 years later, Hattusas requires some imagination on the part of the visitor. Hittite occupation of this now ruined city, with white stone foundations and rubble walls spreading over a thinly-

grassed hillside, began during what is classified as the Old Kingdom, between 1740 and 1460 B.C. The city experienced its second heyday during the "Younger Kingdom" (1375-1180 B.C.).

In the upper city stands the **Lion Gate** dating back to the reign of King Antilles I at the start of the 16th century B.C. At that time, the lions, with their delicately chiselled manes, had eyes inlaid with gems which were supposed to frighten hostile invaders. Invaders tried six times to conquer the city, but were foiled on each occasion by the huge wood and bronze doors that stood in the gateway. The walls also were strong – held together by metal staples, some of which still exist.

But the Hittites remained a nervous people; they constructed massive artificial ramparts to ensure better security. The upper city is only "upper" because

Above: The lions of Hattusas guard the entrance. Right: The fascinating Hittite reliefs near Yazilikaya.

the Hittites made it that way. There was no hill there before. They also constructed secret tunnels, like the one which extends for 70 meters from the **Yerkapi Gate,** through which soldiers could leave the city undetected. Two sphinxes stood above this tunnel – a third sphinx sat at the exit.

Further down the slope is the **King's Gate**, dating from around 1400 B.C., home to the finest surviving Hittite sculpture until its removal to the Ankara museum. Now there is a plastercast of the figure, which is most likely a god. Nearer to the lower city is a large rock, part of the wall of an administrative building, which features a series of intricately carved hieroglyphics. In the Hittite alphabets, these hieroglyphics list the Hittite rulers up to 1300 B.C.

Those rulers lived in the **citadel,** a complicated palace of many rooms and offices linked by corridors. In its center is the royal library, originally divided into two chambers: One for storage, the other for reading. About two hundred scribes were employed here. The masters worked on clay and the apprentices on wood. Several thousand clay tablets have survived and have become the principal source of our knowledge about the Hittites. Behind the citadel is a gorge across which a bridge once provided easy access to one of the city's major temples, known as **Temple I.**

The city below the citadel was a mass of tiny workshops and offices – the heart of the vast imperial bureaucracy. Tablets found here have shown trading connections as far away as Iraq and Syria, while excavations revealed a sophisticated system of "price hedging" through the storage of large quantities of grain in amphorae with capacities up to 3000 liters.

In the middle of the lower city is the **Great Temple**, dedicated to the storm god and the sun goddess. Originally a statue of the god stood in the middle of the roofed sanctuary, which held as many

as 3000 people. Outside the temple is a small bath in which worshippers washed themselves before praying.

The real center of Hittite religion is in nearby **Yazilikaya**, a massive rock shrine that is lined with over 40 reliefs of gods, goddesses and favored rulers. Noteworthy is the representation of the storm god, Teshub, to the far left of the large gallery. In the smaller gallery is a portrait of the 12th-century B.C. monarch Tudhaliya IV, who was probably the builder of the shrine.

Alaca Hüyük is about 25 kilometers away and was the source of some of the finest articles of Hittite jewelry and bronze sculpture. It is also host to a standing gate guarded by two sphinxes and carved with the characteristic relief of an eagle. The site is most famous for the Bronze Age tombs here. These were constructed by the Hatti, a race who inhabited this area before the Hittites, but about which very little is known.

From Alaca Hüyük it is about 50 kilometers to **Çorum**, famous for the al-leged untrustworthiness of its residents ("Not even a man from Çorum would have done that" is a familiar Turkish rebuke) and for its roasted chick peas.

Although Çorum is a town which has been inhabited since the Bronze Age, little of its history remains – partly a result of persistent earthquakes. Çorum's main mosque, **Ulu Cami,** was built in 1307. Several earthquakes later, in 1905, the unusual five-domed roof was added. The pulpit, which dates back to the early Ottomans, is among the finest examples of wood carving in Turkey. In the center of the town is the **Ottoman Castle,** within whose walls are dozens of tiny, typical Anatolian houses painted lilac, sky blue and rust red, with their second floors bulging precariously across the tiny cobbled thoroughfares.

Amasya is a town of rare romance set in a steep and narrow gorge of the Yesilirmak river. Located about 90 kilometers northeast of Çorum, the town was once a favorite place for the political and diplomatic education of the sons of the sultans.

Traditionally, a prince who was capable of governing here was assumed to be capable of governing the empire.

On account of its numerous mosques and theological schools, Amasya is sometimes casually referred to as "the Oxford of the Ottoman Empire". One of the most impressive mosques is the 15th-century **Sultan Beyazit II Camii** on the banks of the river. It is distinguished by the unique "birds' nests" under its dome and engraved wooden doors of the Ottoman period. The adjacent *medrese* is justly proud of its series of glazed wall reliefs. Outside the entrance to the main mosque is a sign which reads: "After you sacrifice the sheep, leave your wife and pray. Whosoever does that will have a wish from God". This is an attractive promise to the townsfolk who rely on apple and okra farming to sustain them. There is high unemployment and no major industry in the area.

Above: The Camii of Sultan Beyazit II dominates the cityscape of Amasya.

A reminder of a greater past is the **fortress** which overlooks the town. It was first built in the Hellenistic period by the most famous and wily King of Pontus, Mithradites, when Amasya was the capital of the Pontic Empire. The famous Greek historian and geographer Strabo, who first described the castle and the town, was also born in Amasya. The castle was reconstructed by the Ottomans. A number of Roman and Pontic tombs are caved into the rock face.

Below the castle is the **Ethnographic Museum**, located inside the carefully restored **Hazeranlar Konak,** typical of 9th-century Ottoman domestic architecture. On the other side of the river is Amasya's main **museum.** The pride of the collection are six 13th-century mummies, all members of the family of the provincial governor during Ilhanid domination of the region. Less ghoulish is the worth-seeing display of finely engraved Ottoman wooden mosque doors.

Tokat, 115 kilometers to the southeast on a good road that trails through endless sunflower fields, was once one of the great trading centers of Anatolia. The **meydan** in the center of the town was for 2500 years a key stopover for caravans traveling from the west of Turkey to Antioch or Aleppo. It is still an important social center for the modern town and is located next to the 15th-century **Hatuniye Camii.**

The Seljuks endowed the town with architecture of great and enduring quality. The 13th-century Hidirlik Bridge, which straddles the Yesilirmak river at the western entrance to the town, and the several dervish lodges, like the Halef Gazi, are good examples.

The unusual concentration of Ottoman houses in the city is clear evidence that the town retained its commercial importance after the Seljuks. The recently restored **Latifoglu Konak**, built in the 9th-century by a wealthy Jewish businessman, is a fine tribute to the skill of Ottoman architects and wood carvers, while the privately-owned **Madimagin Cemal** in the Muftu quarter is distinguished by unusual ceiling frescos.

Tokat is also known for its handicrafts. Local fame for the manufacture of silk and wool carpets, enhanced after 1982 by the arrival of nearly 1000 Afghan refugees, has not diminished with time. Nor has expertise in the making of *yazma* – cloth hand printed with natural dyes – or copper engraving dwindled. The local covered bazaars, like the one on **Sulu Sokak**, are full of inexpensive examples of carpets and kelims.

In culinary terms, the cooks of Tokat are justly renowned for the *Tokat kebab*; a massive concoction embedded in an eggplant. Also worth trying are the award-winning wines of the town.

More famous but less interesting than Tokat is the smaller nearby town of **Zile.** Here, Julius Caesar stood on the ramparts of the castle in 47 A.D. and boasted *"Veni, vidi, vici!"* after a successful five-hour battle against Pharnaces II, King of Pontus. Beneath the castle, built around 2000 B.C. by the Queen of Ninova, is the restored 13th-century **Ulu Cami.**

50 kilometers to the north lies **Niksar,** a well-known hot spring resort as popular with the Romans as with the contemporary residents of Tokat. Niksar is also home to some of the oldest Turkish monuments in the area, including the 12th-century **Yagibasam Medrese**.

To the south of Tokat is the best preserved of the Roman settlements, **Sebastopolis.** The ancient town lies directly beneath the contemporary village of **Sulusaray.** The geographer Strabo maintained that Sebastopolis was built in the 3rd or 4th century B.C. for local merchants, and described it as a "three or four house place". Excavations which so far have revealed public baths and a gymnasium suggest that it was, at some point in its history, considerably larger.

Located 100 kilometers southeast of Tokat, **Sivas** can trace its history back to the Hittites, who called it "Sibasip". The modern town of farmers betrays little of the exotic past that has led Sivas through domination by every great civilization that marched across Anatolia. But it is a rich legacy which has bequeathed to the town, amongst other things, some of the finest Seljuk architecture in Turkey. Most of the buildings are located at the **Konya Meydani** in the center of the town. Although partly in ruins, the **Çifte Minare Medrese**, built by the resident Mongul vizier in the 13th century, boasts magnificent twin minarets and an exquisitely decorated door.

The **Bürüciye Medrese,** also in this district, exhibits typical Seljuk style with an open courtyard and stone portal. It now houses the **Museum of Antiquities.** Close by is the **Sifaiye hospital**, finished, like the Bürüciye seminary, in 1271, and distinguished by the partly decayed but notable tile work that adorns some of the interior rooms. It houses the tomb of its builder, Seljuk sultan Keykavus I. The

Cami and adjacent hospital were constructed in 1228 by the regional Seljuk governor, Ahmet Sah. Most impressive are the doors of the buildings, which are executed with an exquisite attention to detail. As fascinating, though less artistic, is the mass of graffiti carved into the walls on the second floor of the building by bored Ottoman students leaving their names to posterity.

Along the way between Sivas and Divrigi is **Kangal**, a town which has given its name to an internationally-recognized breed of sheep dogs known for their loyalty, speed and size.

The traveler now has the option of proceeding deeper into eastern Anatolia, heading north to the Black Sea, or returning by a circuitous route to the high plains of central Anatolia. If you choose the latter route, you will reach the wonderland of Cappadocia. We will proceed along the latter route.

Lying in the shadow of **Erciyes**, a now extinct 4000-meter-high volcano, **Kayseri** is 200 kilometers to the southwest of Sivas about halfway down the road to Konya. It is a bustling, thriving Anatolian town which was, in Roman times, known as Caesarea, the provincial capital of Cappadocia. Later, in the 4th century, it became famous as the birthplace of St Basil, who was one of the fathers of the early Christian Church.

The town abounds with imposing reminders of its past. The most dominant of these is the great, black stone **Byzantine fortress** which was built by Emperor Justinian during the 6th century in the middle of Kayseri.

Nearby are the **Huant Hatun Medresesi**, part of a Seljuk mosque complex which now doubles as the city's **Ethnographic Museum,** and the **Sahibiye Medresesi**, famous for its impressively carved portal. The 13th-century **Çifte Medrese** is notable as the first medieval school of anatomy. South of the Hudavend complex is the **Döner Kümbet,**

oldest building of historical significance, the 12th-century **Ulu Cami,** a long shallow hall which is dissected by about 50 stone pillars.

For modern Turks, Sivas is famous as site of the National Congress of September 4, 1919, at which Mustafa Kemal, founder of the Republic four years later, decided to liberate the country from the occupying powers, and thus sparked the War of Independence. The seven-day meeting was held in the **Sivas Sultani school** which has been preserved, along with the room in which Atatürk slept and studied, in its original state. From the dinner service to the telephone he used, everything has been maintained as it was.

About 65 kilometers to the southeast of Sivas is **Divrigi,** crowned by a ruined Byzantine castle and home to probably the most extravagant Seljuk mosque complex in Turkey. The well-preserved **Ulu**

Above: Collage of old and new in the town of Kayseri. Right: The bizarre rock towers of Cappadocia.

which was completed in 1276 and literally means the "turning tomb". Even if stationary in practice, it possesses a gorgeously decorated interior.

The **Archaeological Museum** in the Gültepe district of the city displays some of the Hittite artifacts excavated from **Kültepe.** Located about 20 kilometers north of Kayseri, this is one of the most important and oldest Hittite settlements in Anatolia. During its 100-year-long excavation, many cuneiform tablets and seals were found, which revealed much of the scale and character of the empire that dominated this part of the world

Not far from Kayseri, about half an hour back down the road to Sivas, is the restored 13th-century **Sultan Han,** a classic example of the many Seljuk caravanserais in this area. Located nearby is another impressive caravan hostel, the **Karatay Han.**

For climbers and skiers, **Mount Erciyes** is well worth visiting, especially in winter. There are several mountain hotels for those looking for a longer stay.

CAPPADOCIA

Most people come to Kayseri as the departure point for a tour of Cappadocia. Once Cappadocia cut the broadest swathe through Anatolia – bordered by the Black Sea to the north and the Taurus mountains to the south, by the Euphrates in the east and the salt lakes in the west.

Today, the region we know as Cappadocia is less expansive – it is only a strip of land between the lakes and Kayseri. This is an area upon which Mount Erciyes and the lesser volcano, Hasan Dagi, showered vast quantities of mud, ash, and lava during some of the greatest eruptions in history.

Upon contact with the air, this debris was transformed into soft tuff stone, creating an otherworldly landscape made even more fantastic by thousands of years of erosion. Here one finds rough white stone columns that turn ochre when the sun goes down, and fretted valleys marked by the evidence of centuries of human habitation.

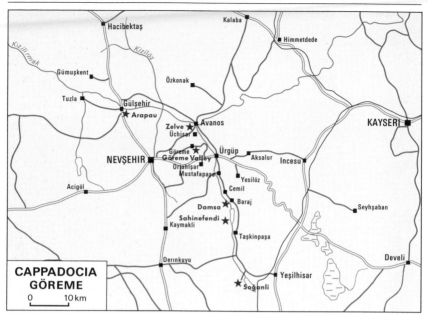

These inhabitants have been of varying lineage. The Bible insists that the Mushki and Tabal tribes living in Cappadocia were the "coarsest people on earth". Other ancient writers noted that the women were of unrivaled beauty. It was an area that attracted diverse migrants. The Tabal Kingdom, which occupied nearly all of the area of modern Cappadocia, fell in the 8th century B.C. to the Assyrians, and later to the Persians. They were drawn to a land of rich resources: gold and silver, as well as sheep, goats and fine horses.

Its most famous residents came not in search of wealth, but of solitude and refuge. Although the horses of Cappadocia are not as numerous or famous as they once were, it is nonetheless fitting that it was on horseback that, in 1907, French cleric Guillaume de Jerphanion rediscovered the monasteries which the Byzantine Christians had left behind.

Right: In Cappadocia a horse-driven cart is not unusual.

The monastic invasion of Cappadocia was set in motion by St. Basil, the 4th-century Bishop of Caesarea, who chose withdrawal into a natural environment. For the next thousand years the region became one of the centers of the Greek church and a destination for pilgrims. The monks first settled in the **Göreme Valley** – an area bordered by the market city of **Nevsehir** and the town of **Ürgüp.** Nevsehir is a modern, uninviting place topped by the ruins of a Seljuk fortress and site of a statue of Ibrahim Pasa, a local man who, in the first half of the eighteenth century, became grand vizier to Sultan Ahmet III.

Much more interesting to visit is **Ürgüp**, where some of the local farmers still live in their traditional rock-cut dwellings above the town. Most of them now inhabit an attractive chaos of beige stone houses that jostle for space along the cobbled roads leading towards the central market square.

In stark, provocative contrast to the ostentatious wealth of the jewelry and

carpet shops that line the arcades of the square is the poverty of the townsfolk themselves – subsistence farmers for whom the donkey, rather than the tractor, remains the most common means of transportation. Many of the locals are vine growers, tenders of the unique Emir grape that has given the wines of the town a deserved international reputation. Every year there is a festival here attended by vintners from many nations.

There are 350 churches in the vicinity of **Göreme**, six kilometers from Ürgüp. Most date from between the 9th and 13th centuries, the heyday of monasticism in Cappadocia: It was a period of tranquillity after continuous Arab invasions and sectarian infighting. Some of the best preserved churches are in the **open air museum** just outside the contemporary town of Göreme. Many feature simple barrel-vaulted naves with an apse and a horseshoe arch.

Most contain frescos; many have sadly been marred by (often piously-motivated Muslim) vandals who have scratched away the faces in the paintings. Even so, these frescos constitute one of the finest collections of Byzantine art in existence.Their style embraces the whole span of medieval Christian art beginning towards the end of the 6th century and reaching its peak during the 11th and 12th. Artists were drawn from the community of monks or imported from Byzantium by wealthy monastic patrons.

It was an exuberant devotion. The beauty and the brilliance of the frescos that adorn the churches betray the monks' commitment to bringing the beauty of holiness into their stone retreats: From the typical portrayal of Christ being crucified against a deep aquamarine sky in the **Tokali Church,** to the detail of the shepherd playing on pan pipes in the **Church of the Virgin**. All these extensive, figurative illustrations amply demonstrate the monks' immense knowledge of the saints of their religion.

In the **Yilanli Church**, probably a funerary chapel, is a rare and highly provocative 11th-century depiction of St.

Onophrius, a woman who, having repented her sins, became a man with a long white beard and breasts. Then there are the portraits of St. George, said to be of Cappadocian origin, fighting with a great white snake rather than the usual green dragon. The soldier is a dominant image in many of the paintings. This is perhaps most striking in the 9th-century Church of St. John above the nearby village of **Çavusin**, where many villagers still live in caves hewn out of rock. They are a reminder that the Byzantine monks, although under the protection of a local, wealthy, warrior aristocracy, were constantly under threat from Arab invaders.

While no one can deny the frightening desolation of the environment in which the monks chose to live, theirs were busy, thriving communities. Perhaps **Zelve,** four kilometers from Çavusin, provides the best insight into the way in which they managed their domestic affairs. The

Above: The customers have already been baited. Right: The crater lake west of Konya.

complex is riddled with interconnecting tunnels which link together churches and monasteries.

From Zelve it is a short journey to **Avanos,** renowned for the skill of its potters. The town lies on the shores of Kizilirmak, the longest river in Asia Minor.

The monks also settled in the **Soganli** and **Ihlara** valleys, to the south of Göreme. On the right side of the Soganli valley is the intriguing **Monster Church**, in which naked women suckling snakes are depicted.

Although many of the monastic settlers left Cappadocia after the Ottoman invasion of the 15th century, the region continued to have a significant Greek population until the foundation of the Turkish Republic in 1923. At that time they were all forced to return to Greece.

Prior to that exchange, the long-standing co-habitation of Greeks and Turks in Cappadocia had for the most part been peaceful. In the Ihlara valley, the 13th-century **Church of St. George** boasts a portrait of the saint flanked by a male and female dressed in Seljuk Turkish costume. The names of the ruling Seljuk sultan and the Byzantine emperor are engraved into the wall next to each other.

Hacibektas, 60 kilometers to the north of Nevsehir, is another tribute to the peaceful coexistence of Muslim and Christian. It was the home of the Bektasi dervish order, founded in the 13th century by the mystic Haci Bektas Veli. His mausoleum and the seminary of his order have been beautifully preserved.

The small hamlet of **Mustafapasa** is an example of peaceful ethnic relations. Before Atatürk, the village known as **Sinasos** was dominated by the presence of Greek farmers and traders. In the center is *Little Istanbul*. Now a hotel, it was formerly the home of a rich Greek jeweler who spent much money and effort lining the interior with vibrant fresco decoration. The Greek villagers also made efforts to decorate their own houses

with smaller paintings, perpetuating the old traditions of the first monastic arrivals. Every year, eldery Greeks return to Sinasos from Greece to visit their former homes, now inhabited by Turks. The 9th-century monastery of **Aya Vasilos** is on the edge of the small, lazy village.

But conflict was also widespread in Cappadocia. The underground cities of **Derinkuyu** and **Kaymakli** were both places of refuge for the local community. The rock chambers were fitted with great millstones that could be rolled across entrance ways to block the path of aggressors like the iconoclasts, marauding Arabs or Mongols. Kaymakli was last used in the early 9th century during the invasion of the Egyptian army. It is an eight-level city complete with chapels, funereal chambers and carefully constructed air shafts.

KONYA

In the guise of a modern city, set alone in the midst of fertile Anatolian steppe-lands about 220 kilometers southwest of Nevsehir, is **Konya**. This is one of the oldest and most conservative places in the whole of Turkey.

Konya was first known and inhabited as "Kuwanna" by the Hittites 4000 years ago, and has been an important provincial trading center since ever then. The Romans knew it as Iconium – a city in which the Apostle Paul once preached. In the 13th century it achieved political maturity as the capital of one of the self-governing states within the Seljuk empire, the Sultanate of Rum.

The city's religious reputation, which has persisted to the present day (Konya is the stronghold of current religious political parties and administered by a fundamentalist mayor), was inspired during the sultanate. At that time it became home to one of the most famous of the Islamic "Sufi" mystics, Mevlana Celaleddin Rumi (1207–1273), the founder of the Order of Whirling Dervishes, whose influence quickly spread throughout the entire Muslim world.

Dervish worship consisted of a dance, the *sema,* which symbolized the unity of man and God. Disciples would whirl, accompanied by a music of the drum and *ney* (a reed flute) or sometimes a bigger orchestra with a choir. Atatürk banned the order in 1923 as part of his secular reforms, although every December a Dervish festival commemorating Rumi's death takes place. Officially, it is a "cultural" and not a religious exercise.

Rumi's presence still dominates the modern city. Built originally as a mausoleum by the Seljuks, the **Mevlana Museum** in the center of the town is also the site of his tomb. Secular or not, it remains a shrine in character. On the tomb itself, shrouded in thick green velvet, is an extract of Rumi's poetry:

Come, Come! Whoever Whatever you may be, Come! Heathen, Fire Worshipper, Sinful of Idolatry,

Above: The greenish "türbe" crowning the tomb of Mevlana. Right: The turquoise waters of Lake Beysehir.

Come! Come even if you have broken your vows a hundred times – Ours is not the Door Of Misery and Despair, Come!

At the entrance to the tomb is exhibited the oldest manuscript of Rumi's most famous work, the epic *Mesnevi*, and other collections of his lyric poetry.

The *sema* itself was performed in the **Semahane**, an Ottoman structure to the north of the **Green Dome.** It now houses a fine collection of dervish paraphernalia ranging from music instruments to calligraphy. Across the street from the museum are the sprawling slum tenements and the market center of the city, which is worth strolling around.

From the museum it is not far to the impressive 13th-century **Alaettin Camii**, and the **Büyük Karatay Medresesi**. The latter was finished in the middle of the thirteenth century and today houses a remarkable collection of ceramics and wall tiles from the Seljuk and Ottoman periods. Just as magnificent is the blue-and-white marbled portal of the school.

Close by is the Seljuk **Ince Minare Dar'ul Hadis** which features another extravagant door and houses the **Museum of Seljuk Stone and Wood Carving**. The most interesting displays are the figurative stone decorations and bas-reliefs taken from the **Konya Castle**, which include depictions of animals such as rhinoceros and elephants. Technically, at least, these break strict Islamic bans on the drawing of creatures possessed of souls as idolatry. On Ressam Sami Sokak is the **Archaeological Museum**, which displays a Roman sarcophagus with an immaculate stucco frieze of the twelve labors of Hercules.

Fifty kilometers to the south along the Silifke/Mersin road is **Çatal Hüyük** which is said to be the site of the earliest human urban habitation on earth, dated back to around 7500 B.C. Not much remains for those who are not professional archaeologists. The road south continues

through the flat plain, punctuated only by the town of **Karaman** (named after the Karamanid Turkish clan who were the last rivals of the Ottomans) and then plunges over the 1600 meter **Sertavul Pass** towards the town of **Mut**.

Suddenly, there are trees again. Mut is a debarkation point for rafts along the Göksu River, which empties into the Mediterranean at **Silifke**. Those traveling by car might like to stop off at **Alahan**, a Byzantine monastery with a dramatic view over the southern slopes of the Taurus Mountains.

Several westward options are also available from Konya. **Beysehir** and the lake of the same name lie about an hour by car over lower mountain passes. Nearly hidden by the muddy streets and general gloom of the contemporary town is the 13th-century **Esrefpasa Cami**, with elegant, carved wooden columns within and a splendid tile *mirhab*, which alone is worth a detour.

South of the lake, a new highway leads to the Mediterranean coast through the forests of the Taurus Mountains. A curiosity along the way is the town of **Huglu**, where the entire population devotes its energy to the manufacture of quality shotguns.

Turkish Lakes

Another trunk road cuts north of Beysehir Lake through lovely farm and apple orchard country towards Isparta and Afyon, and into Turkey's lake region.

Egridir is an old Seljuk city with the ruins of a grand mosque and bazaar located near the shore. A causeway in the middle of town heads to a small island where there are a number of *pansiyons* and small hotels.

More a swamp than a lake is **Ebir Gölü,** between the towns of Sultandagi, Çay and Bolvidin. Bird watchers in summer and hunters in winter make use of flat-bottomed boats that are similar to British punts to wend their way through the two-meter reeds of the bird and duck filled marsh.

ANKARA

(Telephone area code for Ankara: 4-)

Accommodation

LUXURY: **Büyük Ankara**, Atatürk Bul. 183, Tel: 125 6655. **Büyük Sürmeli**, Cihan Sok. 6 Sihhiye, Tel: 231 7660. **Dedeman**, Büklüm Sok.1, Tel: 117 6200. **Hilton**, Tahran Cad. 12, Tel: 168 2888. **Içkale**, Gazi Mustafa Kemal Bul. 89, Tel: 231 7710. **Pullman Etap Altinel**, Gazi Mustafa Kemal Bul, Tel: 231 7760. **Pullman Etap Mola**, Atatürk Bul. 80, Tel: 117 8585. *MODERATE:* **Bulvar Palas**, Atatürk Bul. 141, Tel: 117 5020. **Büyük Ersan**, Selanik Cad. 74, Tel: 117 6045. **Karyagdi**, Sanayi Cad., Tel: 310 2440. **Metropol**, Olgunlar Sok. 5, Tel: 117 3060. **Turist**, Çankiri Cad. 37, Tel: 310 3980. **Yeni**, Sanayi Cad. 5, Tel: 310 4720. *BUDGET:* **Akman**, Opera Meyd., Tel: 324 4140. **Basyazicioglu**, Çankiri Cad. 27, Tel: 310 3935. **Çevikoglu**, Çankiri Cad., Tel: 310 4535. **Elit**, Olgunlar Sok. 10, Tel: 117 4695. **Güleryüz**, Sanayi Cad. 37, Tel: 310 4910.

Restaurants

Chez Le Belge, Konya Asfalti Üzeri, Tel: 184 1478. **China Town**, Köroglu Cad. 19, Tel: 146 0355. **Italyan Restaurant**, Hosdere Cad. 193, Tel: 138 0935. **Kanyon**, Hosdere Cad. 193, Tel: 138 0908. **Marco Polo**, Hilton Hotel, Tahran Cad. 12, Tel: 168 2888. **Washington**, Bayindir S. 22, Tel: 131 2218. **Yakamoz**, Köröglu Cad. 38, Tel: 136 0903.

For a great city panorama, try the restaurant in the **Atakule Tower**, Cinnah Cad.

Nightlife

Ankara enjoys a lively restaurant and bar scene catering to the legions of diplomats, bureaucrats and hangers-on of that particular scene. Many of the better clubs are difficult to find – hidden away on the second floors of residential buildings or down quiet streets.

BARS: **Black and White**, Kavaklidere Sok. 372, Tel: 128 0274. **Checkpoint**, Tunali Hilmi, Segmenler Çarsisi 96/68, Tel: 126 6779. **Galleri Nev**, Horsan Sok. 14, Gaziopasa, Tel: 127 3832. **Karpic** (live Jazz), Guvenlik Cad. 97, Tel: 126 0525. **Maya**, Abdullah Cevdet Sok. 30, Tel: 140 5123. **Park**, Karyagdi Sok. 20, Çankaya, Tel: 188 1616. For "traditional" entertainment, try the **Sehrazat**, Selim Sok 20c, Tel: 230 1643.

Museums / Sightseeing

Atatürk Mausoleum, Anit Cad., Tandogan, closed Mon and Tue. **Ethnographic Museum**, Talatpasa Bul. Opera, closed Mon. **Museum of old Anatolian Cultures**, Kadife Sok., Hisar, Tel: 324 3160, closed Mon. **Roman Baths**, Hisarlar, Tel: 324 3160.

Tourist Information / Other

Tourist Information, G. Mustafa Kemal Bul. 33, Tel: 292930. **British Council**, Adakale Sok. 27, Kizilay, Tel: 131 7788. **Turkish-American Association**, Cinnah Cad. 20, Kavaklidere, Tel: 126 2644. **Port Authority**: Tel: 133 1273. **American Hospital**, Balgat, Tel: 139 1680.

THE NORTH

Accommodation

BOLU: *LUXURY:* **Abant Palace**, Abant Göl Kenari Bolu, Tel: 4642-5012. *MODERATE:* **Emniyet Motel**, Ayrilik Çesmesi Mev., Tel: 461-12075. **Yurdaer**, Belediye Mey., Tel: 461-12903. *BUDGET:* **Çizmeci**, Kiliçarslan Köyü, Tel: 461-11066. **Dogander**, Ismetpasa Cad. 26, Tel: 461-16960. **Menekse**, Izzet Baysal Cad. 1, Tel: 461-11700.

KIZILCAHAMAM: *MODERATE:* **Cam Hotel**, Milli Mark Içi, Tel: 4531-1065.

SAFRANBOLU: *MODERATE:* **Havuzlu Konak**, Haci Halil Mah., Tel: 464-12883.

The **Yedi Göl National Forest** is situated northeast of Bolu. Rustic accommodation is sometimes available from the forestry officials.

THE NORTHEAST

Accommodation

ÇORUM: *MODERATE:* **Turban Çorum**, Çepni Mah., Tel: 469-18515. *BUDGET:* **Kolagasi**, Inönü Cad. 97, Tel: 569-15451.

SIVAS: *BUDGET:* **Kösk**, Atatürk Cad. 15, Tel: 477-11150. **Madimak**, Eskibelediye Sok 4., Tel: 477-18027. **Sicak Çermik**, Ankara Karayolu Üzeri, Tel: 477-11042. **Sultan**, Belediye Sok. 18, Tel: 477-12986.

SUNGURLU: *MODERATE:* **Hitit Motel**, Hacettepe M., Tel: 4557-1042. **Ocakli Motel**, Ankara Cad., Tel: 4557-1746. *BUDGET:* **Gündogan**, Çankiri Cad., Tel: 4557- 3636.

TOKAT: *LUXURY:* **Büyük Tokat**, Demirköprü Mev., Tel: 475-15426.

Flesh Eating Fish

One of the strangest phenomena in the northeastern region is the "flesh eating fish" of the *Balikli Kaplica*, outside of Sivas. Here one dips into the hot mineral baths where tiny minnows nibble away at the outer layer of skin. Locals swear by this treatment. Be sure to keep your bathing trunks on, though!

CAPPADOCIA

Accommodation

AKSARAY: *MODERATE:* **Ihlara**, Kiliçarslan Mah., Tel: 481-11842. *BUDGET:* **Özeller**, Karasu Mev., Tel: 481-11390. **Vadi Oteli**,

Ankara Cad. 17, Tel: 481-114326. **Agaçli Motel,** Ankara-Adana Highway E 5, Tel: 481-14910, **HACIBEKTAS:** *BUDGET:* **Yeni Haus Hotel,** Karsi Hamam Mev., Tel: 4867-1171.
KAYSERI: *BUDGET:* **Hattat,** Osman Kavuncu Cad., Tel: 35-119331. **Konfor,** Atatürk Bul. 5, Tel: 35-200184. Turan, Millet Cad., Tel: 35-112506.
NEVSEHIR: *LUXURY:* **Nevsehir Dedeman,** Ürgüp Yolu, Tel: 485-19900. *MODERATE:* **Altinöz,** Kayseri Cad., Tel: 485-15305. **Sehir Palas,** Nevsehir Camiikebir Cad. 41, Tel: 485-15369. **Sekeryapan,** Gülsehir Cad. 8, Tel: 485-14253. **Viva,** Yeni Kayseri Cad. 45, Tel: 485-11760. *BUDGET:* **Epok,** Hükümet Cad. 39, 485-11168. **Sems,** Atatürk Bul. 29, Tel: 485-13597.
ORTAHISAR: *LUXURY:* **Lapis Inn,** Tel: 4869-1470. *MODERATE:* **Yavuz,** Tel: 4869-1995. **Yükseller,** Kayseri Yolu, Tel: 4869-1450. *BUDGET:* **Burcu,** Koyiçi Mev., Tel: 4869- 1200.
ÜÇHISAR: *LUXURY:* **Club Med Kaya,** Tel: 4856- 1007.
MODERATE: **Kapadokya Robinson Lodge,** Tel: 485-19945. **Pasa Motel,** Tel: 4856-1301.
ÜRGÜP: *LUXURY:* **Dinler,** Kayseri Yolu Üzeri, Tel: 4868-3030. **Perissia,** Kayseri Yolu Üzeri, Tel: 4868-2930. **Cappadocia Merit Holiday Village,** Kayseri Yolu, Tel: 4868-1256.
MODERATE: **Arkadas,** Avanos Cad. 12, Tel: 4868-2395. **Tassaray,** M. Pasa Cad. 10, Tel: 4868-2344. *BUDGET:* **Boytas Tepe,** Kayseri Cad., Tel: 4868-1154. **Sarnic,** Avanos Yolu Çicisi, Tel: 4868-2340.

Festivals / Sightseeing

An interesting time to visit the region is during the *Hacibektas Festival* on August 14-17, when Alevi Turks from all over the country descend on the town. *Haci Bektas Veli* – possibly an apocryphal character – is credited with bringing Islam to the local Christian population in the Seljuk period. In Mustafapasa near Ürgüp, one of the most colorful carpet shops in Turkey offers its wares in an Ottoman caravanserai: Kapadokya Kervansarany, Tel: 48689.

KONYA
Accommodation

MODERATE: **Balikçilar,** Mevlana Alani, Tel: 33- 112969. **Dergah,** Mevlana Cad. 19, Tel: 33-110116. **Özkaymak Park,** Otogar Karsisi, Tel: 33-133770. **Selçuk,** Alaaddin Cad. Tel: 33-111259. **Sema,** Yeniyol, Tel: 33-171510. *BUDGET:* **Basak Palas,** Hükümet Alani 3, Tel: 33-111338. **Bey,** Aziziye Cad., Tel: 33-120173. **Konya,** Mevlane Mey. 8, Tel: 33-116677. **Sahin,** Hükümet Alani 6, Tel: 33-113350.

Whirling Dervishes

A good time to visit Konya is between December 10-17 for the *sema*, or whirling dervish ceremony, which is performed in the local gymnasium – a rather curious venue for a religious occasion. Book well in advance if you intend to be in the city at this time, as the festival attracts thousands.

THE WEST
Accommodation

AFYON: *BUDGET:* **Oruçoglu,** Bankalar Cad. 3, Tel: 491-20120.
ESKISEHIR: *MODERATE:* **Büyük,** 27 Mayis Cad. 158, Tel: 22-112162. *BUDGET:* **Dural,** Yunusemre Cad. 97, Tel: 22-111347. **Emek,** Otogar Yani, Tel: 22-112940. **Has Termal,** Hamamyolu Cad. 7, Tel: 22-117819. **Sultan Termal,** Hamamyolu Cad. 1, Tel: 22-118371. **Sale,** Inönü Cad. 17, Tel: 22-114743.
EGIRDIR: (Isparta) *MODERATE:* **Egtur Hotel Egirdir,** Kuzey Sahil Yolu 1, Tel: 3281-1219. *BUDGET:* **Egtur Egirdir II,** Güney Sahil Yolu 1, Tel: 3281-1219.
KÜTAHYA: *MODERATE:* **Erbaylar,** Afyon Cad. 14, Tel: 231-36960. *BUDGET:* **Bakir Sözer,** Çinigar Cad., Tel: 231-23338. **Yüksel,** Cumhuriyet Cad., Tel: 231-15297. **Gülpalas,** Belediye Mey., Tel: 231-11751.

Poppies

In the five provinces of Konya, Burdur, Isparta, Afyon and Kütahya poppies have traditionally been grown for centuries. Illegal traffic in the raw product led to the association of heroin and Turkey in the 1960s, when Turkish morphine supplied the so-called French Connection and various refining centers of the deadly trade.

Under great pressure from the United States, Turkey forbade the cultivation of poppies in 1970, thus cutting off illegal gathering of raw opium, which in turn handicapped the legal trade in pharmaceutical products made from alkaloids. Cynically, a number of Western nations, notably Australia and New Zealand, decided to take up the slack and began their own poppy production. Turkey's response was to reallow cultivation under strictest police control.

To walk through the poppy fields, the time to be in the region is late June or early July, when the beautiful purple and yellow buds start to dry. It goes without saying that one should not attempt to pick them or buy any from farmers.

For the traveler, the important lesson is this: Do not accept parcels from strangers to be taken to "good friends in Europe" nor involve yourself in any way in the illegal trade.

EASTERN ANATOLIA

TRABZON / SUMELA
TURKISH GEORGIA
ERZURUM / ANI
MOUNT ARARAT
LAKE VAN / AKDAMAR
NEMRUT DAGI

The Black Sea Coast

The coastal road to the east of Samsun is surprisingly better than the one in the west. Heavy tank truck trains from the (former) Soviet Union on their way to Turkey thunder along well into the night, carrying oil supplies to the northeastern region. The Pontic Mountain Range has spectacular steep drops to the sea in places, so that the people living in this area have settled on a very narrow coastal strip running parallel to the road.

Hazelnut bushes grow on the beautiful Pontic slopes, a little to the west of Sürmene. To the east of this, Turkish tea is planted right down to sea level. While Turkey is the world's largest hazel nut exporter, its tea is used solely for domestic consumption.

Even in the 1970s, the journey along the Black Sea's east coast was quite spectacular. After all, it was completely different here from elsewhere in Turkey. The rich green countryside stood in strong contrast to the otherwise barren regions of Asia Minor. The half-timbered houses have now given way to steel and concrete buildings. Workers returning from a profitable stay in such countries as Germany,

Preceding pages: Flowering poppies add a colorful touch to the landscape near Olur.

wishing to live more comfortably, build themselves modern houses once being back at home.

In order to experience the lush nature of the Pontic region, it is necessary to leave the coastal road and make trips into the interior. There are only three paved passes over the Pontic mountains. All the other roads are frequently in bad condition, and barely passable after heavy rainfall. The most important and historically best-known route is the **Zigana Pass**. As far back as 400 B.C., Xenophon chose to cross this pass with his 10,000 strong army. The route from Trabzon to **Erzurum** constitutes only a small part of the old caravan route which went as far as central Asia. It used to be part of the silk route. At that time the goods were shipped from Trabzon to Europe. Even today, passenger ships operating from the Black Sea coast to Istanbul are an important form of transportation since Trabzon has no rail connection.

If you want to get to know the Black Sea coast, the best place to begin is **Samsun**. It was here on May 19, 1919 that Mustafa Kemal Atatürk proclaimed the revolution against foreign occupation. Beyond **Unye**, the coastal landscape becomes picturesque, with many little fishing ports. This region is one of the most beautiful parts of the Turkish Black Sea coast. Via **Ordu**, you reach **Giresun**, once called Cerasus. This town gave its name to the first sour cherries taken to Rome from Pontus by Lucullus after one of his many battles. The excellent fish restaurants here tempt the visitor to stop and sample some of the delicious fare. The little town of **Tirebolu** on the way to Trabzon is an ideal place to take a stroll through traditional streets.

TRABZON

The town was founded in the early 7th century B.C. on a trápeza or tableland, near the now much smaller town of **Sinop**, a Greek colony to the west. Hence, its original name Trapezunt. Xenophon's legendary "ten thousand" sighted the sea again from the surrounding mountains, for the first time in weeks. It is said that they became ill after eating honey: It was the rhododendron honey still sold in this region today – delicious, yet it can be a little toxic for those who are not used to it.

The town's golden era began in 1204, after the crusaders conquered Byzantium. Two sons of the Byzantine Emperor Andronicus I fled to this region, founding a small kingdom protected by the mountains. This area was so well protected that not even the Seljuks had been able to conquer it. When it fell into the hands of the Ottomans in 1461, it had held out 8 years longer than the kingdom on the Bosporus.

Nothing much of the glory of the great Comneni dynasty remains today. The present-day old town of Trapezunt, now known as Trabzon, is a rather dull port city. Occasionally, women dressed in red-and-white striped clothes walk along the street. They belong to the *Laz* tribe, a Caucasian minority group that converted to Islam. You should allow yourself at least two days here: One for sightseeing in Trabzon, and the other to visit the Sumela monastery.

Two deep gorges border the actual town area. The old fortress, once seat of the emperor's government, still stands high up on the cliffs. The middle part of the town was situated inside the town wall and the lower part extended as far as the harbor. The 4000 inhabitants living in Trapezunt at the time of the empire have increased in number to 130,000, and Trabzon has the only university on the Black Sea coast.

Even before you come to Trabzon from the west, you can see its most important cultural landmark, the **Hagia Sophia** ("holy wisdom"), high up on the plateau to the right of the road. The former 13th century monastery was built by Manuel I next to a small Byzantine chapel, the foundations of which can still be seen.

It is a domed church with a narthex, three porticos, and three aisles. The church was used by both Moslems and Christians until 1880, after which time it was painted over and converted into a mosque. Restoration work was carried out between 1957 and 1962 to convert it into a museum. The exterior displays Seljuk motifs, while the porticos show traces of Georgian/Armenian influence. The paintings in the interior of the church are very expressive, and often compared with those in Istanbul's Chora church. In the narthex you can recognise the Annunciation and Miracle of Christ; in the west portico, the Day of Judgement; in the tambour, the apostles and the prophets; in the pendentives the Evangelists, and finally, in the dome, the choir of angels. There is practically nothing left to see of Christ as Pantocrator in the center of the dome.

You will get a good idea of what the old town must have looked like if you go on foot to the **Gülbahar Hatun Camii**. It is thought to have been the first Ottoman mosque in Trabzon, and was built by Selim I for his mother Gülbahar, meaning "spring rose". If you go eastwards from here, through the town gates, you come to

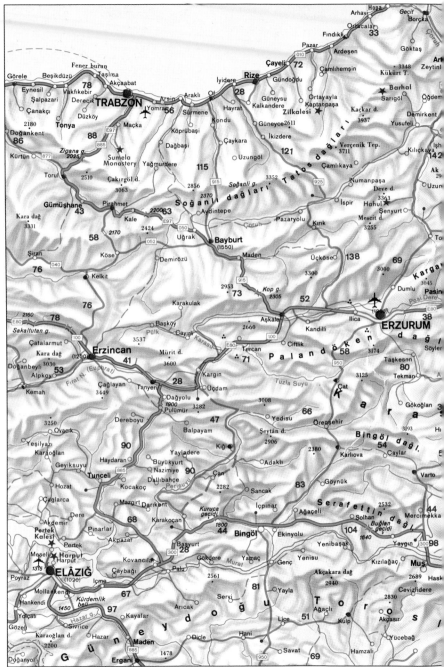

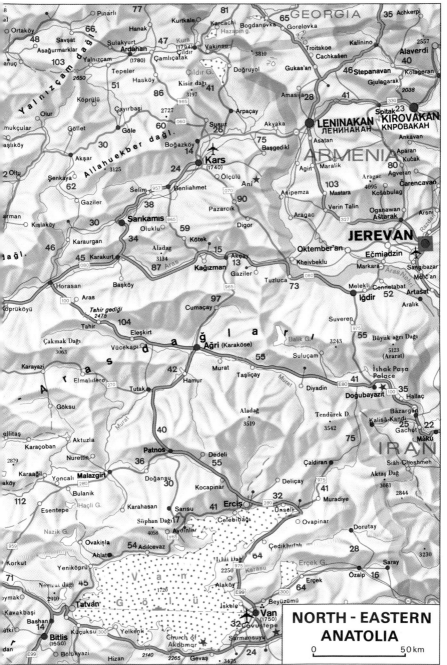

NORTH - EASTERN ANATOLIA

0   50 km

the lower fortress area. The **Zaganos Bridge** spans the west gorge here. Soon you will see the **Fatih Camii**, originally the Byzantine Panaghia Chrysocephalos (Church of the Golden Virgin), thus named on account of its golden dome. Once inside the simple white-washed interior, it becomes obvious that transforming a church into a mosque was not always an easy task. A church altar is always situated in the east, while the *mihrab* always faces Mecca, in this case, almost due south. You can complete a tour of the town by drinking a cup of Turkey's national beverage under the shady trees of a tea garden on **Atatürk Alani**.

SUMELA

It is advisable to visit the **Sumela Monastery** in the morning, since the thick rain clouds that regularly cover the

Above: The monastery of Sumela is both isolated and a bit closer to heaven than most other monasteries.

sky in the afternoon could, literally speaking, put a "damper" on such an unforgettable experience.

You follow the old caravan route to Erzurum in the direction of the Zigana Pass. Passing hazelnut bushes, precarious looking suspension bridges and monumental basalt pillars, turn left in the town of Maçka into the lovely **Altindere Valley**. In late spring, the entire valley is a splendor of blossoms. The rhododendrons are especially beautiful. At the parking lot, first turn left toward the small rock plateau. It is only from here that the monastery can be seen in its entirety.

The strenuous climb up to the monastery takes approximately half an hour. Only half way up are you able to get a good view of the monastery grounds through the trees. When at the top, it is disappointing to find out that thoughtless visitors have broken off pieces of stone as big as your hand from the frescoes, or carved their names in the valuable paintings. The roof of the building, where it isn't formed by part of the cave, has collapsed, leaving the rooms exposed to all kinds of weather.

Unfortunately, numerous arson attempts have added more damage to the ancient monastery. It was only recently that officials recognized its true value, and now they they are doing their best to save whatever they can with funds allocated by UNESCO for this purpose.

Sumela used to be a grotto monastery. It was only as late as the 19th century that the impressive front windows were added. Monks cells, a library and an infirmary were installed here. The name Sumela is derived from the Greek *Hagia Maria tou Mela* (Holy Mary of Mount Mela). The exact foundation date is not known, but it is certain that Sumela existed in the 6th century.

Two hermits, Barnabas and Sophronios, were said to have brought the so-called Luke Icon to Pontus, because they had had a vision of Athens. That marked the beginning of the grotto monastery. Later, the grotto was extended by way of an apse chapel and painted.

The golden era came with the Comneni Empire. A number of emperors were crowned here. Alexios III's coronation is depicted in a fresco on the outer wall of the grotto church, and a number of other frescoes are still recognizable in its interior. The various painting techniques bear witness to the fact that the monastery has been restored many times.

On the roof of the grotto, we see Christ and the Virgin Mary and Child, and on the north wall, the Virgin Mary enthroned (the gold varnish is easily seen from the exit to the grotto). On the south wall, there is a painting depicting the three kings about to commence their return journey.

During the Ottoman Empire the monastery remained relatively secluded and was the center of the Pontic Greeks. When they (about 400 families) were forced to leave Trabzon after Turkey declared independence, the monks also left Sumela. They returned to their home country, where they founded a similar monastery.

The surrounding coutryside is ideal for long walks. It is especially impressive if you climb the mountain on the opposite side to enjoy the view of Sumela, often enveloped in mist.

A small riverside restaurant on the parking lot is open during the tourist season. You can order fresh trout (*alabalik*), meat balls (*köfta*), or lamb chops (*pirzola*) straight from the charcoal grill. Delicious!

A visit to the other two monasteries, **Vazelon** and **Peristera**, is really only worthwhile if your prime purpose is to have a walk. You reach Vazelon by returning to Maçka and turning left towards Erzurum. After 8 km you come to the village of **Kiremitlihan**, where you will have to look for a local guide. After a two-hour walk, you finally arrive at your destination. Don't forget to take along waterproof clothing, since it is essential in this part of the country. You reach Peristera (known as Ayana Monastiri here) if you drive from Maçka back to Trabzon, turn right at the village of Esiroglu (19 km from Trabzon) and continue for 13 km towards Kustul.

Back on the coastal road, the scenery changes. Past **Sürmene** the hazelnut bushes slowly begin to disappear, giving way to an increasing number of tea plantations straddled across the mountain slopes. The region of **Rize** is considered to be the wettest in Turkey, with an annual rainfall of approximately 3000 mm. Large tea factories belonging to the Turkish tea industry begin to appear along the roadside more frequently.

You should ask to be shown around one of the tea factories. If you are lucky, the boss himself might even be willing to give you a tour. At the end, you are certain to be offered a cup of tea.

There used to be coffee plantations in this region, before they were all de-

stroyed by blight. Tea was first introduced at the time of independence. The women and children harvest the almost waist-high tea plants three times a year. Only the uppermost, soft, pale-green leaves are picked and carried in wicker baskets on the women's backs to the collecting point. The climate is so mild (no frost) that even oranges grow here. They are wild, however, rather bitter and not suitable for eating. Now and then you can still see half-timbered houses – a rarity nowadays.

In the little town of **Ardesen** very tasty fish dishes are served in the restaurants just across from the bus station. They are located directly on the waterfront. A small road branches off to **Çamlihemsin** a few kilometers outside the town. From the **Zilli Kale** (fortress) you can go on wonderful hikes.

Above: A married couple in their best clothing, posing for a portrait. Right: Harvesting hazelnuts in a sociable fashion in Giresun.

The small port of **Hopa** is situated approximately 30 kilometers west of the former Turco-Soviet border. The relatively good Hotel Papila is an appropriate place to end your day.

TURKISH GEORGIA

The road winds its way up into one of the most rugged mountainous regions in Turkey (brown bears!). After crossing the watershed at **Borçka**, there is a remarkable change in the vegetation. It gradually becomes arid and quite spectacular. Long, and sometimes precarious, suspension bridges span the Çoruh, a huge, wild river. The countryside seems to be deserted – many narrow paths branch off here and there, appearing to lead to nowhere in particular. Soon you come to the road sign pointing to **Artvin**, the capital of the province. Most visitors to the region find it strange that there is nothing to be seen of the town for miles around. You really have little choice but to follow the road sign to *sehir merkezi* ("Town Center"), until you find yourself on a steep mountain road once again. Like an eagle's eyrie, the town is situated up on the clifftops. The curves are so narrow that larger vehicles often have to reverse, or even turn back. Still filled with suspense, the visitor waits to see where the town is situated until at last it appears.

Most people are surprised to find a comfortable hotel here. Visitors should book into the **Karahan** for at least two nights. It's a real "Turkish delight". The hotel owner not only knows a lot about the region, but is extremely helpful as well. There are maps available, but many places are only accessible on foot and with the help of a local guide. What is of interest here? There are numerous Georgian churches and monasteries dating back to the time between the 10th and 12th centuries. Some are in remarkably good condition, often because they are used as mosques today.

As far back as the middle of the 4th century, Christianity was the state religion, at first conforming with the Armenians in their monophysitic form of belief. Then came the conversion to the orthodox Byzantine model in 6th century. Because of the vast number of monasteries, one even talks about Georgian Athos. In the 8th century, at the start of the rule of the Bagratides, Aschot Bagrationi founded the empire of Tao-Klardshetien. Many independent principalities emerged in the inaccessible mountains during the course of the 9th century. They remained independent until Bagrat III united West and East Georgia for the first time. A golden era followed in the 11th and 12th centuries, before the Mongols (13th/14th century) and Russians (18th/19th century) divided the country again. The country has been divided into two halves since 1923 – Soviet Grusinian and the southern, Turkish part which today has no official name. Unlike the Armenians, the former Georgians in Turkey have accepted Islam.

A number of churches can easily be reached from Artvin. The best place to visit first is **Dolishane**. Together with the well- maintained church of **Porta** and the charming old church of **Yeni Rabat**, this is a full-day trip. To make this excursion you require a car. If you don't have your own transportation, you can always rent a *dolmus* (pick-up taxi). As there are almost no refreshment possibilities on the way, it is advisable to take a substantial packed lunch along with you.

Just beyond Artvin on the road to Erzurum, there is a turnoff leading to **Savsat**. About 10 km farther along the road an old stone bridge spans the river. A quaint tea house is situated at the far side of the bridge. As you approach to the bridge, a dusty steep road branches off to the left, twisting its way uphill to Dolishane (should the road divide again, keep to the right). An unusual church can first be seen after a 15-minute drive, situated in the village of **Hamamli**. Something strange happened to it: In the tambour, the cylindrical construction between the nave and the vault, a wooden floor was installed. In this way, a central building was formed. The mosque is, so to speak, the upper part of the church. Underneath, in the acutal nave, there is a barn today. With a flashlight, you can see some of the saints from the fresco. As unornamented as the church may seem, its few arches, a donor relief, and the statues of the archangels Michael and Gabriel in the tambour actually influenced 10th century exterior design.

After refreshments in the teahouse on the bridge, continue along the road to Savsat. A few kilometers farther along, a cumbersome footpath branches off to the left (ask!). It leads up the steep hill through beautiful countryside to the church of **Porta**. After a good hour's climb, you will enjoy a glass of refreshing spring water and a tasty snack. The view from here of the rugged, romantic landscape is quite breathtaking.

Back on the road again, head towards the bridge that takes you to the other side of the river, to **Ardanuç** and the 9th-century monastery **Yeni Rabat**. This ancient building is situated in a hollow in the forest, approximately 15 kilometers past the town.

The journey from Artvin to Erzurum is considered one of the most spectacular in Turkey. You have the choice of two equally interesting routes. First follow the road signs to Erzurum, passing the turnoff to **Yusufeli** on the right and continuing on until a fork in the road. Both roads lead to Erzurum.

If you drive left towards **Olur**, you get to the town of **Ishan**. Drive through it and turn left onto the gravel road at the sign indicating that you are leaving the town. After a short distance, you arrive at a beautiful 7th-century Georgian church. It is an unusual building. In the 9th century it was transformed from a structure with four conchae into a cross-in-square church with an extended west wing. The paintings in the vault have very vivid colors. The people here are friendly and peaceful, as they are almost everywhere in this region.

Back on the main road, a drive through beautiful scenery lies ahead. Tectonic forces have broken up the earth's crust. Bizarre rock-formations, discolored by oxidation, give the keen photographer much scope.

Leaving Olur behind, follow the road to Oltu, continuing on through splendid scenery. Ruins of medieval Georgian fortresses appear at intervals on both sides of the road. *Oltu-tas* is the name given to a relatively soft, black volcanic stone found here and in Erzurum. It is sold in shops as jewelry.

Sometimes the rocks and hills near **Narman** appear to be bright red, changing to all shades of green and blue. The road winds its way up to the 2400 meter **Kiereçli Geçidi** pass overlooking the valley of **Tortum Çay**. (The word "çay" is also used for the source of a river.) The direct road from Artvin leads off to the right. This road is about 100 km shorter than the road via Olur.

Back to the fork beyond Yusufeli. If you turn right onto the direct road to Erzurum, not only can you admire the beautiful **Tortum Reservoir**, but you also have the opportunity of visiting two more Georgian monasteries.

Just beyond the reservoir there is a tiny roadsign pointing to **Ösk Vank**. After an 8-km drive along the gravel road, you can park your vehicle on the village square in front of the huge 10th-century church. (In case of turnoffs, always keep left.) It's hard to believe that this was one of the most important cultural centers in Georgia in the 10th century. It pays to take a walk through the town. The wooden houses with their balconies are reminiscent of those found in Alpine villages.

Right: Who needs a studio when the street provides the best background.

Going back the same way, continue your journey to Erzurum by always keeping to the left bank of the Tortum Çay. At the small town of **Vihik Kapisi** you can cross the river by way of a modern bridge to visit the monastery of **Hahul** (or: Khakuli, Chachuli, Haho, Heho) along a narrow path. This once famous monastery is made of reddish-gold sandstone, and its Church of Our Lady is still in good condition. This building is also used as a mosque today. The outside wall is not decorated with basket arches as is normally the case, but with ornate sculptures. Eagles, lions, bulls, a large cockerel, and even a whale adorn its exterior

The road to Erzurum soon links up with the road from Oltu at the town of **Tortum** and crosses the Tortum Çay. Poplar trees line the road as it winds its way through the countryside. A final steep climb leads through the **Pass of the Georgians** to the East Anatolian hill and plateau. This almost treeless, almost 2000-meter-high plateau is covered in snow until well into the month of April.

Strange as it may seem, here of all places is East Anatolia's largest town, with 240,000 inhabitants. You can reach it after an hour's drive.

ERZURUM

The city can be seen in the distance, surrounded by the Palandöken mountains (over 3000 meters), the upper reaches of the Euphrates. Its simple houses are blackened by soot and not a very pleasant sight. The old caravan-stop has known much hardship. Erzurum's inhabitants are reserved but friendly, and you can be sure of experiencing the real Turkey here, more than anywhere else. After all, it was here that, around the turn of the century, 40,000 camels a year made their way to Persia along the old caravan route.

The winters in the coldest town in Turkey are quite notorious. The thermometer often drops down to 40 degrees minus. The story of a cat that, during a walk on the roof in November, was exposed to a bout of sudden cold weather

and froze stiff until in the spring, when it thawed and was able to walk again, is indicative of the kind of weather that prevails here during the winter months. There is also an account of wolves seeking shelter from the extreme cold at the Atatürk University campus. This seat of learning was founded in 1958, and for decades was the only university in the east.

As in Ankara, thick clouds of soot hang over the city in winter, making breathing extremely difficult. Despite these ecological problems, Erzurum is famous for its crystal clear water. Earthquakes hit the city at regular intervals, the last one in March 1992, so that buildings should be built for stability, rather than for aesthetic reasons. More than 40,000 people lost their lives in the earthquake disaster of 1939.

Those who have to fight so hard for survival tend to be more religious than

Above: The splendid panorama from the Byzantine citadel over Erzurum, a town with a rich history.

anybody else. Apart from Konya, Erzurum is the most conservative town in Turkey. There are more veiled women on the streets here – despite Kemal Atatürk's prohibition law – than anywhere else in the country. Recently, however, there are girls with very short skirts – generally students from other regions. They provide a strong contrast to the more traditionally-clothed women.

In the 4th century, the town was called Theodosiopolis and was situated directly on the border between Byzantium and Persia. These two empires had divided Armenia between them. In the 6th century, after being conquered by the Sassinids, the town was reconquered for Byzantium and given the name of Anastasiopolis. In the 7th and 8th centuries, Arabs and Byzantines ruled the town alternately. In the 10th century, it became part of the Armenian Bagratite Empire. From then on, it was called Karin until the Seljuk invasions in the 11th century. They conquered the town, rechristening it **Arz er-Rum** (Land of the Romans).

Rum (Rome) was not only a town to the Seljuks, but was synonymous with the Byzantine Empire. Erzurum was, at the time it was conquered, the most westerly part of their territory. Around 1400, Tamerlane invaded and wreaked havoc throughout the town. In 1515, it was finally integrated into Selim I's Ottoman Empire. Erzurum fell victim to Russian invasions on a number of occasions (1829, 1878, 1916).

One should allow at least two days for visiting the town. The best place to stay is the centrally situated, hospitable **Hotel Polat**. You can do all your sightseeing on foot from here. The only older buildings that remained intact are the massive Seljuk masterpieces. The hotel has a map of the town which makes the tour easier. The first impressive building is the **Makutiye Medresesi**, a Koran school built in 1308 by Seljuk craftsmen for the Mongolian emir. The exterior, with blue interwoven Iznik tiles on the minaret, is characteristic of the architectural style found in central Asia Minor.

The rather plain **Lala Mustafa Pasa Camii** situated next to the school was built by no other than Sinan, the famous Ottoman architect. A few hundred meters away is the **Ulu Cami** (Great Mosque). Built in 1179, it has been repaired several times after being damaged by earthquakes. From the outside, it doesn't look very elaborate; its simplicity, however, is attractive.

The most important building in the town, the **Çifte Minaret Medresesi**, the Koran school with the double minaret, is situated across from it. Orders were given by the Seljuk sultan Alaettin Keykubat II in 1253 to have it built. The magnificent entrance at once catches the eye with its double-headed eagle relief (the Seljuk coat of arms), trees of life, as well as numerous geometrical and floral designs. Both of these minarets are also studded with blue Iznik tiles. The enormous building is usually open to the public, so the visitor can get a good idea of what it looks like inside. Four Persian barrel vaults are grouped around a triangular shaped open-air courtyard – extraordinary considering the extreme temperatures. The students' living quarters are on the first floor. The furthermost hall continues into the **Hatuniye Türbesi**, added to the building in 1255 by a daughter of the sultan for herself. It is incorporated on the outside by an arcade of intricate basket arches.

Türbes are tombs where the Seljuks buried persons of high rank. The burial place is nearly always underneath the actual tomb, as the interior is usually a prayer room, very often with a *mihrab* marking the direction of Mecca. They can be seen often in the Eastern Anatolian highland region, between Erzurum and Lake Van. There are three *türbes* standing on open ground within three minutes walking distance to the south of the Koran school, at the **Üç Kümbetler**. (*kümbet* is Persian for *türbe*.) They date back to between the 12th and 14th century. Only the largest and most unusual of them – the Emir Sultan Türbesi – is well known by name. The unusual element here is that the burial place is not underneath the tomb, but in a simple adjoining building. It is also rare that the *türbe* is structured with gable-ended arches under the pointed arch.

A visit to the **Byzantine fortress** is all that remains to be toured in Erzurum. For this you have to cross the road at the Çifte Minaret Medresesi and continue uphill. But before doing so, it's worthwhile to have a look at the *Oltu-tas* jewelery in the nearby shops.

There is a good view of Erzurum and the surrounding countryside from the Byzantine fortress. The **bazaar** area lies to the north of the fortress. The bazaar is still very oriental, with some of its shops situated in a Seljuk caravanserai.

Perhaps you are feeling cold after your tour and have worked up something of an

appetite? In Meram 3, opposite the Polat Hotel, there is a very good place to eat.

After being in the city for so long, the serene beauty of the vast eastern Anatolian countryside is a pleasant change. Heading eastwards, leave Erzurum on the Europe Road 23, the old caravan route. Shortly after **Pasinler**, the Aras River (the Araxes of antiquity) comes into view on the right side of the street, spanned by the six-arched **Çobandede** ("shepherd grandfather") **bridge**.

It is a typical example of Seljuk architecture and was built in the 12th century. On the left hand side of the street runs the railway line that passes through Kars on its way to the (former) Soviet Union. Steam trains still travel along this route. You can find out their departure times at

Above: The painstakingly-ornamented Çifte Minaret Medresesi in Erzurum. Right: The remote little church of Tigran Honentz stands on the bank of the Arpa Çay, at this point the border between Armenia and Turkey.

the station in Erzurum. Between Pasinler and Horasan loose pumice stones cover the ground, reminding the traveler of the Göreme valley.

The road divides at **Horasan** and it is a good idea to leave the E 23 and take the road to Karakurt. Here you are faced with another difficult decision. The road on the left goes to Kars via Sarikamis and continues on to the former Armenian capital town of **Ani**. A visit to Ani is one of the spectacular highlights of a trip to Eastern Turkey. If you turn off to the right in Karakurt and drive towards Kagizman, you will experience the splendid array of colors in the Aras Valley. Depending upon how much time you have, you can drive back to Karakurt for your trip to Ani. The return journey from Ani via Ladikars and Kötek is a good compromise. You will reach the Aras Valley again at Kagizman.

The road from Karakurt to **Sarikamis** twists its way up the mountainside revealing an unexpected change of scenery. Pine forests with an almost Alpine character line the route as far as Sarikamis, only to disappear again. A few kilometers beyond Karakurt, on the left side of the road, obsidian slopes catch the eye. The black specks are noticeable even from quite a way off. Obsidian is volcanic rock resembling bottle-glass that breaks into sharp-edged pieces. If you throw a chunk onto the ground it will splinter into razor-like fragments. Even in ancient times, obsidian stones were used as cutting instruments.

A garrison is stationed in Sarikamis. The former casino has been turned into a remarkably good hotel. Here, as well as in the surrounding villages, the Russian influence up until 1920 becomes obvious – in addition to the older buildings from that era, one spots herds of geese, down quilts and tiled stoves.

Kars is the capital town of the province, with a garrison and a railway station. The colossal fortress looms over the

town. A 10th-century Armenian church stands at the foot of the fortress. The 12 apostles are depicted in the tambour, but the artistic designs are rather clumsy in comparison to Ani's artistry.

You have to apply for a permit to visit Ani. First you have to go to the tourist office, and then to the museum to purchase a ticket. It's another 45 km along a bad road before you reach Ani-Köyü. The ban on photography on the grounds has been lifted since the middle of 1990. It's only a few kilometers to the (former) Soviet border from here. Their lookout towers can be seen at the other side of the river **Arpa Çayi**. The tourist office issues visitors a list of restrictions. Hand signals towards the (former) Soviet Union are not allowed, neither using binoculars, nor picnicking.

ANI

The golden era of this town was in the 10th century during the Bagratide dynasty. It lies on a triangular plateau and was protected very well indeed: On two sides by the deep canyons of the rivers Arpa Çayi and Alaça Suyu, on its third side by a double wall secured with a bastion erected by the Bagratide Smbad II (977-989). During its golden era, the town earned itself the epithet "town of the 1000 churches, 10.000 houses and 100.000 inhabitants." It was not only the center of learning, but of the arts and sciences as well. Under the reign of Gagik I (990-1020) it enjoyed one of the rare peaceful phases in Armenia's history. In 1065, the Seljuks looted the city. After the murder of Gagik II and his sons by the Byzantines, the power of the Bagratides collapsed. After a severe earthquake in the 14th century, this once flourishing city was devastated. From that time, Ani was a ghost town – rediscovered by tourism.

The secular buildings are hardly recognizable today. Thanks to the outstanding achievements of Armenian church architects, many of the churches are still in very good condition. In the middle of a highly volcanic area, it was necessary to develop a special building technique that would give the domes enough stability to withstand severe earthquakes. For this purpose, the sandwich technique was developed. The desired stability was achieved by filling one wall, consisting of two hewn stone slabs, with mortar. This technique was applied with such dexterity that the architect who designed the Ani cathedral, Tiradates, was called to Istanbul to reconstruct the collapsed dome of the Hagia Sophia.

You can enter the grounds at the **Lion Gate** (Arslan Kapisi). The lion sculpture can be seen quite clearly on a stone slab in the wall. A marked path leads to the most important of the churches. Two to three hours should be allowed for the tour, which will give you a good impression of the fundamental principles of Armenian architecture. First you will notice the 11th-century **Redeemer Church**. It's a central building with eight apses, its exterior has 19 sides. The cylindrical tambour is set back and structured with delicate basket arches. The dome has been partly destroyed, so that the building technique can be observed very well. The frescoes still show through the white wash, depicting various images strictly forbidden in Islam.

The very impressive **Tigran Honentz** church is situated only a few hundred meters farther on. It's also known as the "colorful" church. This church isn't noticeable at first, however, since it is situated on a slope on the way to the river. Because the entrance hall has collapsed, some of the interior paintings are now exposed to daylight, showing their brilliant colors in "open-air" fashion. They date back to the 13th century. The fact that the Seljuks had already occupied the city at this time proves that the Muslim rulers

Right: The cathedral of Ani is, unfortunately, increasingly suffering from the sands of time.

were tolerant, and that they co-existed peacefully with the Armenians and their religion. The church is a genuine cross-in-square church with an extended west wing. The basket arches are richly decorated with animal motifs and emphasize the verticality of the exterior structure. Inside the building are scenes from the life of Gregor the Enlightened, who was the founder of the Armeninan Apostle church.

The building which stands out more than any other, however, is the **cathedral**. To reach it we have to climb the slope again and follow the marked path. Tiridates was the brilliant architect of the basilica. Its dome has been destroyed. Before you go inside you shouldn't miss the very delicate, shell-shaped alcoves on the outside of the east front. The interior is very impressive, directing your glaze upwards. Four great compound piers, probably Gothic forerunners, divide the building into three aisles, but unlike in Gothic architecture, they have no supporting function. The alcoves for the apostles are situated in the semicircular apse. Here too, the frescoes shimmer through the whitewash.

Surprisingly, the next building is a mosque. The **Menücehr Camii** mosque has a seven-sided minaret and is built from multicolored stone. The arches are a fine example of Armenian stone masonry. The view back to the Tigran Honentz church is unique. The path leads back towards the city wall.

Following the Alaça Suyu, the 12-sided **Gregor Abugamrenz church** can be seen from quite a way off. The building is a construction with six conchae and is the only one of its kind. It is still in perfect condition. The small amount of floor space reminds us that Armenians remain standing throughout the church service.

The incongruous building only a few hundred meters away is the **Gregor Gagik church**. The Doric capital bears witness to the fact that the Armenians

were influenced by Greek architecture. This dome-shaped building was based on the one in Zwarthnotz, in former Soviet Armenia. The oversized dome collapsed soon after the church was built. Once again the great city wall appears. On the left is the **Kars Gate** that was used mainly as a goods entrance.

You have to take the same bumpy road back – the melancholic atmosphere of Ani lingers. The hotels in Kars are not worth mentioning and extremely expensive. You are compelled to go to Dogubayazit if you want a reasonably comfortable hotel. The accommodation in Sarikamis is a compromise solution. It is definitely cleaner and better than what you would get in Kars.

Return on the same road, but only as far as the little town of Ladikars, where a good road turns left to Kagizman. You have to allow yourself four hours for the drive to Dogubayazit, preferably in daylight. The beauty of the countryside, but also the dangers involved in driving at night, are reason enough. You will ex-

perience a wonderful display of colors on the way to the majestic **Mount Ararat**, the mountain of Noah's Ark, where Turkey, Iran and the former Soviet Union meet. From a 2000 m plateau, it towers a further 3000 m into the sky. The bizarre scenery of the Aras Mountains changes color like a chameleon. The rugged Aras Mountains can be seen in the background, herds of sheep and cattle grazing on the slopes. The never-ending flower fields are an unforgettable sight, especially in springtime and early summer.

The crater-like formations near the 3276 m **Asagi Dagi**, before you come to Tuzluça, are reminiscent of the moon's surface. After a short climb you come to one of the region's main beauty spots – the **Igdir Valley**. It is so sheltered that cotton can be grown in it. The irrigation system has created a real Garden of Eden. Apricots, strawberries, apples, oranges and all kinds of other fruits and vegetables flourish. Only on a clear day you can see and admire Ararat's towering summit (5165 m) from here.

MOUNT ARARAT

(Turkish: Agri Dagi, "Mount of Sorrows"). It has been solely on Turkish territory since 1920. Just when you are sure you are very close to your destination, a tedious climb over the Pamuk Geçedi ("Cotton Pass") through the mountain's lava masses lies ahead.

The few remaining nomads in Turkey have their main camp here. They always come to it in the summer, following the melting of mountain snow. Their summer pastures are called *yaylas*. Only after the summit of the pass you can get a view of the **Dogubayazit Plain**. A few Kurdish villages are situated at various points along the road. The architecture is characteristic for this part of the country – stone houses half underground, the roof of one house often forming the terrace of the adjoining one. The gray pumice stone

Above: Wood is quite a precious commodity in some parts of Turkey. Right: The "Mount of Sorrows", Ararat, is over 5000 m high.

is a harsh contrast to the glistening white Ararat glacier, softened just a little by the green marshes at the foot of the mountain. Kurdish hand-woven carpets, the *kelims*, put out to dry on the roofs of the houses, lend some color to the otherwise gloomy landscape.

Expeditions to Mount Ararat are becoming increasingly popular. An official permit is required, however. As the mountain is often enveloped in cloud, these expeditions can be very disappointing. It's hard to believe that the great flood that carried Noah's Ark supposedly took place in this hilly region, although in both world wars pilots are said to have seen pieces of a ship sticking out of the south side of the glacier in summer. Numerous legends bear witness to this theory. Experts are unanimous, however, that the only place to look for evidence of this event is on the plain between the Euphrates and the Tigris, near Mount Cudi in the town of Cizare, not far from the Iraqi border. It's here that Noah's grave, a rather modest grotto, is revered.

Dogubayazit is a lively border town and makes its living mainly from smuggling. Even on your way into town the local boys try to sell you cigarettes at half price. Those climbing Mount Ararat start out from here, so that the town profits financially by providing guides and equipment to the numerous climbers. Persians also cross the border to have a holiday in Turkey, especially during the Persian New Year (Nevruz). Compared with Iran, Turkey is a liberal country.

Apart from Mount Ararat, East Anatolia has another attraction – the 18th-century **Ishak Pasa Sarayi**. It towers over the city, high up in the mountains on the spot where ancient Dogubayazit, probably destroyed by the Russians at the beginning of this century, once stood. This palace, built at a height of 2200 meters, is on one of the side roads of the silk route. This was always a popular place for building strongholds.

If you stood in front of the richly decorated portal looking over the countryside towards the Ottoman mosque, you would

be able to observe a small cavity in the rock-face with a pair of binoculars. On taking a closer look, you would see that it's a relief depicting an animal being sacrificed to a divinity. This is the first evidence of a settlement in this area, an Urartian rock relief. The Urartian people ruled the country from the 6th to the 9th century B.C.

Pieces of a wall from Seljuk times run along the cliffside. The Seljuks, as well as the Ottomans, had trading posts here. **Ishak Pasa**, the Ottoman governor, was in charge of one of the most important trading routes between Europe and Asia. Like his predecessors, he demanded toll money and taxes. The building has been continually restored, as can be seen from the light gray stone in the first courtyard. This is where the guards' quarters used to be. Another richly decorated portal leads to the mosque. If you turn right after going through the door, you come to the **Selamlik**, the hall used for receiving important guests and for matters of jurisdiction. Originally, the now dilapidated

rooms above were covered by barreled vaults. An adjoining passageway leads through the library into the **mosque**, with a pulpit that has to be entered from the back and is shaped like a flower-basket.

The chains that used to hold the oil lamps still hang from the painted dome. The gallery, at one time used by the ruler and his family, can also be seen from the pulpit. Unfortunately, the entrance to the minaret has been closed. Visitors can no longer admire the unforgettable view from the minaret over the palace grounds and the colorful surrounding hills. There is no adjoining passageway between the mosque and the second largest complex in the palace, the private quarters of the governor.

We have to go back through the library into the large courtyard to the largest of the palace portals, the entrance to the *harem*. But before doing so, the *türbe* of Ishak Pasa is well worth seeing. This

Above: It's a long climb up to the Ishak Pasa Sarayi in the mountains of Dogubayazit.

tomb has a roof shaped like a cone. The rather plain doorway leads to a vault underground and looks like the door of a hut in comparison. The pillared dining hall is on the right, directly after the entrance to the harem.

The very delicate stonework is reminiscent of Armenian-Georgian stone masonry. The ruler had chosen a Georgian to be the architect. After the building was completed, the unfortunate architect was put to death to prevent him from constructing a similar building elsewhere in the country.

On leaving the dining hall, you see the family quarters on the right, each room equipped with an open fireplace and a wooden balcony. The toilets, the *hamam*, and the soot-blackened kitchen are to the left of the dining hall entrance. Their colossal size indicates the kind of banquets that were held here.

From the outside, the palace looks very grand and majestic. If you climb the steep slope opposite the entrance, it will give you an idea of just how large it is. Despite the fact that art experts have criticized the architect's attempt to fuse the various architectural styles, saying that the incongruous assortment makes the palace's aesthetic value inferior, Ishak Pasa Serayi's various styles seem to blend well, making it quite unique. The very ugly telegraph pole at the entrance is surely more incongruous, aesthetically speaking.

If Lake Van is to be your next destination, you have the choice of two different routes. You can either take the Europe-23 route via **Agri**, **Patnos** and **Ercis**, or the shorter and more interesting road via **Çaldiran** and **Muradiye**. Previously, this road was used by too many vehicles and is in bad condition. Since 1990, however, it has been improved and now takes you comfortably through the remote, volcanic, nomad country of the 3548-meter **Tendürek Dagi**. Contrary to what one might expect, there is an excellent place to have an outdoor lunch at the beautiful **Muradiye Waterfall**.

The actual town of Muradiye is only a few kilometers farther on, and the shoddy, tumbled-down houses make it quite obvious that this was all too often the epicenter of severe earthquakes threatening the existence of the population.

LAKE VAN

Very soon, the spectacular **Lake Van** (Van Gölü) comes into sight. Almost seven times larger than Lake Constance, it is more like a sea than a lake. In fact, Van's citizens sometimes refer to it as a sea. Its depth still has not been measured, but it is said to be over 100 meters deep near the edge. It is quite unique in all respects. The saline content of the water is so concentrated that no fish can survive here. Small white fish are found only in the estuary. They are considered very tasty and were traded as dried fish to places as far away as China during the Urartian period.

Neither Urartians nor Armenians, who were always townspeople and earned only some of their living by fishing, live here nowadays. A large number of Kurdish people have settled here now. By tradition, they were always nomads who knew very little about fishing. But things have changed. The majority of Kurds have given up their nomadic lifestyle and settled in the towns. Most of them, however, still don't want anything to do with fishing.

In view of the popularity attached to water sports, it seems quite uncanny that there are no windsurfers or yachtsmen to be seen anywhere on the lake. In fact, there is almost no activity at all here, so that many tourists find their visit to Lake Van to be a rather awesome, if not eerie experience. The only form of activity you will witness are the freight ferryboats, run by the state-owned shipping company, which are used to freight the goods waggons from Tatvan to Van. Here they are unloaded and put onto the railway line for their long journey to Iran. It would have proved too cumbersome to construct a railway line around the 3000 meter spiralling mountain range that surrounds the lake.

Furthermore, Turkey's second highest mountain, the 4058 meter **Süphan Dagi** is situated in the northwestern region of this mountain range. You can enjoy a splendid view of the clear, turquoise-blue lake for almost an hour before you reach Van. On a clear day, the Süphan Dagi can be seen in the background.

Van was the capital of the little-known kingdom of Urartu, existing between the 9th and 6th century B.C. It was established to defend the Urartians against constant attacks by the Assyrians. It quickly became Assyria's most powerful opponent and developed into a prosperous cultural and economic center, world-renowned for its architectural achievements and agricultural skills, as well as metallurgy and horse-breeding. At the height of its power, Van had trading links with China and Etruria (today's Tuscany). It is highly probable that a large section of Tuscany's population may originally have come from this area. It's quite remarkable how much both peoples have in common. Even their legends correspond. The Assyrians and the Urartians declined in strength at the same time. Weakened by the battles they had fought against each other, they finally became allies, unsuccessfully joining forces against the invading equestrian tribes – the Medes and the Scythians.

The capital of Urartu was established on the site of ancient Tushpa on Lake Van. For strategic purposes, palaces were always constructed on exposed mountain ridges. Tushpa of that period is the present-day **fortress hill** in Van. It is approximately one kilometer long, and numerous ruins all along the route bear witness to the various cultures that successively occupied it. Apart from the Ottoman and Seljuk ruins, the **royal tombs** are especially worth seeing. Hewn into the side of the cliff, they are not always easy to get to. One of them that you shouldn't miss visiting, however, is the tomb of **Argishti I** (790 -765 B.C.) The majority of these tombs and cult grounds are covered with inscriptions in the Urartian language, but written in Assyrian cuneiform writing. There is an example of this type of script on Argishti I's tomb. The so-called Horhor Chronicle tells of the king's military prowess. A stairway leads into the empty, looted interior with four chambers branching off it. There are no windows. Although the inscriptions tell us almost everything about the history of the Urartian people, they reveal almost nothing about their burial cult. It is thought that it was derived from the Etruscans.

Right: The Hosap Kale in the stark environment of the Hakkari mountainscape appears impregnable.

If you climb the rather steep fortress-hill, up to the second largest viewing platform, you will be rewarded with splendid panoramas of the ancient ruins and the once prosperous town. Cattle can today be seen grazing among the foundation stones of the crumbled buildings.

Only two mosques are still intact and they mark the spot where the ancient town of Van once stood. At the beginning of this century, Armenians and Turks used to live here in peaceful coexistence. It seems quite incredible that the stable church erected by the town's Armenian community no longer stands.

Two small pillared *türbes* are all that remain of the church. They stand unobtrusively at the side of the gravel road. Because the inscription is missing, they are simply called **Iki Türbe** ("two tombs"). It pays to walk around the fortress hill to the ruins. Only from below can you observe the Urartian rock tombs and stairways. Sunset is an unforgettable experience here.

The present-day town of Van is a bustling trading center. It soon becomes obvious that this is the carpet capital of Eastern Anatolia. Its proximity to the (former) Soviet Union, Iran, Iraq and Kurdistan is evident by the wide variety of goods. You can purchase rare objects here at more than bargain prices.

Unfortunately, an unpleasant competitive struggle to win customers has developed. There is only a handful of shops that sell traditional arts and crafts, and while the other shops sell more modern goods, they are inexpensive too. You should look around for a hand-woven carpet – Van's specialty. There are many varieties, with embroidery, for example. The high quality Turkish hand-knotted carpets are also available.

Van is an ideal place for making trips into the surrounding region. You can find out all about transportation and sightseeing at the comfortable and inexpensive **Hotel Büyük Asur.**

On no account should the visitor miss visiting the **Urartu Museum** in Van. It holds great treasures and is very well laid out. There is an ethnological section on the first floor.

The first excursion takes you to **Hakkari**. As there is a lot of unrest in this province, it's advisable to enquire if the road to Hakkari is open. You can nearly always get as far as **Hosap** (Güselsu) along this road without any danger, however.

On the central Cumhuriyet Caddesi you can leave Van. Heading southwest, you will soon come to eroded open countryside. The Hakkari province is often cut off from the outside world for months at a time in winter. It is very sparsely populated, with four inhabitants to every square kilometer.

After crossing the 2000 meter pass, there is a steep drop in the road and the Güselsu valley appears. Even in Urartian times, people were familiar with hydroculture, and the ancient aqueducts are still there, weather-beaten after years of exposure.

A new dam has been built outside Hosap with the help of principles used in the ancient irrigation system. But before you come to it, a long rock borders the right-hand side of the road. If you take a closer look, you will see Urartian foundation blocks meticulously hewn out of stone. Here, the great fortress of King Sardur II (765-733) was erected. Today the fortress is called **Çavustepe** (Field Marshal Hill), and is the best remaining Urartian excavation. Professor Afif Erzen of Istanbul University has been in charge of the work here for 30 years. Luckily, photography is now permitted.

This double fortress was erected outside Tushpa and had a representative function. The intricate temple inscriptions in black basalt bear witness to this. Three layers were found. The Urartian one (7th century B.C.), a later one (4th century B.C.), and a medieval layer. If you have difficulty determining the chronological order of the finds that can be seen during your tour, one of the guards will be pleased to help you.

There is a walled-in temple area on the left above the parking lot, marking the upper fortress. First walk along a shopping area. The exact stone blocks specially made for the relief can still be seen. You then come to the Uçkale, a formerly tin-covered gate, and from there the store-room is a little farther up. It still contains well-preserved stocks. Grain still capable of germinating was discovered in this area.

The highest point is, as always, the temple area. The sacrifice stone with a specially-made groove for the blood to run into is not far away. Finally, you will come to the palace area situated behind the temple. The wells can still be seen. The Turkish flag is hoisted at the end of the street.

The road leading to Hakkari soon reaches the point where the Güselsu is

Above: These peshmergas are celebrating their successful flight from neighboring Iraq.
Right: The Armenians built the Akdamar Church on the shores of Lake Van.

dammed, and then continues along the reservoir. Leaving the reservoir behind, you will come to a huge fortress in the middle of the rugged, colorful landscape. Five kilometers farther on is the **Hosap fortress** at a Seljuk bridge which is well worth seeing. There are also a few inviting tea houses nearby. The footpath to the fortress goes over this bridge and continues for about 500 meters uphill, where a guard keeps watch. The children here sell wall-hangings made of chick peas, a traditional decoration.

The magnificent fortress with the Persian name of Hosap ("güselsu" or "beautiful water") was built as it now stands on the ruins of a Seljuk fortress in 1643 by the regional ruler Sari Süleyman from the Mahmudiye tribe.

The splendid relief sculpture on the portal dates back to the time of the old fortress. The Hosap fortress is said to have consisted of as many as 360 rooms, three baths, two mosques, a dungeon and a large guardsroom. The fortress was surrounded by two enormous circular walls with crenellation. There is a spectacular view from above of one of the circular walls. From the distance it looks like a lizard with a serrated back.

A 2730 meter pass (Çoh Geçidi) still has to be crossed. However, the trip is only worthwhile if you have enough time to spend a night in this town. After all, you really shouldn't miss admiring the unique mountain ranges. But be prepared for the stringent police checks in this part of the country. You might even be asked to turn back.

Because of political unrest in this region, it is not advisable to go to the eastern region of Cizre, or anywhere farther south than Hakkari. A return journey to Van is therefore unavoidable. The other scenic highlights, the island of Akdamar and the Seljuk burial grounds, are situated there.

Nestorian Christians still lived in Hakkari in this century, leading a secluded

life in the mountain regions. The exterior of their churches is not at all ornate. In fact, they look more like small forts than places of worship. They were, after all, always threatened by hostile tribes. The Nestorian Church separated from the Byzantine Church in the 5th century. The Nestorians used to live on Turkish soil, but in the period of upheaval at the beginning of this century they fled either to Iran or Iraq.

Before you are going to visit the Nestorian churches, you should first apply for a permit. The Hotel Çallih in Hakkari will be pleased to supply you with a local guide and arrange the permit for you. A trip to the village of **Konak** with its patriarch church is only possible with a cross-country vehicle. The last part of the journey has to be done on foot and takes a good few hours.

If you don't want to go all the way back to Van, you can turn left at the forked road after Çavustepe towards Gevas / Bitlis, taking you to the Akdamar Island wharf. You should take a look at the **Halim Hatun** *türbe* in the graveyard in **Gevas**. It is beautifully structured and was built for a Seljuk princess in 1358. Modern tombstones and old ones from the Seljuk period stand side by side. Their intricate stone masonry work is an example of Armenian craftsmanship.

Small boats belonging to the shipping cooperative can be seen at the wharf. The visitor can use this opportunity to eat at the excellent Akdamar restaurant. The boats depart only when they are full, but it's advisable nevertheless to book in advance with the captain. The trip takes about half an hour and is quite an unforgettable scenic experience.

AKDAMAR

The Akdamar (Akhtamar) cross-in-square church from the 10th century is the only one of its kind among the Armenian churches. Its uniqueness lies in its elaborate façade. Contrary to other churches, the interior design plays a less important role here. Gagik I, King of

Waspurakan, had the Holy Cross church built and moved his residence from Van to the island. The fact that it was the seat of the anti-Catholicos contributed to Akdamar's becoming a religious center. Gagik, who paid tribute to the Caliph of Baghdad, broke away from the Bagratide Empire and founded this small kingdom in the Lake Van area. The church is the only building left of this splendid residence. It stands in beautiful scenery. The island was linked to the mainland at one time by a dam 3 km long. The chronicler of that period, Thomas of Ardzruni, reported that the church looked like a second sun from the edge of the lake. Its exterior was gold-plated, the reliefs were painted in bright colors and the statue's eyes studded with precious stones. It must have been a very wealthy kingdom, and this pompous display indicates the lavish lifestyle of the period.

Above: The story of Jonah and the whale, a relief in the Akdamar Church. Right: The view from the Medrese in Mardin.

You should leave yourself ample time to visit the church. Various extensions have been added to the original building over the centuries, so that its symmetrical shape has been changed to the extent that it now is a cross-in-square church with an extended west wing. The entrance is situated on the west side at the belfry – first built in the early 19th century. The relief sculptures on this side to the left of the entrance depict the legends of Jonah, David and Goliath, as well as the royal family in traditional dress.

The 14th-century oratory, the oldest extension, is on the north side. It partly hides the reliefs, but the fall of man, Daniel in the den of lions, St. Theodore, St. Sergius and St. George can be seen to the right of the window. Finally, on the west side, we see King Gagik I holding a model of the church in his hand, being blessed by Christ. The view is a little distorted here as well because of the triple-aisled, 18th-century ante-church.

The nearest acceptable hotel on the way to the southeast is the new Hotel

Selçuklu in **Ahlat**. The only thing that remains of this historical town is the expansive Seljuk **graveyard**. The town was in the hands of the Urartians, Alexander the Great, the Parthians, Romans, Armenians, Arabs, Kurds, Seljuks, Mongols, Turcomens and Ottomans, respectively.

As you enter the town, the filigree-adorned **Ulu Kümbet** *türbe* dating back to the year 1273 can be seen at the edge of the lake opposite the museum. After looking at it, enter the cemetery, where many decorative tombstones, once collapsed, have been erected again. At the end of the expansive graveyard there is a pillared *türbe* (**Bayindir türbesi**). It contains a prayer room. More *türbes* can be admired to the east and west, are all within walking distance.

Before leaving for southeast Anatolia, a walk in the crystal-clear mountain air of the over 3000 meter high **Nemrut Dagi** (not to be confused with Nemrud Dag in Commagene) is an appropriate way to complete this part of your tour. Several lakes are situated in the crater of the vol-

cano, including one with warm water. In this area you often come across friendly nomads who have set up their summer camp here. Their dogs are less friendly, however, often barring their sharp teeth to approaching strangers.

It's worth stopping at Tatvan. The Ottoman caravanserai, **Alaman Han**, is situated in a hollow to the left of the turn-off to Mus a few kilometers from Bitlis. Caravans are said to have still camped here at the beginning of the 20th century. There are two more buildings for storing provisions a few kilometers farther on, on the right side of the road. The road leads downhill to the watershed between Lake Van and the tributaries of the Euphrates (Firat, in Turkish) and the Tigris (Dicle).

The rather gloomy, but quaint town of **Bitlis** is the provincial capital. It lies snugly in the Bitlis Çay canyon, dwarfed by a mighty Byzantine fortress. The town was in the hands of Kurd landowners until the 19th century, able to defend itself against the Ottoman rule until 1848. The bustling tobacco market makes a

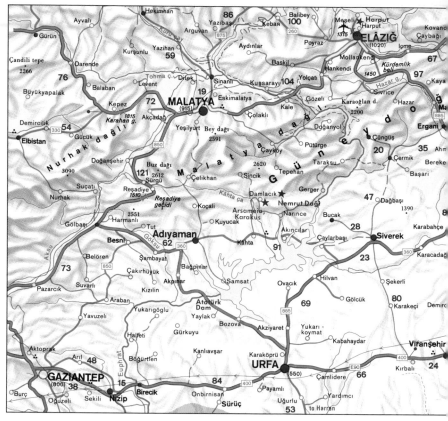

short walk through the small town center worthwhile. You can also buy the famous Turkish honey with honeycomb here.

The Southeast

As the road winds its way continually downhill, the sun becomes more intense. A rise in temperature is already noticeable in **Baykan**. Dwarf oaks and mulberry bushes indicate a complete change in vegetation. Very shortly, you will cross the first tributaries of the Tigris and come to a road junction. The direct road to Diyarbakir is on the right. If you turn left, it will take you on a roundabout route that is very worthwhile. You should take the trouble at all costs to visit the 12th-cen-

tury Ortokidic **Malabad Bridge** 3 km to the right.

Batman is the center for Turkey's oil industry. It is situated in one of the poorest and most troubled regions in Turkey. The struggle to find work in the petro industry creates a lot of social unrest. The sinister-looking black pumps work lethargically, bringing the oil above ground, and the tank track trains transporting the oil to the picturesque town of **Hasankeyf** irresponsibly race alongside the Tigris meadows at top speed. A *türbe* stands out on the right side of the road. It is studded with blue Iznik tiles, characteristic of Central Asia. The view from the new bridge across the Tigris towards the remains of the old bridge is exactly

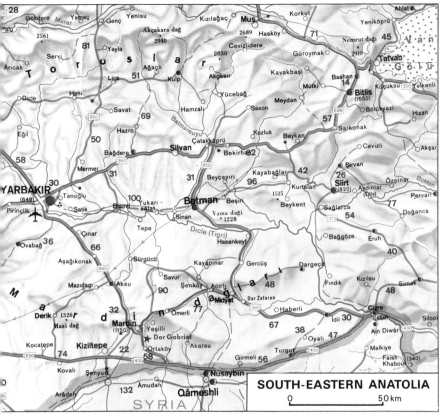

SOUTH-EASTERN ANATOLIA

0   50 km

how one might have envisaged Mesopotamia as a child.

The Romans founded Hasankeyf on the frontier to the Persian empire. It got its name from the Arabs in the 7th century – they called it Hisn Kayfa. As you see it today, so it was during the time of the Turcoman Ortokides (12th century). You can see the ruins of a palace in the rock face.

From now on, the road continues through the province of Mardin, crossing an arid region called **Tur Abdin** (in Aramaic "the Mount of God's Servants"). The capital of the province is **Midyat**. It is strange to see as many church towers as minarets in this region. The reason for this is that Tur Abdin has been a place of

retreat for Syrian Orthodox Christians (Jacobites) for several centuries.

The present-day seat of the metropolitan is the **Mar Gabriel** monastery. You can get to it quite easily from Midyat on the road to **Cizre**. There is a turnoff to the left after 25 km, leading to the monastery. The friendly monks are willing to give you a guided tour and more than pleased to receive a donation. Although these Christian monasteries are officially protected by the state, some of the monks spend all their time working abroad in order to finance them.

There is a very good road from Midyat via Savur to the elegant provincial capital of **Mardin**. The town has an Arabic flavor, and is located on a plateau. From

here you can see from northern Mesopotamia to Syria. Apart from Turkish, the country's official language, much Arabic is spoken. The whole way of life here is influenced by Arabian culture.

The old town with its ornate limestone houses streches its way uphill in the shape of an amphitheatre, adorned by the Byzantine fortress at the top of the hill. A NATO radar screen controls the surrounding air space at the moment.

The *medrese* built by Sultan Isa in 1385 is situated just below the fortress. You get the best view of the town from the roof of this Koran school, as well as a very close perspective of the fluted dome on the sultan's *türbe*. You can also spot the Ulu Cami mosque. Its round, fluted minaret is decorated with Kufi inscriptions. If you want to find a good hotel, you will have to put up with the one-hour

Above: Friday prayers in Diyarbakir. Right: The watermelons of Diyarbakir have the reputation of being the biggest and best in all of Turkey.

journey to Nusaybin (excellent Nezirhan Hotel) or Diyarbakir. The establishments in Mardin cannot be recommended.

The center of the old caravan town of **Diyarbakir** is still surrounded by an ancient **city wall**. It is 5 km long and made out of black basalt. It was erected in the year 349 by the Byzantine Emperor Constantine to keep out the Persians. It has been restored many times, the last time by the Turcoman Akkoyunlu ("white ram") dynasty. You get the first and best view of the medieval town coming from Mardin at the arched **Tigris bridge**. The hot summers here are notorious, and you are advised to take a look at the town in the early morning. The city wall is still cool from the night air, so it's best to begin your sightseeing at the **Kiçi Burç** tower near the Mardin gate. The view from here takes in the Tigris Valley, the bastions of the city wall, as well as the dark basalt minarets.

The watermelons grown in Diyarbakir are famous all over Turkey. They grow on the banks of the river and are fertilised with pigeon dung. They reach an enormous size and may weigh up to 70 kilos. You can sample the quality of these melons at dinner in one of the rooftop restaurants.

On entering the **main mosque** in the center of town, directly next to the bustling bazaar, you will notice that its architecture and decor are a mixture of both Christian and Islamic styles. At one time it was the Church of St. Thomas, which was turned into a mosque during the Islamic period, making it the first mosque in Anatolia.

For a long time, however, it was used by both Christians and Muslims. Much extension work was carried out by the Turcomans after a fire. There is still an old altar to the right of the entrance, and straight ahead two fountains for the traditional washing ceremony (*sadirvan*). The mosque, the aisle of which runs parallel to the *quibla* wall (the wall in which the prayer niche is embedded), is usually closed. You are advised to show respect for the customs of the conservative and sometimes intolerant inhabitants.

The 16th-century **Hasan Pasa Hani** is situated on the other side of the road. It is named after the grand vizier who built it. The second largest caravanserai building is used more and more by carpet dealers. The Diyarbakir bazaar reflects the various cultures of southeast Anatolia. The dominant culture is that of the Kurds, with Muslim and Christian Arabs and Turks in the minority. It is understandable that the police have to be very vigilant here in their attempt to keep the peace.

To make matters worse, American soldiers from the radar station at Pirinçlik have often behaved disrespectfully towards Islamic customs, making the inhabitants of Diyarbakir even more aggressive towards strangers.

Urfa, the old Edessa, is a more hospitable place. There is probably no other town that has been subjected to so much unrest than this, and none that has had to

reassert itself so frequently after being attacked and looted by aggressors. **Sanliurfa** – "famous Urfa" – is what the town is now called. The town's history probably goes back some 3700 years to the time of the obscure Hurrian kingdom, the capital of which is said to have been here. But hardly anything of that remains today – only the **Byzantine citadel** with its belfry and some mosques from the same period, as well as Abraham's pond, **Birket Ibrahim** with the **Halil ur-Rahman mosque**. According to legend, the heathen king Nimrod ordered Abraham to be burned at the stake here. But at the crucial moment, a miracle happened – a spring appeared and put out the fire. The glowing embers of the stake were turned into carp which still swim in the pond today and are considered holy. According to legend, whoever touches them will become blind. Since both Christians and Muslims are descended from Abraham, the holy carp pond is respected by believers of both faiths. The spring water is said to have healing powers.

The **Sanliurfa Bazaar** is considered to be one of the most original in Turkey. Not only are goods sold here, they are also made. Most of the bazaar is covered by a roof, and an Ottoman caravanserai constitutes the main part.

The construction of the new Atatürk Reservoir will guarantee Urfa a prosperous future. The whole region is to be transformed into a flourishing agricultural zone. Even the arid ground around Abraham's town Harran (modern: **Altinbasak**) is to profit from this plan. Large water pipes have already been laid; pistachio trees and cotton are beginning to grow. The Biblical town is reached after a 40 km drive on the road to Akçakale on the Turkish-Syrian border.

Abraham lived here for a few years on his way from Ur in Chaldea to Canaan. His youngest brother was actually called

Above: The evening sun casts its glow on an idyllic scene. Right: The Karakus Hill, the sepulchral hill of three women of the royal house of Commagene.

Harran. The present insignificant town is one of the oldest settlements in the world. Evidence has been found that there was a settlement here as far back as the year 3000 B.C.

It was near here that Rachel and Jacob first met. The Assyrian empire came to an end in Harran in 606 B.C., and a significant temple of the moon god Sin was situated here as well. The Greeks named the place Karrai and the Romans called it Carrhae. They were defeated by the Parthians here in 53 B.C. Emperor Caracalla died here in A.D. 217 in a battle against the Parthians, and Justinian had the city wall re-erected in the 6th century. In 639, the Arabs conquered the city.

You can still see the Byzantine city wall. Its **Aleppo Gate** forms the entrance to the city. The **fortress** is built on the spot where the old cedar temple used to stand, and the Arab **Ulu Cami** is to the left on the level ground. The *trullis* are unique to Turkey. It is now against the law for the Arabic speaking, once nomadic population to build these beehive-

shaped mud houses, although they are ideally cool in this intense heat. Furthermore, they can be built at a very low cost. Instead, evermore ugly concrete buildings mar Harran's biblical character.

The road to Diyarbakir takes you through expansive pistachio fields, olive groves and vineyards. If you want to go to Nemrut Dagi, you will have to take a new route, since the old Euphrates bridge between Kahta and Urfa is covered by the water level of the Atatürk reservoir. There is a ferry for small vehicles. The new route is even shorter, however, and gives you the chance to visit the reservoir. It takes you via Bozova and Adiyaman to **Kahta**, the starting point for ascents to Nemrut Dagi.

NEMRUT DAGI

If you want to spare yourself the journey by car, you can go to Nemrut Dagi by way of public transportation. The road to the summit has improved a great deal, but the upper part is still very bumpy. You can see the summit of the 2000-meter mountain looming in the distance from Kahta on a clear day. The first tumulus appears on the left side of the road after 20 kilometers. This is **Karakus Hill** ("Eagle Hill"), where the royal family of the house of Commagene buried three of their women. The mound was surrounded by three double pillars. Only the one surmounted by the sculpture of an eagle is still in good condition. The Romans under Septimius Severus discovered the tombs, looted them and used parts of the pillars to build **Cendere Bridge**. It spans the broad river Cendere a few kilometers further on. You can enjoy a refreshing swim in the cool gorge.

You come to **Arsameia** after passing the village of Eski Kahta with its medieval Mameluke fortress. The last part of the way is a footpath. After a few hundred meters, you reach a stone relief of the Commagene Emperor Mithridates, Antiochus I's father. He is holding out his hand to Hercules – a typical pose in Commagene. The relief is still absolutely in tact. A little farther down there is a 158-meter-deep tunnel stairway cut into the rock. Its exact function is not known. It may have led to a Mithras cult place. There is a Greek inscription at the entrance. Professor Doerner from Germany, who has been supervising the excavation work at Eski Kale since 1951, translated it. It tells about the fortress town of Arsameia, its emperor and his political objectives. There is a detailed report about the cult and the holy laws.

The town of Arsameia was situated above the tunnel on a plateau. There is nothing much left of the town, as Christians condemned it as the work of heathens and used it as a quarry for their own purposes. All that remains is part of a stairway, a few pillar bases, an oversized sandal, and rainwater cisterns. The fantastic view over the sun-parched countryside and the Mameluke fortress makes the steep climb worthwhile.

The road winds its way around the mountainside, and 20 minutes away from the tumulus are a few guest houses and hotels. Some of them have been built in traditional style, blending in well with the landscape (e.g. Hotel Euphrates); others are rather ugly concrete buildings. The road soon becomes bumpy and steep. It takes you to almost 300 meters below the summit. When you get off the bus at the tea house, the steep climb to the top begins. You won't be able to see the heads of the gods and kings until the very last minute. It was only in 1881 that a German engineer, Karl Sester, discovered the ruins on Nemrut Dagi. Until then, shepherds kept a watchful eye on the mountain's secret. The actual excavation work was done by Professor Doerner and Theresa Goell after the Second World War with American funds.

Antiochus I broke up the peak of the mountain into fist-sized stones and had his tomb built in the exposed rock. After his burial, the stones were piled 50 meters above his grave to form a new summit. A mammoth job. The mystery attached to the tomb has never been solved because until now, nobody has dared to set foot inside. Readings taken with modern equipment also fail to supply exact information. There are only the inscriptions on the back of the throne to tell about the gods and Antiochus' royal objectives. The mountain is surrounded by three terraces – the east and west terrace are still fairly good condition. Originally, they looked exactly the same. While the throne and the torsos of the statues are still in good condition on the east terrace, the colossal heads have remained intact on the west terrace, giving us a rough idea of what the complex must have looked like in its original form.

The actual height of a statue was eight to nine meters, made up of eight stone slabs. Antiochus I is situated on the extreme left and is beautifully carved. The only woman's head is set back a little. The father of the gods – Zeus-Ahura Mazda, situated in the center – is a little bigger than the others.

Finally, we have Apollon Mithras (similar to Antiochos I) and Hercules, also known as Artagnes. The row of gods is flanked on both sides by eagles and lions with noticeably human expressions. This is a synthesis of the Greek and Persian pantheons, tracing the ancestors of Antiochus back to Darius I (Persian – paternal) and to Alexander the Great (Greek – maternal).

It's surprisingly cold up here, making people return sooner than planned to the tea house. But the return journey to the valley brings the warm weather again all too soon.

Certainly, Nemrut Dagi will linger in your memory for a long time to come, and there is surely no better way of completing a trip to Eastern Anatolia than at the spot where Occident and Orient meet.

Right: Nemrut Dagi, where an entire mountain was turned into a temple.

BLACK SEA COAST

THE WEST
Accommodation

GIRESUN: *BUDGET:* **Çarikçi**, Osmanaga Cad. 6, Tel: 051-20628. **Gedikali**, Bulancak, Tel: 051-41081. **Giresun**, Sultanselim Mah, Tel: 051-13017. Tel: 051-13017. **Karagöl**, Bektas Yaylasi, Bulancak, Tel: 051-41069. **Kit-Tur**, Arifbey Cad. 2, Tel: 051-20255.

ORDU: *MODERATE:* **Belde**, Kirazlimani, Tel: 371- 13987. *BUDGET:* **Turist**, Atatürk Bulvari, Tel: 371-19115.

SAMSUN: *LUXURY:* **Turban Büyük Samsun**, Atatürk Bulvari, Tel: 361-10750.

MODERATE: **Yafeya**, Cumhuriyet Meydani, Tel: 361-5113134.

BUDGET: **Vidili**, Kazimpasa Cad., Tel: 361-1605051. **Burc**, Kazimpasa Cad., Tel: 361-1547981. **Tugra**, Irmak Cad., Tel: 361-5114143.

SINOP: *MODERATE:* **Belediye Yuvam Tes**, Gelincik M., Tel: 3761-2532.

BUDGET: **Melia Kasim**, Gazi Cad., 3761- 4210.

THE EAST
Accommodation

ARTVIN: *BUDGET:* **Karahan**, Inönü Cad.16, Tel: 0581-1800.

FATSA: *BUDGET:* **Dolunay Motel**, Çamlik Mev., Tel: 372-11528.

HOPA: *BUDGET:* **Cihan**, Ortahopa Cad. 7, Tel: 0571-1897. **Papila**, Tel: 0571-3641.

PERSEMBE: *BUDGET:* **Vona**, Gacali Mah., Tel: 3717-1755.

RIZE: *BUDGET:* **Keles**, Sahil Mev. Palandöken Cad. 2, Tel: 054-14612. **Findikhan**, Findikli, Tel: 0567-1368.

TRABZON: *MODERATE:* **Büyük Liman Tesisleri**, Sahil Cad., Vakfikebir, Tel: 0451-1725. *BUDGET:* **Best**, Sahil Cad. Besikdüzü, Tel: 0453-1944. **Horon**, Sirimagazalar Cad. 125, Tel: 031-11199. **Özgür**, Atatürk Alani 29, Tel: 031-11319. **Sümela**, Akçaabat, Tel: 041-48067. **Usta**, Iskele C. Telegrafhane S. 3, Tel: 031-12195.

ÜNYE: *MODERATE:* **Belediye Çamlik Motel**, Çamlik Mev., Tel: 373-11085. *BUDGET:* **Kumsal**, Gölevi Köyü, Tel: 373-14490.

The Laz

The people of the eastern Black Sea coast have a very distinctive character of their own, and their fellow countrymen frequently refer to them as *Laz*. This is merely verbal shorthand, for the Laz are only one of the many ethnic groups in the area, although their native dress – headscarf, vest, and trousers stuffed into knee-high boots – has been adopted with variations, by all. The residents are a fascinating tangle of Turks, Türkmen, real Laz, Circassians, Georgians and the elusive Hemsin and Of tribes.

Until the compulsory exchange of populations between Greece and Turkey in 1923, there were also Pontic Greeks whose ancestors settled in the coastal cities as early as the 8th century BC. In certain mountain villages, a derivation of Greek is still spoken by the inhabitants despite their obvious devotion to Turkey and Islam.

To the visitor, whether from abroad or another part of Turkey, the residents of the Black Sea coast seem overwhelmingly hospitable and welcoming, as well as stubborn and proud.

Festivals

Unique to the Black Sea region are the summer fesivals held in the mountain meadows, or *yaylas*. The most important of these are the *Kadirga*, above Tonya, and the *Kafkasör*, a bull-wrestling match (bull versus bull) above Artvin, both take place in late June.

The *Aksu Festival* on Giresun Island is celebrated on May 20, and the *Vartavar Festivities* in the highlands of Çamlihemsin take place in late June and August.

Access / Transportation

Samsun and Trabzon airports have regular service to Ankara and Istanbul. Buses provide cheap, frequent service. There are weekly ferryboats between Instanbul and various Black Sea ports. Rental cars and jeeps are available from the Avis office in Trabzon.

EASTERN ANATOLIA
Accommodation

DOGUBEYAZIT: *MODERATE:* **Sim-Er Hotel**, Iran Transit Road, Dogubeyazit-Agri. Tel: 0278-1601.

BUDGET: **Isfahan**, Eminiyet Cad. 48, Tel: 0278-1139. **Ishakpasa**, Emniyet Cad. 10, Tel: 0278-1243. **Memo Camping**, Tel: 0278-2393.

ERZINCAN: *MODERATE:* **Roma**, Ordu Cad. 102, Tel: 023-11016. *BUDGET:* **Urartu**, Cumhuriyet Mey., Tel: 0231-11561.

ERZURUM: *MODERATE:* **Büyük Erzurum**, Ali Ravi Cad. 5, Tel: 011-16528. **Oral**, Terminal Cad. 3, Tel: 011-19740. *BUDGET:* **Buhara**, Kazim Karabekir Cad., Tel: 011-15096. **Polat Oteli**, Kazim Karabekir Cad., Tel: 011-11623. **Sefer**, Istasyon Cad. 7, Tel: 011-16714.

KARS: *MODERATE:* **Anihan Motel**, Tel: 021-17404. *BUDGET:* **Yilmaz**, Kücük Kazimbey Cad., Tel: 021- 11074.

IGDIR: *BUDGET:* **Latif**, Karadag Cad., Tel: 0227-2509. **Parlar**, Irfan Cad. 39, Tel: 0227-2509.

VAN: *MODERATE:* **Akdamar Hotel**, Kazim Karabekir Cad. 56, Tel: 061-18100. **Büyük Urartu,** Hastane Cad. 60, Tel: 061-20660. *BUDGET:* **Asur,** Cumhuriyet Cad., Tel: 061-18792. **Tekin,** Kuçük Camii, Tel: 061-11366.

If you want to hire a vehicle or boat in Van, contact Orhan Tekin, Old Tusba Turizm, Tel: 061-14561.

Mount Ararat

Permission is needed to climb the mountain where Noah's Ark allegedly came to rest. Climbers who go directly to Dogubeyazit without prior authorization to climb will be disappointed. Arrange your climb with adventure travel agencies (see section below) well in advance. In addition to Ararat, there are other peaks in the region such as the **Kaçkar** in the Pontus chain. Skiing is starting to catch on here, with Turkey's best runs on the **Palandöken Mountain** outside of Erzurum. There are several decent hotels less than ten minutes away in town, and flights to the city's airports from Istanbul and Ankara allow for weekend ski trips.

Adventure Travel Agencies

Aloha Turizm: Cinnah Cad. 39/8, Çankaya, Ankara, Tel: 4-1401201. **Tempo Turizm,** Izmır Cad. 57/15, Kizilay, Ankara: Tel: 4-1254037. **Natolya Turizm:** Abdülhakhamit Cad.70/5, Taksim, Istanbul, Tel: 1-1552466. **Gençtur Turizm,** Yerebatan Cad. 15, Istanbul, Tel: 1-5205274.

Access / Transportation

There are regular flights to the airports at Erzurum and Van, and bi-weekly flights by small craft to Erzincan and Kars. The northern railway line enters the Soviet Union at Kars via Erzincan, Erzurum and Sarikamis, the southern route leads to Iran at Van via Elazig and Tatvan.

SOUTHEAST ANATOLIA
Accommodation

ADIYAMAN: *MODERATE:* **Bozdogan,** Atatürk Bul. Tel: 878-13999. *BUDGET:* **Serdaroglu,** Turgutreis Cad. 20, Tel: 878-13331.
DIYARBAKIR: *LUXURY:* **Demir,** Izzetpasa Cad. 8, Tel: 831-12315. *BUDGET:* **Kristal,** Inonü Cad., Tel: 831-40297. **Turistik,** Ziya Gökalp Bul. 7, Tel: 831-12662.
ELAZIG: *BUDGET:* **Beritan,** Hurriyet Cad. 24, Tel: 811-14484. **Büyük Elazig,** Harput Cad. 9, Tel: 811-22001.
GAZIANTEP: *BUDGET:* **Alfin,** Hürriyet Cad. 27, Tel: 85-119480. **Kaleli,** Hurriyet Cad, Tel: 85-13417.
KAHTA: *BUDGET:* **Nemrut Tur Tesisleri,** Adiyaman-Kahta Road, Tel: 8795-1967. **Zeus**

Motel, Tel: 8795-2428. **Kommagene Oteli,** on the main road. Along the way to Nemrut Dagi: Village inn **Eski Kahta**. Nemrut Dagi: **Euphrat Hotel,** Tel: 8795- 2428.
MALATYA: *BUDGET:* **Kent,** Atatürk Cad. 151, Tel: 821-12175.
SANLIURFA: *MODERATE:* **Köran,** Ipek Yolu, Tel: 871-31809. **Harran,** Atatürk Bul., Tel: 871-34743. **Mirkelam Tur Tes Motel,** Karsiyaka Mev., Birecik, Tel: 8761-1272.
BUDGET: **Turban Urfa Oteli,** Köprübasi Cad. 74, Tel: 871- 13520.

Cuisine

This region boasts some of the best food in Turkey, especially the spicy chops and grills. The dried fruits, walnuts and pistachios are of excellent quality. The cheeses of the region are well known too, the most famous being the *Otlupeynir*, made from goats milk, garlic and herbs.

Access / Transportation

There are regular flights to the airports of Diyarbakir and Gaziantep as well as small craft landing strips at Urfa, Malatya and Elazig. A train line skirts the Syrian border, connecting through Urfa and Diyarbakir to points west. Additionally, local buses serve all the towns of the area. The **Haci Yuksel Taksi Service** in Diyarbakir (Tel: 831-13433) provides cars and drivers.

Security

Southeastern and eastern Anatolia are for the most part inhabited by Kurds. This people, the fourth largest in the Middle East, traces its origins to the Medi, and still speaks a western Iranian language. Ever since the founding of the Turkish Republic, the Kurds have been referred to officially as "Mountain Turks". The new government of President Demirel decided to loosen some of the restrictions placed on the Kurds. For example, they are supposed to be allowed to speak Kurdish in public and to sell recordings of Kurdish music. Whether this will become law remains to be seen.

The growing self-confidence of the Kurds has manifested itself in greater political and cultural activities. The PKK, Kurdistan's Worker's Party, has also been waging guerilla warfare against the Turkish government that could affect any travel to eastern Anatolia. Army control has increased ever since one kidnapping action in 1991, during which German tourists were abducted and later released unharmed. Wilderness camping is by no means recommendable; hotels can be considered as safe. People are by and large very friendly and hospitable. In order to avoid any conflict it would be wise not to get involved in any political discussion.

TURKEY À LA MODE

"Do re mi fa sol la ti.....do!"

Standard fare for the serious music student, but few laymen know that each of the above syllables serves as the point of departure for a distinct musical mode (or scale) with its own internal structure of half and whole steps.

The roots of these modes can be traced back to the ancient societies of Anatolia and beyond, to the 4000-year-old Karnatic music of the Hindus.

The names Ionian, Dorian, Phrygian, Lydian, Mixo-Lydian, Aeolian and Locrian have their origins in pre-Hellenic Anatolian societies, mostly in the areas of the western edge of Asia Minor where classical civilization later took root. But the modes predate Greek civilization by centuries, and were regarded as having the power to influence certain moods.

Preceding pages: Modern life and the ancient dignity of the Hagia Sophia. Above: Street music in Urfa. Right: A belly dancer.

One of the first concrete references to this function of early music appears in the third book of Plato's *Republic*, where Socrates suggests that the Lydian and Ionian modes be banned from the ideal state as they are conducive to indolence or despair. Other modes, such as the Dorian and Phrygian, were desirable for inspiring the proper qualities in citizens.

Sadly, it is impossible to know for sure how these modes actually sounded: No notation survives, and recording studios are a 20th century invention. Still, many Western music theoreticians employ the names "Byzantine" major and minor (sometimes "Gypsy" or "Persian"), to describe scales related to the modern "Phrygian", which Spanish *flamencos* and Portuguese *fadistas* call "Moorish", the Moroccans call "Egyptian", and Turks call "Arabesque". These are distinguished by a half step leading downward to the bottom of the scale, with a perfect fifth above – as in the interval between the first two words of *My Favorite Things*: "Rain drops on roses..."

Much of Europe's medieval sacred music was inherited from Byzantine Turkey and distilled through the Roman church, which explains why musicians refer to the early scales as the "church modes". All the modes were explored with the exception of the Locrian: Due to its unresolved structure it was said to contain the "Devil's interval" and therefore avoided by pious composers.

Gregorian chant was the beginning of notation in Western European music, a revolutionary development leading to the intricate polyphony and counterpoint of medieval church composers like Palestrina and Josquin des Prés.

Modal music was composed throughout the Renaissance, with a growing emphasis on the new science of counterpoint and a preference for the Ionian (major) and Aeolian (relative minor) modes.

By the Baroque era, modally-inspired music had given way to harmony and a new pitch system, the tempered tuning. "Easternisms" such as heavy ornamentation, maintaining a single mood or "effect", and the use of augmented seconds remained in Bach, but by the mid-18th century, Western music had become totally dominated by the major-minor key system perfected by W. A. Mozart. Discoveries in chromatic harmony during Beethoven's time led to emotional rollercoaster rides in the music of Johannes Brahms, Richard Wagner and Gustav Mahler, and it was only in the early 20th century that composers such as Claude Debussy and Maurice Ravel began to re-examine the possibilities of the ancient modes again.

In the West today, the best expression of modal music is in modern jazz, with its roots in the blues strains brought to the New World by black slaves from Africa, and from there it started its triumphant advance across Europe. Influential jazz figures such as John Coltrane and Miles Davis have experimented with a myriad of world music modes in an attempt to

break free of the structures imposed by Western European court music.

In Turkish conservatories, meanwhile, musicians can still study the "eastern" subdivisions of the modes – nine gradations of the whole step – using non-fixed pitch instruments such as the *ud* and violin, which are suitable for the intricate variations once played by their Anatolian ancestors.

Nonetheless, it is questionable how long this tradition will last. Atatürk went so far as to actually ban classical Turkish court music, which he thought was decadent and not fitting for the ears of the ideal citizen of his new Republic of Turkey. Violin concertos were to be heard instead. The performance and study ban was not lifted until well after his death, with much lost during the long hiatus. Even today, efforts to extirpate "eastern" music continue, with many politicians bent on weaning the nation away from "Arabesque" towards that most popular modern expression of the Ionian mode – disco-music.

A TOUR OF THE POLITICAL LANDSCAPE

Whether a member of a Hittite royal family, Byzantine peasant, Ottoman officer or student in one of today's many universities, the people of Anatolia have never been apolitical. All members of the various cultures which make up the mosaic of today's Republic have examined contemporary events and political developments – often at their own peril.

Today, *siyaset*, or politics, continues to dominate the daily life of nearly all citizens of the Republic. This concern (or even obsession) manifests itself in the way that people dress and wear their hair. The zealous leftists sport unkempt mustaches like those of Stalin or Gorky, while the neo-fascists tend to trim their facial hairs into artistic creations some-

Above: On the anniversary of the founding of the Turkish Republic. Right: Soldiers on the Bosporus.

how reminiscent of Ghengis Khan. Most easily identified are the religious fanatics, thanks to their flowing beards, skull caps, wide trousers and prayer beads. Among the ladies, the only easily identifiable group belongs to the last class, distinguished by *turban*, or head scarfs, and wide coats worn summer and winter to hide every trace of hair and flesh from the intruding eyes of the outside world. The most extreme expression of this religious devotion is shown by a small group of women who wear the entire veil, even in the larger cities.

No sooner do two Turks come together than one will ask the other the familiar question of "what will become of the country?" Then the discussion revolves around how the nation is going down the drain and can only be saved from disaster if a new (or old) leader takes power.

The concept of the "leader" as the object of a personality cult has long antecedents in Turkey, made all the more remarkable by the strange fact that so many of the leaders who continue to rouse admiration and passion throughout the land might be termed abject failures elsewhere, or have been victimized by circumstance so often that a different body politic would reject them in hopes of following someone with a greater prospect of success.

The first name to come to mind in this regard is that of the irrepressible Süleyman Demirel, who has twice been cast from power. Known as "Bey Effendi" to the masses due to his tendency to give generous price supports to farmers and job insurance to the legions of civil servants with little regard for the impact on the state budget, Demirel won the election at the end of 1991, once again becoming Turkey's Prime Minister.

Another old timer, around since the mid-1960s, is Bulent Ecevit, the "Poet Prime Minister". He got on quite well with the leaders of other nations, but fared much worse with his own people.

Dr. Necmettin Erbakan continues to draw crowds of "fundis" (mostly Turkish workers from Germany) who demand the return of Islamic Law. Alparslan Türkes still manages to excite the virulently nationalistic fringe with his unique brand of pan-Turkism. Erdal Inönü of the Social Democratic Populist Party rekindles the memory of his father Ismet Pasa, who skippered the ship of state through the delicate days of World War II at the head of the Republican People's Party.

The man who has dominated Turkish politics for the past decade, however, is Turgut Özal, the founder of the center-right "Fatherland Party", or ANAP, which controlled parliament throughout the 1980s. Özal climbed to the presidency in 1989 amid accusations that he had usurped the highest office in the land by means of a gerrymandered election, but he seems determined nevertheless to push through his Friedmanesque program of economic reform despite criticism from all quarters. But most often the "spiritual" leader is still Atatürk, the man

who departed from the political scene more than 50 years ago, but whose long shadow continues to influence the nation today.

There is an Atatürk for every political persuasion: a leftist Atatürk for the reds, a rightist Atatürk for those of a nationalist bent, a free-market Atatürk and even a devout Atatürk for Muslim fundamentalists (although this is admittedly a difficult argument to make). There is also the Atatürk of the army, whose martial memory has been invoked as the primary cause for three military coups effected against civilian governments since the country entered the period of multi-party democracy in 1950: The most recent coup took place in 1980.

Conspicuously absent from the political roll call in both the pre and post-coup periods are the Communists. Although semi-legal since the 1970s under a variety of different party names, the followers of Lenin and Mao have had a hard time in Turkey. They have come to regard prison as their most common home.

A MAGIC CARPET RIDE

It is a rare tourist who is not drawn into one of Turkey's thousands of carpet shops to sit spellbound as the dealer literally spins a yarn, rolling out one exquisite rug after the other until a mountain of woven wool is piled at one's feet.

But, however entertaining the experience may be, one should be aware of certain basics concerning quality and design before making a purchase.

The first thing to look for (assuming you like the pattern and color!) is the number of knots per square inch/centimeter. This might seem time-consuming, but the higher the density of the knotting, the more durable the rug will be and the greater the detail in the design. Turn the carpet over and check the number of knots on the reverse side. The back of the carpet should also have the same colors

Above: "Cultivating" rugs on a rug farm near Bodrum. Right: A prayer niche is covered with fine rugs in the Eski Cami in Edirne.

as the front: Any difference in tone strongly suggests that chemical dyes have been substituted for natural dyes, or worse. Refuse to accept any argument to the contrary: Scraps of 500-year-old, naturally-dyed carpet in museums still maintain their original tones, and your one or two-year-old carpet should as well. The only "antique" looking carpets on the market are those which have been scorched with blow torches, dipped in acid baths, or "contoured" by having the black and brown wool strands clipped out of them to make them fit some strange preconception of what looks old.

Turkish carpets can be divided into four essential groups according to the material used: silk, floss (synthetic silk), pure wool and wool on cotton. Carpets are further divided according to their tradition or place of origin, as each region of the country has its own characteristic patterns and colors.

Leading the pack are *Hereke* silk rugs, known for their tight weave and floral designs. An ordinary *Hereke* has 36 knots per square centimeter; if the knot/centimeter density is higher, the rug becomes a "Super Hereke" and the price rises accordingly. Although a very popular carpet, the floral designs can seem just a little rich for some tastes.

Comparable in quality to the *Hereke* carpets are *Kayseri* silk and wool rugs. These also feature detailed floral patterns as well as the familiar medallions. Also comparable are the "prayer rug" *Mihrabs* – representation of the *qibla* niche in the wall of a mosque denoting the direction of the Holy City of Mecca. The Tree of Life is also a popular design. Other highly-prized generic types of carpet are the *Kula* (noted for its tightly-woven, geometrical patterns) and the *Kars*, or Caucasian type of carpet, with large, geometrical figures and a strongly dominant brown color.

Konya-Ladik carpets are identified by central design patterns with an integrated fringe and soft colors. A similar rug is the "nomad" *Yaglibedir*, usually cheaper than the Konya-Ladik. Sometimes called "Bergama", these are characterized by the dark blues and deep reds of the background and the rigid, geometric motifs dominant in the rug.

Other so-called nomad carpets are the *Yahyali* (Kayseri), *Dösemealti* (Antalya/Mediterranean), *Kozak, Taspina* and the ever popular *Milas*, the generic type of carpet from the extreme southwest of the country in the region of Mugla and Bodrum.

However romantic the notion of buying a "real" oriental carpet from the loom of the weaver via a tale-telling carpet dealer may be, there are now two options for the prospective customer wishing to know exactly what he or she is buying. The first of these is the *DOBAG,* or Natural Dyes Research and Development Project, set up in the early 1980s in the village of Ayvacik in the Çanakkale province. Only natural dyes are used, the exception being synthetic indigo for the

blues: Chemical indigo has been in use for 100 years and is chemically identical to extremely rare, natural indigo. A far as the other colors go, DOBAG uses madder root for red and its derivatives, and wild daisies for yellow and its various tones. The prospective customer will be disappointed to hear that the only DOBAG sales outlet is in Ayvacik; all the so-called DOBAG carpets in the bazaar are fakes. So be careful!

An interesting spin-off of the DOBAG is the *Computer-Generated Classic Carpet* project supported by the Ministry of Tourism. Bringing DOBAG a step further, the project has taken dozens of classic designs found in carpet museums (and even the paintings of the great masters) throughout the world, created computer models and then let village weavers work with state-supplied, natural dyed thread. The main outlet is in the Haseki Hürrem Sultan Hamami near the Hagia Sofia Museum on Sultan Ahmet Square in Istanbul, where samples are on display and orders are taken.

THE GREAT OUTDOORS

Turkey offers a surprising number of moderately difficult peaks for climbers in various parts of the country.

Undoubtedly the most evocative climb by far is the 5137-meter Agri Dagi, the Mount Ararat of Biblical fame. According to tradition, Noah's Ark is buried somewhere beneath a crown of perennial snow and ice. The climb itself is more a long uphill walk than a crampon and rope affair, although the Ahora Gorge on the north slope facing the town of Igdir provides a fairly stiff challenge, and there are occasional fatalities.

Closer to the main tourist centers along the "Turkish Riviera" are the Taurus Mountains, with the favorite climbs located in the Aladaglar range, a 1000 square kilometer wonderland between Kayseri to the north, Nigde to the west

Above: Setting out for the hunt in winter.
Right: Climbing a cliff of the Kaçkar.

and Adana to the south. Their highest point is the 3205-meter Alaca Peak. While climbing and trekking are possible all year round, June is the favorite month due to the amount of potable water from the spring run-off. The screes and summits are still covered with ice and snow, however, and ice-axes, ropes and crampons are advised. July and August present less of an equipment problem, but have a drought factor which becomes acute in late August and September.

Another favorite climb in the eastern part of the country is the mist-enshrouded peak of the Kaçkar Tepe, rising to 3971 meters within 50 kilometers of the Black Sea coast. Expeditions consist of a north-south trek from above the town of Çamlihemsin to Yusufeli on the Anatolian side of the range, or vice versa. Here, climbers wend their way along slopes covered with a sea of wild flowers, between majestic spruce and *Rhododendron Ponticum*, all crisscrossed by countless springs collecting the run-off from the peak. Unhappily, the cause of the fecundity is also the curse of the trekker or climber: Rain, and even more distressing, fog. The southern face lacks the richness of nature found on the northern slope, but the weather is better.

The craze to defy the odds and shoot down uncharted rapids and waterfalls in *kevlar kayaks*, canoes and rubber rafts has reached Turkey, where the best white water streams and rivers are found either in the Taurus Mountains or the Pontic Range.

The waters of the Taurus run slowly but surely, tamed by dams and reservoirs. Yet devotees can still find challenging kayak runs on both the south and north branches of the upper Göksu, as well as suitable canoeing in the lower reaches of the same river. The entire way is characterized by cathedral mountains and deep gorges. Rumors have been heard of exciting stretches of white water above the dam on the Manavgat river east of Antalya, as well as on the upper Seyhan River, which flows down from the slopes of the Aladaglar before emptying into a reservoir north of Adana. Rafters, and in some cases even kayakers and canoeists, are best advised to plan their trips during April and May, since water levels after that time turn the upper reaches into boulder fields, and the lower stretches into sluggish ponds.

Black Sea rivers are characterized by extremely steep courses and generally high flow levels, and thus attract the most adventurous: The water level fluctuates wildly throughout the year, and reaches a dangerous point in April and May. Most of the streams are best navigable in late June, although there is often sufficient water well into August. The Firtina is the favorite for courageous kayakers of the suicidal persuasion.

Tamer than the smaller rivers is the Çoruh, which gathers the waters of the southern slopes of the Pontus and is a sufficiently broad and regular float to attract canoeists of a less daredevil sort.

The long stretch between Ispir and Yusufeli is considered world-class kayaking and rafting water, especially during spring run-off.

The Yusufeli-Artvin section is also recommended and has easier vehicle access. Although most of the shoreline is sheer canyon walls, there is usually a beach every kilometer or two that is large enough to pitch your tent on for the night. Be careful, especially during times of rainy weather, to make camp well above the water line since levels can rise several meters overnight. The last real rapid of the river is about 15 kilometers above Artvin, after which the Çoruh becomes navigable enough for even the most neophyte canoeist, while still retaining a brisk enough flow to carry along an inflatable raft at a good clip. Boaters are advised not to attempt continuing beyond the town of Borçka, where the Çoruh takes a turn to the east and heads into the (former) Soviet Union. Maybe it will soon be possible to do a little cross-border canoeing.

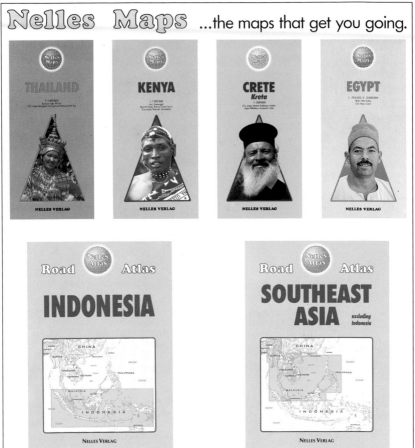

Nelles Maps ...the maps that get you going.

- Afghanistan
- Australia
- Bangkok
- Burma
- Caribbean Islands 1 /
  Bermuda, Bahamas,
  Greater Antilles
- Caribbean Islands 2 /
  Lesser Antilles
- China 1 /
  North-Eastern China
- China 2 /
  Northern China
- China 3 /
  Central China
- China 4 /
  Southern China
- Crete
- Egypt
- Hawaiian Islands
- Hawaiian Islands 1 / Kauai
- Hawaiian Islands 2 /
  Honolulu, Oahu

Nelles Maps

- Hawaiian Islands 3 /
  Maui, Molokai, Lanai
- Hawaiian Islands 4 / Hawaii
- Himalaya
- Hong Kong
- Indian Subcontinent
- India 1 / Northern India
- India 2 / Western India
- India 3 / Eastern India
- India 4 / Southern India
- India 5 / North-Eastern India
- Indonesia
- Indonesia 1 / Sumatra
- Indonesia 2 /
  Java + Nusa Tenggara
- Indonesia 3 / Bali
- Indonesia 4 / Kalimantan
- Indonesia 5 / Java + Bali
- Indonesia 6 / Sulawesi

- Indonesia 7 /
  Irian Jaya + Maluku
- Jakarta
- Japan
- Kenya
- Korea
- Malaysia
- West Malaysia
- Manila
- Mexico
- Nepal
- New Zealand
- Pakistan
- Philippines
- Singapore
- South East Asia
- Sri Lanka
- Taiwan
- Thailand
- Vietnam, Laos
  Cambodia

GUIDELINES

FREQUENT QUESTIONS ABOUT TURKEY

What do they call turkeys in Turkey?

Believe it or not, the Turks call that bird a *hindi,* or "Indian". They call their own country *Türkiye,* meaning "Land of the Turks". This is a fairly new concept, dating only back to the founding of the Republic in 1923. Prior to that, a citizen of the Ottoman empire referred to him or herself as an *Osmanli,* and then by religious designation – Jewish, Christian or Muslim. Strangely enough, the word "Turk" used to be a term of derision, and referred only to the tribal nomads of the country. Equally curiously, the label "Turk" has become a common tag for many people in Central and South America. Most of these "Turks" are Lebanese Arabs who migrated from the former Ottoman Empire to the western hemisphere in the 19th century.

Just who are the Turks?

The citizens of today's Republic are the product of a cultural and ethnic melting pot. Just ask a Turkish friend about his or her ancestors, and you will probably receive an answer like this: the maternal grandmother came from Hungary and her husband from Bulgaria, while the paternal grandfather is a Kurd who married an Egyptian woman. There are blonde Turks, black Turks, tall Turks, short Turks. It is difficult to give a physical description of your basic Turk, just like it is impossible to give a physical description of North Americans. Perhaps the definition is best captured by Atatürk's famous quote *"Ne Multum Türküm diyene"*, or "Happy is he who calls himself a Turk", which encompasses all races, ethnic origins and religions of the citizens of today's Turkish Republic.

Who was Atatürk?

Mustafa Kemal Atatürk was an outstanding politician who steered Turkey away from the East and oriented the nation towards the West by introducing the Latin alphabet and "Western-style" clothes. Refer to the history chapter for more information about him.

As you will notice, statues of the great leader adorn the main square of every town in the country, and his picture is de rigeur in all offices – official or other – throughout the land. Airports, dams and avenues are named after him as well, all amounting to a cult of personality that one tampers with at one's own peril.

What is a Muslim?

A Muslim is someone who follows Islam, an Arabic word meaning "submission to God". The Islamic religion began in Arabia in the mid-7th century when Mohammed began receiving messages from Allah, which means "The One God". Mohammed collected the messages in a book, the Koran, the holy book of the Muslims.

The difference between the Koran and the Bible is quite simple: while the Old Testament is the history of the Jews and the New Testament the life of Jesus, the Koran is believed by Muslims to be the literal word of God transmitted to earth via Mohammed. That's why the Muslims call him their prophet, because God spoke through him. For that matter, Muslims also regard Jesus as a prophet to be held in great esteem.

Statistically, 98 percent of the population of Turkey is Muslim, with the other two percent being a mixture of Turkish Jews and Turkish Christians. But it is one thing to profess a religion, and another thing to practice it. The vast majority of Turks are Muslims more by culture than by practice.

Can one visit a mosque?

Of course, but in the same way you would visit any house of prayer: Modesty and respect are the key words. Women will be asked to drape a scarf over their heads, and both sexes will have to take off their shoes. Shorts and T-shirts will be frowned upon, so it is a good idea to wear appropriate "mosque" clothes.

Also, most mosques are closed to visitors during prayer time. Mosques are open places. Instead of benches or pews, the floors are covered with lovely carpets on which believers say their prayers facing Mecca.

Because the Islam forbids the representation of human and animal forms, most walls are decorated with elaborate geometric and floral designs.

Are women still in the harem?

Of course not. Turkish women received their universal rights of suffrage long before Western women did. Atatürk might be called a one-man women's liberation movement. But there is a difference between theory and practice. Turkish women may be the most liberated in the Muslim world and active in all professions, but on the practical level there are still many changes to be made, particularly in the rural areas.

Why are men kissing each other?

The Turks are kissers. From youth, they are taught to kiss the hands of their elders as a mark of deference. Pecking the cheeks of friends on arrival and departure is standard among both men and women.

The sense of space is also different here, and conversations are conducted at much closer range than in the West. It is not unusual for people to touch each other while talking, or for two heterosexual men walking down the street holding hands.

What about *Midnight Express*?

Let's be candid. For those who have never visited Turkey before, the first image associated with the country is that film. Turks are justifiably outraged by this malicious portrait of their country.

But however awful the image of Turkish prisons may seem on the silver screen, the reality – yourself behind bars – is far worse. The simple way to avoid it is not to break the law. This can be surprisingly easy if you follow these guidelines:

Don't assault or murder anyone.
Don't use, carry or smuggle drugs.
Don't enter restricted military zones.
Don't treasure hunt for antiquities.
Don't become involved with
stolen goods.

With the exception of the last two, this may sound surprisingly similar to the does and don'ts in your own country. There are very few nations in the world who go out of their way to welcome killers, dopers and spies.

The antiquities law is different. Turkey is heir to a stunning level of cultural activity throughout the millennia, but has seen its ancient treasures stripped from its soil and carted away to foreign museums and private collections for centuries.

Like it or not, the official attitude is this: If you dig for antique treasures you are a thief, and if you buy them from someone else you are an accessory to a crime. It is just like purchasing stolen goods from a fence. Avoid the issue by steering clear of temptation, and you will find security personnel surprisingly friendly, even docile. A smile from a foreigner can make a traffic cop forget the fact that you were speeding. However strange it might seem, don't be surprised by the level of airport security, multiple pat-downs and spot checks of identity papers on the highway. These may be an inconvienence, but this is how things are in Turkey.

TRAVEL TIPS

Before You Go

Visas: No visas are required from the following nationalities upon entering

Turkey with a valid passport for the following periods of time:

Three Months: Federal Republic of Germany, Finland, France, Iran, Ireland, Lichtenstein, Malta, Morocco, Portugal, United States of America.

Two Months: Australia, Austria, Canada, Denmark, Hong Kong, Italy, Jamaica, Luxemburg, Mauritius, Pakistan, San Marino, Spain, Sweden, Trinidad, Tunisia, Uganda, United Kingdom.

Seven Weeks: Afghanistan, Romania, (up to now) Yugoslavia.

Six Weeks: Belgium, Iceland, Japan.

For additional information, call the Turkish Tourism Office associated with the nearest Turkish Embassy or Council in your country.

Health Regulations and Precautions

No vaccinations are required to enter and most medicines are sold at pharmacies *(eczane)* throughout the country. It is a good idea to bring any special medication with you. In terms of health hazards, the situation is generally good, although there are still periodic cases of rabies reported, as well as an outbreak of cholera in the southeast where vast stretches of land are under irrigation. Malaria and typhoid are not unheard of. Common sense suggests caution as regards drinking water (use bottled water when possible) and fresh fruit and vegetables: Make sure they are washed well.

Climate

Turkey enjoys a Mediterranean climate similar to that of Greece, Italy and Spain. With long, hot summers and rainy winters in coastal areas, there are dry, temperate summers and cold, snowy winters in the inland mountains and central plateau. Winter in the eastern part of the country can be bitterly cold, with many villages literally cut off from the world for the duration. Heavy rainfall all year round is typical near the Black Sea, whereas the southeast approaches one's preconceived ideas about the Middle East in summer.

Electricity

With the exception of a few pockets in Istanbul and the American embassy residences, Turkey is entirely on the 220v-50 hz system.

Weights and Measures

Turkey uses the metric system and clothing measurements are those used in continental Europe.

Business Hours

Working and shopping hours are usually from 9:00 a.m. -7:00 p.m. Monday to Friday, with half days on Saturday; banking hours are 9:00-12:00 and 1:30 p.m. - 4:00 p.m.

Holidays

Sunday is the official day of rest. National holidays include: April 23 - Independence Day; May 19th - Children's Day; August 30th - Victory Day; October 29th - Republic Day. The Muslim feasts of *Seker Bayrami* and *Kurban Bayrami* fall at a different time every year, due to the shorter Islamic calendar. They will be celebrated in April and June throughout the 1990s.

Getting There

International Air Connections: Most international airlines fly to Turkey and the country is increasingly serviced by charter companies as well. The national carrier *Türk Hava Yollari* (Turkish Airlines) has flights to most points in Europe and the Middle East, and has recently expanded its operations to include New York, Singapore and Tokyo.

Arrivals and departures have become a relatively painless affair via Istanbul's Atatürk International Airport, Turkey's window on the world. It is a modern and secure air terminal with the whole range of duty-free facilities.

In addition to Istanbul, international connections are made through Ankara's Esenboga and Izmir's Adnan Menderes international airports, both new and with all the requisite services, ranging from banks to rental car agencies and duty-free shops. Two other airports offer international charter flights as well as local connections – Antalya and Dalaman, both strategically located in the tourist sun-belt. A new international airport at Bodrum has been open since the spring of 1991.

Istanbul Airport	(1) 5732920
Ankara Airport	(4) 3122820
Antalya Airport	(31) 216009
Izmir Airport	(51) 371188

Domestic Air Connections: In addition to international flights from the above-mentioned terminals, domestic flights also serve all major cities in the country via the national carrier THY or through an expanding net of independent airlines. Airports include Adana, Bursa, Diyarbakir, Elazig, Erzurum, Gaziantep, Samsun, Trabzon and Van, while there are small-craft airfields now at Bodrum, Erzincan, Kars and Malatya, with others being built or planned. Helicopter rentals are also available through such firms as Sanuk and Sancak.

Istanbul (Telephone code: 1)

THY	5733525
Bodrum Airlines	5744818
Air Inka (to Bodrum)	5747878
Sönmez (to Bursa)	5739323
Sancak	5742720
Sanuk	1514439
EMAir	5744318
THT	5743119

Ankara (Telephone code: 4)

THY	3126200
THT	1191492
THK	3104840

THE COUNTRY

Turkey is spread over a large peninsula of 779,452 square kilometers, with 97% of its land mass in Asia (Anatolia) and 3% in Europe (Thrace). Bounded by three seas – the Black Sea to the north, the Aegean to the west and the Mediterranean to the south – Turkey also has borders with the (former) Soviet Union to the northeast, Iran to the east, Iraq and Syria to the south, and Greece and Bulgaria to the northwest. The population of 56 million lives in 71 provinces, with some 55% of the population involved in agriculture. The population growth rate is approximately 2.2%, with a disproportionately high number of citizens under the age of 20. Literacy is officially set at 88% of the population, but is probably a little lower.

The country is 98% Muslim, of whom most are Sunni. Minorities include a large Alevi population and tiny pockets of Shiites in the extreme northeast, and Yezidies in the southeast. The only officially recognized minorities are the small groups of Greek Orthodox, Armenian Christians and the Sephardic Jews.

The form of government in Turkey is parliamentary democracy, with the president playing a particularly important role. Scheduled elections are held every five years for the 450 seats of the former, while parliament elects a new president every seven years.

Turkey is a member of the United Nations, Council of Europe, NATO, OECD, IMF, World Bank, International Committee of the Red Cross, International Atomic Energy Agency, and an associate member of the European Community.

ACCOMMODATION

The lists of hotels and pensions in the respective Guideposts are not exhaustive, and only represent the editors' choice of accommodation in different price ranges in various parts of the country. For further information, check with the local Tourist Information Office or with a travel agency. A list of the major international tour agencies is given under "Tour Operators".

SHOPPING

Everybody knows about Istanbul's famous Grand Covered Bazaar, where carpet merchants will fill you with wonderful stories about their wares, but there is a plethora of other interesting self-indulgent or gift shopping ideas as well. Travelers are advised to bring an empty bag for all the goodies they will want to lug back home.

Fashion leather ware – jackets, coats, skirts, etc. – are available everywhere in the country; many of the shops in the resort towns along the Mediterranean coast seem to specialize in selling winter attire! Prices are very cheap compared with those in Europe.

Fashion fabrics are also a great buy in Turkey, which has long been one of the main producers of ready-to-wear in Europe, even if it is sold under different brand names due to EC-imposed quotas. The upmarket boutiques include *Vakko* and *Beymen,* although prices in these shops tend to be high.

Those with a little more time might like to have a hand-tailored suit made; Turkish wool and cotton fabrics may be exported to Europe, but tailors are not.

Copper and brass also are a very good buy, if a bit bulky: Favorite purchases here are the large round, hand-worked tables *(sehpa)* which stand on wooden legs. Meerschaum pipes, carved into really bizarre shapes and better for decoration than for smoking, are unique gifts, as are the (heavy) onyx candle holders sold around Cappadocia. Other nice gift items are hand-knit socks and mohair blankets, especially those produced in the southeastern town of Siirt.

This is also the land of the world-famous Smyrna fig and sultana raisin, not to mention the hazelnut, pistachio and walnut. Buy a couple of pounds for a song and look like a big spender back home!

TRANSPORTATION

Road Transport
Those with their own vehicles will enter the country via the Kapikule border gate outside Edirne on the Bulgarian frontier or via Huduk/Ipsala on the Greek border. Others may arrive via the Ro-Ro ferries from Rumania or the car ferry from Venice to either Izmir or Istanbul. Insurance and ownership documents should be in order upon arrival (have your insurance confirm that it is also valid in the Asiatic portion of Turkey); the vehicle identification number will be stamped into the owner's passport and difficulties will arise if one attempts to leave the country without the vehicle, or without having placed it on the customs farm. Other valuables such as cassette recorders, cameras and even fur coats may also be noted in your travel documents, and you must have them with you when departing the country.

Regular, super, high-octane and diesel fuels are readily available at numerous state and private gas stations throughout the country. The lead-free fuels required by catalytic converters are now making their way onto the Turkish market as well. Diesel fuel is about 1/3 cheaper than gasoline due to state supports for farmers and truck drivers; otherwise, prices are somewhat less per liter than in most European countries.

E-5, the major trunk route connecting Europe to the Middle East via Edirne, Istanbul, Ankara and Adana, is crowded with trucks and can be very dangerous. Pass with care. Other roads require equal attention. Statistics speak for themselves: With 40 fatalities for every 10,000 vehicles on the road, Turkey's roads rank among the most dangerous in the world.

Rental Cars

Car rental agencies have sprung up like mushrooms in the wake of the recent tourist boom; in addition to Hertz, Avis and Europcar, a plethora of completely obscure agencies now offers vehicles. The majors have offices in all international airports and most cities, as well as in areas of high tourist density. Demand is high in the summer, so book well in advance. None of the agencies allow their cars to be taken over international borders. Here are Istanbul headquarters of the majors:

Avis: Tramvay Cad. 72, Kuruçesme; Tel: 1577670, Fax: 1575632, Tlx: 26704.

Hertz: Cumhuriyet Cad. 295; Tel: 1412336, Tlx: 26019.

Europcar: Cumhuriyet Cad. 47/2, Taksim; Tel: 1508888; Fax: 1507649, Tlx: 24175.

Buses

For those who are looking for economical transportation, air-conditioned buses are the norm for intercity travel. Scores of companies vie for the honor of being regarded as the most "modern" by the public; drivers maintain the air of pilots, and attendants walk up and down the aisles seeing to one's every need. Here are the Istanbul headquarters of the majors; scores of others are available at the bus station *(otogar)* in every town:

Varan: Taksim, Tel: 1517474; Topkapi: 5821090.

Ulusoy: Taksim, Tel. 1441271; Topkapi: 5826845.

Kamilkoç: Taksim, Tel: 1452795; Topkapi: 5822930.

Pamukkale: Taksim, Tel: 1452946; Topkapi: 5822935.

Trains

Turkish trains are not up to European standards: With the exception of the sleepers between Istanbul and Ankara and Ankara and Izmir, they are slow and crowded. Recently attention has been given to upgrading the lines throughout the country and promoting the old steam trains which are still in use on some routes. Enthusiasts will be delighted to hear that such trains now run along the Black Sea and that a special steam locomotive runs every weekend from Izmir to Selçuk/Ephesus. Here are the main station numbers:

Istanbul Sirkeci . . . . . . (1) 5206575
Haydarpasa . . . . (1) 3383050
Ankara Station . . . . . . (4) 3106515
Izmir Basmane . . . . . . (51) 335897

Inner City Transportation

Taxis are readily available. All are equipped with meters and surprisingly inexpensive. Be sure to note whether the day or night meter *(gece)* is on, because the night surcharge will increase the rate by 50%. Some drivers have been known to flick the night switch at noon if they think the passenger is green.

Inner city buses, however, are a different story: If your idea of a good time is to be packed like a sardine in a diesel-belching monster during the summer heat of downtown Istanbul, be our guest–a better idea is to take a taxi, *dolmus* (route taxi) or just walk.

TELECOMMUNICATION

It is a rare village that does not have international direct dialing and even a rarer hotel that does not have a fax. Nearly all hotels have a surcharge for local, intercity and international dialing, however. On the street, just look for the yellow PTT sign of local post offices, which provide a variety of services – from currency exchange to money transfers, *post restante* and same-day delivery *(acele posta)*.

Mobile post offices now roam areas of high touristic density. Recently, plastic cards have begun to replace the standard *jetons* used for call boxes, so it is a good idea to purchase a couple of these to have on hand. A list of both local and international codes is usually found attached to telephone boxes. Put in the coin (or card), dial 9 for trunk calls or 99 for international, followed by the country/city code and the number. Local Information: 011; Intercity: 031; International: 032.

CURRENCY AND CREDIT CARDS

The Turkish Lira (TL) is moving towards full convertibility: In effect this means that there are no regulations about the importation of any amount of TL or any other currency, and that a black market no longer exists. Daily exchange rates are published in newspapers, and one can change money at one's hotel, in a bank or at the numerous exchange offices set up in areas of heavy tourist traffic.

Denominations are as follows: 10, 25, 50, 100 and 500 TL coins and 1000, 5000, 10,000, 20,000 and 50,000 bills. Be careful with the 10,000 and 50,000 bills which are both green and the same size. A 100,000 TL note is said to be under consideration.

All major credit cards are accepted nearly everywhere in the country, save for roadside diners and the cheapest hotels and pensions. The usual conditions and surcharges apply.

EMBASSIES AND CONSULATES

Australia: Nenehatun Cad. 83, GOP, Ankara, Tel: 1361240-3. **Austria**: Atatürk Bul. 189, K.dere, Ankara, Tel: 134 2174. **Belgium**: Nenehatun Cad. 109, GOP, Ankara, Tel: 136 1653. **Bulgaria**: Atatürk Bul. 124, K.dere, Ankara, Tel: 1267455; Istanbul Consulate: Zincirlikuyu Cad. 44, Ulus/Levent, Tel: 169 2314. **Canada:** Nenehatun Cad. 75, GOP, Ankara, Tel: 1361275-7. **Denmark**: Kirlangiç Sok. 42, GOP, Ankara,

Tel: 1275258. **Egypt:** Atatürk Bul. 126, K.dere, Ankara, Tel: 126 6478. **Finland**: Galip Dede Sok. 1/10, K.dere, Ankara, Tel: 1265921. **France**: Paris Cad. 70, K.dere, Ankara, Tel: 1261480; Istanbul Consulate: Istiklal Cad. 8, Taksim, Tel: 1424387. **Germany**: Atatürk Bul. 114, K.dere, Ankara, Tel: 1265465; Istanbul Consulate: Inönü Cad. Taksim, Tel: 1450705. **Greece**: Ziya Rahman Sok. 9/11, GOP, Ankara, Tel: 1368861; Istanbul Consulate: Turnacibasi Sok. 32, Galatasaray, Tel: 1450596. **Holland:** Köroglu Sok. 6, GOP, Ankara, Tel: 1361074. **India**: Cinnah Cad. 77/17, Çankaya, Ankara, Tel: 1382195. **Italy:** Atatürk Bul. 118, K.dere, Ankara, Tel: 1265460. **Iran**: Tahran Cad. 10, K.dere, Ankara, Tel: 1274320. **Iraq**: Turan Emeksiz Sok. 11, GOP, Ankara, Tel: 1266118. **Israel**: Farabi Sok. 43, K.dere, Ankara, Tel: 1263904; Istanbul Consulate: Valikonagi Cad. 73/4, Nisantasi, Tel: 1464125. **Japan**: Resit Galip Cad. 81, GOP, Ankara, Tel: 1361290; Istanbul Consulate: Tontonkaptan Sok. 15, Beyoglu, Tel: 1431024. **Norway**: Kelebek Sok. 20, GOP, Ankara, Tel: 1379950. **Poland:** Atatürk Bul. 241, K.dere, Ankara, Tel: 1261698. **Portugal**: Cinnah Cad. 2873, Çankaya, Ankara, Tel: 1275055. **Saudi Arabia**: Abdullah Cevdet Sok. 18, Çankaya, Ankara, Tel: 1366921. **Spain**: Abdullah Cevdet Sok. 8, Çankaya, Ankara, Tel: 13. **Sweden**: Katip Çelebi Sok. 7, K.dere, Ankara, Tel: 1286735; Istanbul Consulate: Istiklal Cad 497, Tünel, Tel: 1435770. **Switzerland**: Atatürk Bul. 247, K.dere, Ankara, Tel: 1380392. **Syria**: Abdullah Cevdet Sok. 7, Çankaya, Ankara, Tel: 1388704. **United Kingdom**: Sehit Ersan Cad. 46/q, Çankaya, Ankara, Tel: 1274310; Istanbul Consulate: Mesrutiyet Cad. 26, Galatasaray, Tel: 1498874. **United States of America:** Atatürk Bul. 110, K.dere, Ankara, Tel: 1265470; Istanbul Consulate: Mesrutiyet Cad. 104/08, Tepebasi, Tel: 1513602. **CIS:** (up to now) Karyagdi

Sok. 5, Çankaya, Ankara, Tel: 1392122; Istanbul Consulate: Istiklal Cad. 443, Tünel, Tel: 1441693. **Yugoslavia:** (up to now) Paris Cad. 47, K.dere, Ankara, Tel: 1260236.

TOUR OPERATORS

Airtour: Istanbul office: Cumhuriyet Cad 271/3, Harbiye, Tel: 1462021, Tlx: 23553; Kusadasi office: Atatürk Bul., App B, Tel: 3633; Marmaris office: Yat Limani 7/A, Tel: 1557, Tlx: 53847; Antalya office: Feyzi Çakmak Cad. 2, Mahmut Cil Apt 75/33, Tel: 31108, Tlx: 560 92; Alanya office: Iskele Cad. 22, Tel: 10 41, Tlx: 56665. **Albatros:** Istanbul office: Yerebatan cad 20/6, Cagaloglu, Tel: 5285510, Tlx: 22615; Bodrum office: Neyzen Tevfik Cad. 72, Tel: 2309, Tlx: 52979; Marmaris office: Barbaros Cad. 11, Tel: 1033, Tlx: 53080. **Bodrumtour**: Istanbul office: Cumhuriyet Cad. 16, Kahan, Elmadag, Tel: 1401850, Tlx: 27853; Ankara office: Kader Sok. 6/3, GOP, Tel: 1670711, Tlx: 42368. **Camel Tours**: Istanbul office: Opera Ishani 41/5, Tel: 143 8020, Tlx: 24446; Antalya office: Feyzi Çakmak Cad. 57, Tel: 13845, Tlx: 56007. **Duru Tourism:** Istanbul office: Istiklal Cad. 365, Beyoglu, Tel: 1437659, Tlx: 24343; Ankara office: Atatürk Bul. 83/4, Tel: 134 4844, Tlx: 43415; Bodrum office: Karantina Cad. 31, Tel: 1431, Tlx: 52976. **Esin Tourism:** Cumhuriyet Cad. 47/2, Taksim, Tel: 150 88888, Tlx: 24175; Izmir office: Sehit Fethibey Cad. 122, Tel: 31083, Tlx: 52277. **Miltur**: Istanbul office: Cumhuriyet Cad 135, Elmadag, Tel: 1464020, Tlx: 23576; Ankara office: Tunus Cad. 6/4, Tel: 118 2015, Tlx: 42512; Izmir office: Kizilay Cad. 1/b, Tel: 218731, Tlx: 53587. **Setur:** Istanbul office: Cumhuriyet Cad. 107, Elmadag, Tel: 1300336, Tlx: 22718; Ankara office: Kavaklidere Sok. 5/b, Tel: 1277113, Tlx: 46190; Izmir office: Atatürk Cad. 294/a, Tel: 215595, Tlx: 52183; Antalya office:

Feyzi Çakmak Cad. 26/a, Tel: 16938, Tlx: 56045; Marmaris office: Atatürk Cad. 16, Tel: 4608, Tlx: 533816.

TURKISH LANGUAGE

Turkish is a member of the Ural-Altaic family of languages, which includes a variety of Central Asian dialects such as Uzbek and Kirghiz.

There are approximately 100 million Turkish speakers in the world. Entirely different from Indo-European as well as Semitic languages of the Middle East, in Turkish information is created by attaching new particles to the end of a word:

House . . . . *ev*
My house . . . . *evim*
In my house . . . . *evimde*
He/she is in my house . . . . *evimdedir*
He/she was in my house . . *evimdeydir*

The following lexicon does not pretend to provide the traveler with anything more than the very basics, and those inclined to learn more should look for a grammar book. At the very least, learning how to pronounce the several peculiar Turkish letters will lead to much greater understanding when reading road signs, etc.:

C/c=j as in "just"
Ç/ç=ch as in "chat"
Ş/ş=sh as in "shot"
ğ=extends the sound of the preceding vowel as in "ought"
ı=undotcd "i"
as in "sing"

SURVIVAL TURKISH

Please . . . . *lütfen*
Thank you . . . . *teşekkür*
Yes . . . . : . *evet*
No . . . . *hayır*
To not be so . . . . *değil*
Hello . . . . *merhaba*
Good-bye . . . . *güle güle*
Good morning . . . . *günaydın*
Good day . . . . *iyi günler*

Good night	iyi geceler
Excuse me	affedersiniz
Welcome!	hos geldiniz!
(Reply)!	hos bulduk!
How are you?	nasılsınız?
Fine, thanks	iyim, sagol
How much?	ne kadar?
Where?	nerede?
When?	ne zaman?
How?	nasıl?
What time is it?	saat kaç?
Money	para
Expensive	pahali
Cheap	ücüz
Beautiful	güzel
Ugly	çirkin
There is	var
Is there?	var mı?
There isn't	yok
Food	yemek
Room	oda

Time

Second	saniye
Minute	dakika
Hour	saat
Day	gün
Night	gece
Morning	sabah
Noon	yarım
Afternoon	ögle den sonra
Evening	aksam
Today	bugün
Tomorrow	yarin
Yesterday	dün
Week	hafta
Month	ay
Year	yil

Days of the Week

Monday	Pazartesi
Tuesday	Salı
Wednesday	Çarşambe
Thursday	Perşembe
Friday	Çuma
Saturday	Cumartesi
Sunday	Pazar

Numbers

Half	yarım
One	bir
Two	iki
Three	üç
Four	dört
Five	beş
Six	altı
Seven	yedi
Eight	sekiz
Nine	dokuz
Ten	on
Eleven	onbir
Twelve	oniki
13-19.....etc	
Twenty	yirmi
Twenty one	yirmibir
Twenty two	yirmiiki
23-29......etc	
Thirty	otuz
Forty	kirk
Fifty	elli
Sixty	altmiş
Seventy	yetmiş
Eighty	seksen
Ninety	doksan
One hundred	yüz
Two hundred	ikiyüz
300-999....etc	
One thousand	bin
Two thousand	ikibin
One million	bir milyon
One billion	bir milyar

Please note: Due to technical difficulties, the uniquely Turkish characters "Ş","ğ" and "ı" have only been used in this language guide. The publishers apologize for the absence of the characters in the rest of the book.

AUTHORS

Heike Brockmann wrote the chapter on the Mediterranean Coast.

Eddie Goltz, jazz musician and continental wanderer, contributed the feature on the link between the ancient modes of Anatolia and contemporary jazz.

Tim Kelsey, the Turkey correspondent of the *Independent* newspaper, wrote the chapter on Central Anatolia with its emphasis on the Hittites.

Hans and **Ingeborg Obermann** both graduated with a MA in Middle Eastern archaeology, geology and ethnology. They have published several scientific papers, their favorite subjects being art, religion and philosophy. They work as translators, freelance writers and lecture in adult education institutes on art history, scientific study of religion, antique and medieval literature.

Waltraud Schuster discovered her affinity to Turkey during her intensive studies of geography in Munich. Since 1984, she organizes study trips to Turkey, her favorite country. She is the author of the chapters "City on the Bosporus", "Thrace, Sea of Marmara, Northern Aegean" and "The Aegean Coast".

Jochen Steinhardt has studied geography. Since 1982, he works as a freelance photographer and tour manager for an agency specializing in study trips to Islamic and Buddhist countries. He has contributed texts and photographs for several *Nelles Guides* and various other publications.

Laine Stump, itinerant computer wizard and rubber raftor, wrote the feature on "The Great Outdoors".

Nezih Tavlas, who has monitored political events in Turkey for the *Günes* and *Sabah* newspapers, wrote the feature on the contemporary political landscape.

Asli Uler wrote the feature on Turkish carpets and kelims, "A Magic Carpet Ride". She also assisted **Cem Aydin Tas** with the Guideposts and Travel Tips.

PHOTOGRAPHERS

Archiv für Kunst und Geschichte, Berlin	82
Becker, Frank S.	18, 154, 178, 182, 209, 211, 218
Bondzio, Bodo	233
Bondzio, Zdenka	126
Çakir, Nevzat	39, 40/41, 48, 91,138, 159, 165, 188, 230/231, 234
Çatak, Manuel	85, 118, 158, 161, 162, 167, 219
Demirkol, Mehmet	238
Gönendik, Funda	166
Goltz, Thomas	80
Guynup, Sharon	55, 120, 121, 127, 137, 222, 232
Hackenberg, Rainer	45, 106, 146, 149, 157
Henninges, Heiner	122, 141, 148
Hinze, Peter	93, 98, 117
Hühn, Holger	50, 51, 52, 74, 186, 210
Huntt Mason, Karen	1, 44, 89, 96/97, 109, 111L., 143
Kacmpf, Bernhard	151
Kafagil, Sabit	25
Kaya, Mustafa	111R.
Keribar, Izzet	57L., 57R., 187, 237
Kulahçi, Necmettin	152, 216
Poblete, Jose F.	8/9, 63, 70, 71, 139, 198
Roth, Hans-Georg	14, 31, 54, 60, 235
Schneider, Günter	58, 170/171, 179
Schuster, Waltraud	114, 115
Schwarz, Berthold	112, 125
Skupy, Jitka	136, 155, 183, 206, 212
Steinhardt, Jochen	10/11, 19, 20, 61, 76, 116, 130/131, 164, 180, 185, 192/193, 200, 204, 207, 215, 223, 224, 225
Thiele, Klaus	23, 147, 153, 176, 189, 203, 217
Timoçin, Tulgar	16
Tuvi, Jusuf	90, 107
Unbehaun, Horst	66/67, 77
Werner, Hans A.	Cover
Yesilay, Zeynel	78, 79, 104, 113
Zaman, Ibrahim	12/13, 24, 88, 145, 201, 227

INDEX